I0892393

El Paso

Globalization and Community

Dennis R. Judd, Series Editor

Volume 13
El Paso: Local Frontiers at a Global Crossroads
Victor M. Ortíz-González

Volume 12
Remaking New York: Primitive Globalization and the Politics of Urban Community
William Sites

Volume 11
A Political Space: Reading the Global through Clayoquot Sound
Warren Magnusson and Karena Shaw, editors

Volume 10
City Requiem, Calcutta: Gender and the Politics of Poverty
Ananya Roy

Volume 9
Landscapes of Urban Memory: The Sacred and the Civic in India's High-Tech City
Smriti Srinivas

Volume 8
Fin de Millénaire Budapest: Metamorphoses of Urban Life
Judit Bodnár

Volume 7
Latino Metropolis
Victor M. Valle and Rodolfo D. Torres

Volume 6
Regions That Work: How Cities and Suburbs Can Grow Together
Manuel Pastor Jr., Peter Dreier, J. Eugene Grigsby III, and Marta López-Garza

Volume 5
Selling the Lower East Side: Culture, Real Estate, and Resistance in New York City
Christopher Mele

Volume 4
Power and City Governance: Comparative Perspectives on Urban Development
Alan DiGaetano and John S. Klemanski

Volume 3
Second Tier Cities: Rapid Growth beyond the Metropolis
Ann R. Markusen, Yong-Sook Lee, and Sean DiGiovanna, editors

Volume 2
Reconstructing Chinatown: Ethnic Enclave, Global Change
Jan Lin

Volume 1
The Work of Cities
Susan E. Clarke and Gary L. Gaile

El Paso

Local Frontiers at a Global Crossroads

Victor M. Ortíz-González

Globalization and Community / Volume 13
University of Minnesota Press
Minneapolis • London

Chapter 1 contains excerpts from *North American Cities and the Global Economy: Challenges and Opportunities,* by Peter Karl Kresl (Thousand Oaks: Sage Publications, 1995); reprinted by permission of Sage Publications. Chapter 1 contains excerpts from *Border Matters: Remapping American Cultural Studies,* by José David Saldívar (Berkeley and Los Angeles: University of California Press, 1997). Chapter 2 contains excerpts from "The Unbearable Ambiguity of the Border," by Victor M. Ortíz-González, *Social Justice* 28, no. 2 (2001); reprinted by permission of *Social Justice,* SocialJust@aol.com. Chapter 2 contains quotations from "Let's See Some Papers," by Tina Plaza, *The Progressive* 57, no. 4 (April 1993): 18; reprinted by permission of *The Progressive,* 409 East Main Street, Madison, Wisconsin 53703. Chapter 2 contains excerpts from "Sealing Our Borders: The Human Toll" (1992) and "Operation Blockade: Sealing Our Borders" (1994); reprinted by permission of the American Friends Service Committee. An earlier version of chapter 3 was published as "Latinas on the Border: The Common Ground of Economic Displacements and Breakthroughs," by Victor M. Ortíz-González, in *Gender's Place: Feminist Anthropologies of Latin America,* edited by Rosario Montoya, Lessie Jo Frazier, and Janise Hurtig (New York: Palgrave Press, 2002), 197–215; copyright 2002 Rosario Montoya, Lessie Jo Frazier, and Janise Hurtig; reprinted with permission of Palgrave Macmillan. Parts of chapters 3 and 4 were originally published in "NAFTA and Emergency Subjects in the Border City of El Paso," by Victor M. Ortíz-González, in *Dialectical Anthropology* 23 (1998): 31–54; reprinted with permission from Kluwer Academic Publishers. Parts of chapters 3 and 4 were originally published as "Only Time Can Tell If Geography Is Still Destiny: Time, Space, and NAFTA in a U.S.–Mexican Border City," by Victor M. Ortíz-González, in *Human Organization* 58, no. 2 (1999); reprinted with permission from the Society for Applied Anthropology. Parts of chapter 4 are reprinted from *Dreaming the Future and Living the Unity: El Paso Makes Strategic Choices* by permission of Joe Old/Unite El Paso.

Published by the University of Minnesota Press
111 Third Avenue South, Suite 290
Minneapolis, MN 55401-2520
http://www.upress.umn.edu

Library of Congress Cataloging-in-Publication Data

Ortíz-González, Victor M.
El Paso : local frontiers at a global crossroads / Victor M. Ortíz-González.
p. cm. — (Globalization and community ; v. 13)
Includes bibliographical references and index.
ISBN 0-8166-4076-9 (hardcover : alk. paper) — ISBN 0-8166-4077-7 (pbk. : alk. paper)
1. El Paso (Tex.) 2. El Paso (Tex.)—Ethnic relations. 3. Mexican Americans—Texas—El Paso. 4. Globalization. I. Title. II. Series.
F394.E4 O78 2004
976.4'96'063—dc22

2003018066

Printed in the United States of America on acid-free paper

12 11 10 09 08 07 06 05 04 10 9 8 7 6 5 4 3 2 1

A mis padres, Guadalupe González y Ernesto Ortíz,
a mis abuelos, Manuela Orozco y Marcos Carrasco, y a mis tíos,
Alicia González y Luis Pisaña, que como muchos otros crean hogares
en el ir y venir de Ciudad Juárez y El Paso.

To my parents and grandparents, who, like many others,
make homes in the coming and goings of Ciudad Juárez and El Paso.

Contents

Preface: Who Owns the Border? ix

Introduction: Otherness and Globalization on the U.S.–Mexican Border and Beyond xv

1. Between an Image and a Hard Place 1

2. Undermining Reality 31

3. La Vista Grande: The Common Ground of Displacements and Breakthroughs 73

4. Local Democracy and Global Demography: New Parameters of Community 103

Conclusion: El Paso as an Eternal—Yet Not Final—Frontier 141

Works Cited 161

Index 169

Preface

Who Owns the Border?

The lights had just been turned off as I rushed into the auditorium. I took the first seat I managed to spot with the help of light from the stage. It was a one-man performance art show about the U.S.–Mexico region, "Border Brujo." A Mexican man in his late twenties engaged in a self-conscious over-dramatic parody presenting the region through stereotypes. The scenario featured an altar made from a pastiche of corny paraphernalia, including a colorful serape, religious candles, a bottle of Herbal Essence shampoo, and a megaphone. In the actor's monologue, statements about interethnic conflicts and binational entanglements were juxtaposed in a blur with exaggerated gesticulations and cartoonish emulations of characters ascribed to the border. The first character was a long-haired, heavily made-up sorcerer who underwent various transformations and monologues, ranging from a solemn priestlike transfiguration uttering sordid denunciations of the political asymmetries between the two countries to a Mexican street vendor speaking in circuslike, syncopated singsong. The play was almost entirely in English, purposefully delivered with a heavy Mexican accent, but the monologues were sprinkled with Spanish and gibberish incantations. With no concern for boundaries, as it were, the grotesque and the bizarre were indulged heavily to highlight, ostensibly, transgression and chaos as the quintessential features of the region. This aesthetic characterization served as the conduit for political snippets, aesthetic defamiliarization tricks, and parodic clichés about Euro-Americans, Mexicans, and the border.

The play appeared as a jaded theater of the absurd, self-consciously recycling tricks from the counterculture scene in Mexico during the 1960s and 1970s, a mixture of Alejandro Jodorosky and Alfonso Arau. What I found most striking, however, was not the play, but the response of the audience, who celebrated the entire performance with cheers and laughs, keeping pace with its frenetic style. At the end of the performance, after the applause ended and the lights came up, I eagerly looked around for the friends who had told me about the performance. What I saw was an audience that was overwhelmingly Anglo, mostly in their early to mid-twenties, and ostensibly middle class, judging from their trendy, urban, artsy outfits and demeanor. For the most part, in short, it was the typical audience for performance art. Stunned and oversaturated by the excesses of the performance, I slowly followed the crowd out of the auditorium, still looking for my friends. As I did so, I tried to listen for an interesting conversation about the performance that I could join. My hope was to talk with someone so I could make sense of the shock I had experienced. This hope soon dissolved. None of the conversations I overheard concerned the play. Most were just brief greetings or inquiries about where to hang out next. While the performance had captivated the audience's attention as it took place, it had seemingly slipped out of their minds once it was over. Maybe they were postponing such discussion for a more convenient time and place. I could not help but notice, however, the contrast between my immediate reaction and theirs.

I had a nagging feeling for some days after the performance. In time the play became more popular, adding to a trendy representation of the border region as a "no-man's-land," an image that gained particularly commanding appeal as NAFTA (1993 trade agreement signed by Canada, the United States, and Mexico) brought intense attention to the region. I found most of the accounts of the border in academia, arts, and the mass media heavily based on the spectacular and the bizarre. Having grown up in the border area and researched it for years, my impression was that these tendentious accounts mischaracterized the region at a time when major developments, with complex human consequences, demanded a sober understanding. I felt that the momentary thrill of an art performance and other representations, for example, contributed more to fomenting crossborder drinking escapades for underage teenagers than to an understanding of border cities.

A couple of years later, upon completing my dissertation, I embraced the task of correcting the misrepresentations. An opportunity presented itself when I was invited to give a talk at the school where I had just accepted a postdoctoral position. I particularly welcomed the invitation because of my indignation over a new draconian measure being deployed by the border patrol in El Paso to stop undocumented crossings. The measure, which in my view worsened the hardship and tensions in that city and in Ciudad Juárez, posted border patrol officers on permanent guard along the entire extension of the boundary between the two cities. The morning of my presentation, I called a friend in El Paso to check on the latest effects of the measure. My friend told me that the measure was apparently losing its initial effectiveness given that Raquel, the undocumented maid who cleaned her house, had shown up that week, after a two-week absence. My friend said Raquel had arrived very scared and exhausted. She had crossed the river at the desolate outskirts of the city and had had to walk a long stretch before she could get public transportation to my friend's house. Yet, she had managed to cross.

After I hung up the phone, a question flared in my mind: who owns the border? I had met Raquel at my friend's house a few summers before and I could painfully picture that alert middle-aged woman putting herself at great risk of being raped or murdered by crossing the boundary in a desolate area and then enduring the hardship and disorientation of having to find her way to her place of work. Does she own the border? Wasn't she able, this time at least, to bypass the stringent guard? Yet what about those people imposing or supporting the new measure? Did they own the border? Or were they attempting to prove that they did? As I pondered this question, I realized that my simplistic claim of "correcting" the so-called mischaracterization was also an attempt to claim ownership of the border. I then recognized the absurdity of my undertaking.

My initial certainty that the border was rightfully owned by its local residents crumbled as I recognized their evident displacement. Raquel's hardship, as an undocumented worker, was obvious and severe. But what about the long waits in idling cars at the crossing bridges? What about the pollution and waste of fuel that these delays produced? What about the intrusive searches by customs agents and immigration officers? What about the periods of crisis that each of Mexico's recurrent devaluations created in El Paso? What about the region's high unemployment and make-believe economies of second- and third-rate tourist traps and foreign-owned firms that determined the number of local jobs? Who owns the border? I asked myself again as I walked to the classroom for the presentation, panicking because my prepared notes no longer made any sense to me.

As I faced the audience, the answer crystallized with poignant clarity: the border is owned by no one, and thus it is owned by everyone. In other words, no one owns the border because everyone has open access to it. It is an open space with multiple claims made on it. Contested by everybody, the border remains a frontier, a division reinforced and transgressed again and again. Even in the case of some of the most vulnerable inhabitants of the area, the undocumented workers, this condition stands. In the case of Raquel, her mixture of desperation and audacity led her to prevail, at least temporarily, over those self-perceived "legitimate" residents of El Paso who sided with exclusionary policies for their own immediate, particular frontierlike reasons. Audacity and desperation are classical attributes of the frontier, in which individual will and resilience prevail over the physical setting, be it barren, wild, or "civilized."

Yet, not everyone has equal access to the border. For example, with NAFTA, some people and transactions have gained greater access, while for others access has been curtailed, making it difficult, for example, to visit relatives on the other side of the divide. In this persistent frontier, this open space for recurrent colonizations, newcomers and institutional bodies based elsewhere command greater influence than most local residents. These powerful "invaders," such as directors of bank branches and INS deputies (who are seldom from the area), also alter or circumvent the "law of the land" to suit their own agendas, a "law" that stipulates that the last to come enjoy special treatment due, for some, to their more direct contacts with the absent owners of local resources, or, for others, to sheer desperation. Yet local residents make and remake their options and delineations as well.

If no one owns the border then anyone can represent it as bizarrely, sordidly, or romantically as they wish—as the artist in the one-man performance was doing when he proclaimed himself to be an emblem of the region. My undertaking can only be one more such claim. Yet, some claims or descriptions are more comprehensive than others. My account in this book is neither a complete nor a corrective one. My immediate aim is to underscore the persistent frontier character of the region—its overwhelming and pervasive subordination of local concerns to nonlocal interests. At the same time, my aim is also theoretical.

My original attempt to disprove the persistent myth of the border region as a "no-man's-land" remains absurd. As a zone of tolerance or transgression, and more recently as an emblem for hybridity and multiculturalism, the region's appeal as a liminal zone is powerfully seductive. At first sight, I merely provide a "native view" by considering the actions and situations of people who engaged with the frontier condition of the region when its intermediary function between Mexico and the United States was being altered through NAFTA and related events. Beyond this focus on the region, I also examine the appeal of its representation as an emblem crystallizing the dislocating effects of globalization in other settings. In this respect, my aim is to elicit an epistemological reflection regarding the reconfiguration of boundaries and parameters due to globalization and the multiple transformations it implies with contradictory and inconclusive effects.

In discussing the compelling appeal of representations of the border region to sort out these reconfigurations, I point out that we face perplexing times not only because greater and more expedient transit, traffic, and communication link country to country, but because parameters of all sorts, both operational (time, space, symbols) and social (gender, class, nationality, age, sexual preferences, and so forth) are being redrawn. Baffling juxtapositions of the old and the new, the rich and the poor, and the West and the rest of the world, including both the advancements and regressions in civil rights, challenge our sense of order in the world and in our society, lending intense appeal to the overshadowing use of the image of the border as an allegorical figure. Thus, as we are confronted by perplexing contrasts, such as bell-bottoms mingling with punk outfits and saris in expensive shopping malls minutes away from dilapidated neighborhoods, we need to stop the frenzy and ask: Are we winning? Are we losing? Who are we? Are the rich better off when the magnitude of ostentation and comfort reaches unprecedented levels at the same time that their social well-being shrinks, constricted by violent and chaotic urban settings? What about when those settings are gentrified? Are the poor worse off when they can afford to sport the trendy tennis shoes of the month? These rather absurd questions obviously miss the point. However, by their blatant and simplifying excess, they dramatize pervasive analytical pitfalls. One such pitfall is the celebration of "border" or "hybrid" identities, while the dramatic worsening of regional poverty is trivialized and the asymmetrical character of "blendings" ignored. I hope my effort suggests a new way to look at how old and new parameters of these diverse dimensions overlap and fragment.

Many individuals have played very important roles in this manuscript and its writing. I start with the hundreds of people in Ciudad Juárez and El Paso who provided information or were participants in crucial experiences for my formulations of the insights I describe and analyze. I appreciate the help of Joe Old, Rick Rios, Charlie Ponzio, Cecilia Rodríguez, Cindi Arnold, Guillermo Glenn, Donald Michie, Marta Tovar, Cookie Mapula, Carlos Marentes, Willibaldo Delgadillo, Debbie Nathan, Susan Kern, Hector Holguin, Denise Bixtler-Márques, Alton Gilbert, Pete Duarte, Jeffrey Brannon, Donald Nibbie, Victoria Perea, Lucinda Vargas, Alicia Chacon, Ray Caballero, Elliot Sheppley, Manny Aldana, Homero Galicia, Tanny Berg, Barbara Péres, and Rudy Ortíz. I acknowledge the fraternal and crucial support of Leticia Hernandez-Ausbach and Walter Ausbach, as well as my soul sisters Caroll Fitzgerald, Leticia Ramos, Irma Reyes, Marta Berlanga, and my carnales Rene García, Enrique Reyes, and Daniel Postel. I recognize my heartfelt debt, never to be paid, to Beverly Ruth Taub and Amalia Cabezas. Likewise, my father, Ernesto Ortíz Jasso, and the spirit of my mother, Guadalupe

González, are always with me. Thanks to my brothers and sister for their love and their children. I am grateful for the support of Kristine Bartyzel, Kamilla Romaszewska, Janise Hurtig, Rodrigo Carramiñana, Robert Alvarez, Marc Zimmerman, Refugio I. Rochin, Dennis Nodin Valdés, George Collier, George and Louise Spindler, Jose Cuellar, Sarah Hoagland, Laura Lopez, Sylvia Puente, and Maricela Garcia. Special thanks to Manuel Arellano for his tireless assistance in the final phase of the editing of this book. My students MariCarmen Moreno, Susan Sabastian, Jose Munoz, Toni Medina, Andrew Bogan, and Sam Pastorello helped me with tedious and vital tasks, as well as inspiring me with their alert minds and friendship. I thank Dennis Judd for his faith in this work and Carrie Mullen and Anna Pakarinen for carrying it through the editorial board of the University of Minnesota Press.

The completion of this book could not have happened without diverse grants that the University of Illinois at Chicago gave me through the years. In particular, I acknowledge the crucial benefits I gained while a fellow at the Great Cities Institute and as a mentor in the McNair Program.

Muy especialmente, agradezco a Abigail y Edgardo Aguayo, cuyo amor abierto y grande mantiene a mi padre vivo y en mí la certeza de que la generosidad sin límites existe más allá de mi madre. Indeed, this book has been a wonderful opportunity to witness that people—beyond such artificial characterizations as class, race, ethnicity, nationality, gender, and age—are much bigger than their circumstances would seem to allow.

Introduction

Otherness and Globalization on the U.S.–Mexican Border and Beyond

Specter of Change

A specter of change roamed the border city of El Paso at the end of the 1980s, perhaps a specter of revolution such as Marx and Engels proclaimed in Europe a century and a half earlier. As Marx recognized, nevertheless, human beings make history, but not under conditions of their choosing. To begin with, in El Paso few if any of the revolutionary activities were inspired by a communist ideology. Instead, the movements arose in response to challenges and opportunities characteristic of globalization: the intensified interconnection of local settings with nonlocal flows. In an ambiguous climate of urgency about local challenges and excitement about global opportunities, the city's pervasive dislocation reached new plateaus. As a site of transit right at the center of the U.S.–Mexican border, this Texas city has always been global. Steady streams of people, trade, culture, and technology have shaped and reshaped local conditions in overwhelming ways. In the late 1980s, however, as the integration of the United States and Mexico intensified with the advent of the North American Free Trade Agreement (NAFTA), the city flirted with the possibility of transforming its intermediary function from within. Dictated not by outside forces and interests but promoted by emergent local leaders, collective alternative paths were tested to transform—"revolutionize"—the overriding subordination of the site to nonlocal processes.

At the westernmost point of Texas, at the edge of New Mexico and the Mexican state of Chihuahua, El Paso was the twenty-third largest city in the country with over 600,000 inhabitants. It was also one of its ten poorest cities, with only 58 percent of the national average per capita income figure. Attempts to control critical local developments were related to this mixture of economic and demographic growth in the midst of worsened poverty. Altered—if not necessarily new—interaction patterns emerged in terms of gender, ethnic, age, class, and national divisions, defining the contours of the spectral impression of revolutionary changes. New economic fortunes and success stories arose. Many of these stories involved women and people of Mexican ancestry or origin. Altering their traditional exclusion from positions of affluence and influence in the city, these individuals gained access to unprecedented opportunities for business and political prominence. In tandem with new technological innovations, the young also found enhanced occupational avenues. Similarly, a new sense of the interaction between the two countries, as manifested by NAFTA, prompted a new relation with the neighboring Mexican city of Ciudad Juárez.

All of these changes, as vivid and significant as they were, remained fragmented and precarious—leading to their spectral character. Some women, Mexican Americans, and Mexicans promoted and benefited from this "revolution," but they remained a numerical minority within their respective groups, which make up the majority of the total population. In turn, conditions for this largest group of residents worsened as poverty increased, along with unemployment and urban chaos. These proportional imbalances drastically mitigated the excitement about individual breakthroughs, despite their symbolic significance as markers of transcended barriers for the groups as a whole. Accordingly, new opportunities enjoyed by the young eluded most of their parents, condemning them to an even more impoverished labor market of dead ends, instability, and low pay. The individual successes paralleled the selective nature of the economic integration of Mexico and the United States, which in El Paso and the entire border region manifests itself in a dislocating coexistence of intensified trade exchanges and harsher measures to prevent the flow of people that the integration process uproots.

The specter of revolution in El Paso suggested in these fragmented changes points to complex transformations of social and economic relations in an environment of sharp local polarization and intensified global integration. How to assess these changes? How to make sense of fragmented outcomes and polarized effects? How to formulate effective democratic responses that enhance the breakthroughs and minimize unevenly distributed costs—which are increasingly defined by nonlocal events?

These questions are crucial for many cities around the world. Displacements and dislocations are not exclusive to El Paso, nor are they isolated events. On the contrary, because of the global character of the developments conditioning local challenges and opportunities, El Paso merely reflects with drastic clarity predicaments that have become common in most other urban centers. Multiple migratory waves, the relocation of factories by transnational corporations across the world, and intensified exchanges of products and services across boundaries reshape the meaning of national demarcations, as well as local social and cultural landscapes. All of these developments have overtaken El Paso, and thus are manifested in it with dramatic clarity. For more than four centuries the city has been shaped by a sequence of major transformations related to regional, national, and international integrations. From its origin as a resting point for Spanish explorers in the sixteenth century to its current state as a region transformed by post-NAFTA operations, the contiguous cities of El Paso and Ciudad Juárez have played instrumental roles in shaping the complicated intermediary character of the border region.

The Local, the Global, and the Blurs of a Postmodern Icon

The border region crystallizes the stunning ambiguities of globalization with blinding clarity. This international boundary links and divides the United States, an economic and military superpower, and Mexico, an industrializing country of rich cultural dimensions and many young people in need of opportunities for social mobility. To begin with, the region is in fact two regions: it is made up of two contiguous yet divided and asymmetrical national regions that overlap and, at the same time, distance each other. On the U.S. side, you have small cities such as Brownsville and Nogales, along with the large concentrations of El Paso and San Diego. On the Mexican side, you have cities like Matamoros, Ciudad Juárez, and Tijuana, which have grown at an even more accelerated pace than their U.S. counterparts in the past half century. All border cities serve as the stages for multiple flows of people, goods, materials, technology, and capital. Millions of people cross the border in both directions. Yet the flows reflect significant contrasts and contradictions. Some cross with official permits and some without them. In addition, the motives of the migrant coming north are different from those of the migrant going south. Trade between the two countries shows complexity and rapid growth. It encompasses a complicated range of products, from basic consumer goods to illegal drugs and from semimanufactured items to toxic waste. These multiple flows, agents, and agendas crisscross at the border region, which serves both as a bridge and a barrier. It is a transit ground as well as an interdiction site.

Global integration intensifies these fragmenting flows. In turn, the direct impacts of these exchanges and migrations are distinctly felt beyond the border with various degrees of clarity and intensity. Cities far away from the international boundaries increasingly experience cross-cultural contacts and multilocal relations involving the two countries. In Mexico, many rural towns and urban centers depend on remittances sent by transnational workers in the United States. In addition, more and more localities increasingly rely on U.S. products and technology. In the United States, Mexico plays an integral social and economic role. About 8 percent of the U.S. population has an ancestral or immediate connection to Mexico. Predominantly young, this group makes a visible imprint in education requirements, political balances, and labor markets. Southward flows differ strikingly from this group in geographical, generational, and class respects. For example, U.S. retirees relocate to Mexico's warm weather and concentrate in areas of Baja California, Guanajuato, Jalisco, and Oaxaca. Also moving southward, U.S. businesses cross the national boundary to use Mexican labor. In the past, the use of this labor pool took place only through the migration of workers to the United States. Since the mid-sixties, factories have relocated to Mexico through the maquiladora program, which allows foreign companies to establish manufacturing operations there.

In 1990, the two federal governments officially recognized this accelerated integration of migratory, production, and consumption flows through their negotiation of the North American Free Trade Agreement. The agreement eliminated trade barriers among Mexico, the United States, and Canada. For the United States and Mexico, NAFTA built on previous phases of economic integration. Their commercial exchanges even predate the establishment of the current international boundary. As early as the seventeenth century, a trade route, the Santa Fe Trail, linked Santa Fe, the largest settlement in the northernmost explorations of the Spanish Colony in the region at the time, with Mexico City (Timmons 1990, 29). Soon after the war the United States waged against Mexico, which finally established the current boundaries in 1850, Mexican workers were recruited to work in U.S. agricultural fields and in the construction of its railroad system. The boundary delimitation was not officially enforced until 1929 with the creation of the border patrol. A few years later, in 1942, Mexico and the United States signed a binational labor agreement, commonly known as the Bracero Program, to regulate the already established flow of Mexican workers. Two decades later, the United States unilaterally rescinded that agreement and the Mexican government implemented the maquiladora program. The program attempted to alleviate the mounting unemployment rates that the high concentration of prospective "braceros" generated in border cities. At first, the program provided fiscal incentives to companies in the United States and other countries to run manufacturing operations only in these cities. Since the early 1970s, foreign companies have been allowed to establish production plants in the entire country. Constant growth in these operations has translated into ever stronger links between the Mexican economy and U.S. industry.

NAFTA introduced new parameters into this sequence of expanding linkages. At the national level, it recognized the increasing volume of commercial and industrial transactions and provided a legal framework for regulating them. At the regional level, it paid heed to voices pointing to the disproportionate brunt of increasing flows on border cities. Beyond mere declarations, it established funds for a North American Development Bank with special provisions for the region. These measures, however, failed to fully acknowledge the character and extent of the exchanges, the role of the region, and the impacts of the flows on it. Instead, working from a neoliberal perspective, NAFTA negotiators treated economic exchanges as isolated from sociopolitical factors. Initial discussions left out immigration, environmental, and labor considerations. Eventually, as last-minute compromises, provisions were added to address only environmental and labor concerns. The reluctance to recognize the inherent impacts on immigration stems from the ambiguous role of the border region as both a bridge and a barrier. As a bridge, the border region was expected to experience a more manageable flow of people because of the increased employment opportunities that NAFTA would generate in Mexico. As a barrier, the border would witness curtailed immigration flows because of the existing policy of stricter border controls.

In its restricted optic, NAFTA further complicates the already complex intermediary role of the border. It has increased the volume of commercial transactions, as well as manufacturing and transportation activities. In addition, and contrary to unidimensional expectations, immigration has also increased because of the economic restructuring implicit in trade liberalization. In turn, measures to stop the flow at the border have only become harsher, without becoming more effective (Suro 1998, 329). Attempts to establish or implement effective official regulations have been overridden by the persistent imbalances between the two countries. Consequently, and typical of the times of spectral transformations in which we live, attempts to regulate exchanges have produced sharper irregularities in the border region through intended and unintended results. The regional dislocation becomes ever more costly in human terms.

The Production of the Border as an Eternal Frontier

Increased volumes of transactions and transit, on the one hand, and more obtrusive operations by border patrol and customs agents, on the other, deepen the border region's ambiguous role as a bridge and a barrier. At first sight, this dislocating situation can be seen as inevitable given the region's geographical position: the border is on the way to somewhere else. It happens to be a line of demarcation in a journey or an exchange. But is the region inherently or exclusively a transit area? We can easily attribute its intermediary function to geography alone. A closer look, however, leads us to realize that there is nothing inherent in any point on the map that alone determines the place's function. In fact, the intermediary function of El Paso, the oldest settlement in the region, was established in 1581, long before the republics of Mexico or the United States. History, as much as geography, gives the city its defining role. Yet it is also history as it occurs, not just in terms of past events and actions. For example, the ongoing NAFTA negotiations had immediate impacts on the region as they developed. To understand the nature and meaning of the region's intermediary function, we need to expand our understanding of the city beyond well-established assumptions that the border is inherently a transit zone. To start, we need to realize that the border is also the place of residence for millions of people who must contend with the dislocating condition of the region.

Henri Lefebvre provides an insightful conceptual scheme that can be applied to our assumptions about the border region. With the counterintuitive title *The Production of Space* (1991), his analysis rattles our firm tendency to see spatial arrangements as givens, as inert settings where history occurs. Instead, he shows that places are as much products of historical events as they are factors in those events. Space, Lefebvre says, is not a given but is "produced" by the social interactions that it conditions and that, in turn, transform it. This formulation disrupts the common-sense perception of space as a "container" in which history takes place (Soja 1989). Capturing the interactive dynamics of space and social dimensions, Lefebvre discusses the ways that multiple actions, approaches, and symbols mingle, with different forms of logic and diverse levels of influence, to "produce" space. Dramatic examples of the production of space are the Aztec city Tenochtitlán on the land-filled lake of Anahuac and the San Joaquin Valley in Southern California, which was transformed by irrigation from a desert to one of the most profitable arable regions in the world. Space does not lie inert, however. A disturbing example of the interaction of actions and approaches is the greenhouse effect, which is altering the Earth's temperature and climate.

According to Lefebvre, "Every society . . . produces . . . its own space" (31). In his scheme, space is both a social outcome and a factor composed of an interrelated triad of concepts referring to actions, ideas, and experiences. Actions involve "spatial practices." Ideas are "representation of space," and experiences occur in "representational spaces" (38). By "spatial practices" he means actions related to the physicality of space: its extensions, environmental conditions, availability of resources, accumulated buildings and constructions, demographic density, pathways, and so forth. He uses the notion of "representation of space" to refer to its designing as a mental construction, as a conception. This design and representation encompass urban policies, trade routes, real estate developments, industrialization projects, military plans, architectural designs, gardening projects, travel accounts, emblematic representations, and more. As a conception, space is designed, surveyed, imagined. He uses the third and last notion, "representational spaces," to refer to the existential meanings ascribed to space. As such, space functions as a code. It symbolizes and inspires through its deployment and its embodiment of historical events or particular attributes related to ethos or natural/material attributes: Philadelphia as the site of the signing of the Declaration of Independence, Middle Eastern countries as oil producers, Hawaii for its recreational beauty, and, currently, the border as a site of transit and transgression.

Although Lefebvre refers to these three analytical categories as "moments," from the Hegelian underpinnings of the analysis, their relationship is not linear. They are not necessarily either congruent or incongruent, complementary or contradictory. With either diffused or direct interrelations, they refer to different engagements. "Spatial practices" are operational, as in the practical dimensions of survival and everyday routines. "Representation of space" is transformative, as in the conceptualization of projects, regulations, and depictions. "Representational spaces" encompass the existential, as in the experiential connotations of sites: the relaxed enjoyment of the patio, the frantic excitement of the stadium, the solemnity of the church, or the chaos of the border. In a cryptic yet evocative way, Lefebvre refers to spatial practices as the perceived, to representation of space as the conceived, and to representational space as the lived (40).

The three categories can be readily illustrated in terms of El Paso. In fact, they can be teased out in the very name of the city. As previously mentioned, the initial settlement received its name over four centuries ago from its function as a conduit. In Spanish, the name *El Paso* can be translated as the passway and the step. Prophetically, it seems, Spanish explorers proclaimed much of its future spatial practices. The settlement remained a staging area for further explorations into the Spanish northern colony for a number of decades. Later, it also became a transit point on the Santa Fe Trail, which eventually linked Saint Louis, Missouri, to Mexico City. During the gold rush, thousands of hopeful miners passed through the city, already part of the United States, on their way to California (García 1981; Timmons 1990). In the 1880s the arrival of railroad lines made the city a hub for mineral and agricultural shipments between the two countries (García 1981). A few years later, during the Mexican Revolution, the city became a very important entry port for refugees and workers coming to the United States. The labor flows expanded, making El Paso an important source of labor for various industries and regions of the United States. This movement of workers was sanctioned by official provisions that exempted Mexican immigration from the restrictive measures of the 1917 and 1924 U.S. Immigration Acts. Two decades later, Mexico and the United States negotiated a labor agreement in effect from 1942 to 1964 (Martínez 1978), allowing temporary work permits to be granted to Mexican workers. These ever-expanding labor flows intensified the intermediary function of the city. In the past five decades, global rearrangements of manufacturing production have increasingly transformed the local economy of the city: first nationally, mainly through garment production, and then internationally, with the maquiladora industry. These developments were accompanied by increasing trade between the two countries, which, with NAFTA in place, has escalated to unprecedented levels.

This brief enumeration of important moments in El Paso's history highlights transit and transactions as the foremost spatial practices of the city. These practices perpetuate the condition of the city as an eternal frontier, an open space exposed to subsequent takeovers of diverse and expanding flows. Central to these takeovers are successive arrangements that entail the manipulation of the boundary in the use of Mexican labor. A mere transit point until the bracero program after World War II, El Paso became a major garment-manufacturing center when manufacturing operations were relocated from traditional industrial areas of the United States—the Rust Belt—to the southwest. This industry employed mostly women on both sides of the border. The contiguity of these populations, the relatively easy access to jobs in El Paso for Ciudad Juárez residents, and the comparatively higher wages on the U.S. side, created an abundant labor pool and pushed down wages. By the mid-1960s, a modification in the use of Mexican labor came about with the maquiladora industry. Companies relocated operations directly to Ciudad Juárez. Yet as rapid as the growth of the industry has been in that city, there have not been enough jobs to meet an unending flow of migrants from the interior of Mexico.

An abundant pool of workers remains a common feature in both cities. Unemployment in El Paso, which has been higher than in most other parts of the country, has fluctuated between 10 and 13 percent since the beginning of the 1980s. However, it acquired a particularly bitter twist in the early 1980s, when garment plants started to relocate operations to Mexico and Asia. With occasional and temporary recoveries, the garment industry finally dwindled by 1999. As garment workers were laid off, new economic activities in support of industries for maquiladora plants have created opportunities for other sectors of the city's population. Lawyers, accountants, engineers, and many business people have enjoyed unprecedented opportunities, while garment workers and less skilled workers have faced acute hardship. Again, the spatial practices generate the frontier condition of El Paso: an open space, a region defined by successive reconfigurations brought about by waves of immigrants and other transient flows and exchanges.

As with the suggestive coincidence between spatial practices and the name *El Paso* as a passway, the image of the frontier as a representational space also appears in the second meaning of the name, "the step." The city can be seen as a step in a progression, as the frontline of an impending fateful integration of the two countries. In the mass media, this conception was suggested by journalist Joel Garreau, who saw the border region as the epicenter of a blending of the two countries he called MexAmerica. Two years later, this impression was echoed by Bill Moyers in a special documentary he produced for PBS. Throughout the program, Moyers insistently repeats the central tenet stated in the title of the documentary: "The U.S.–Mexican Border: One River, One Country." Again and again, he states that the region is neither Mexico nor the United States, but an emergent geopolitical entity all its own. A few years later, the announcement and discussions of NAFTA gave tangible credence to this impression of ongoing integration. The image has outlasted the intense discussions over NAFTA. A similar characterization was revived by *Time* in a front-cover article on the region with the title "Welcome to Amexica" and the subhead "The border is vanishing before our eyes, creating a new world for all of us" (June 11, 2001).

Artistic and academic representations also foster a sense of dramatic blending. In the arts, Gloria Anzaldúa and Guillermo Gómez-Peña pioneered the depiction of the region as a site of hybridity and cross-fertilization. In academic circles, anthropologist Renato Rosaldo coined the notion of "border crossings" to address the undefined interaction patterns emerging in the multicultural condition of the United States. The celebrated Argentinean anthropologist Néstor García Canclini owes much of his current fame to his catchy formulation of Tijuana as a laboratory of postmodernity, one that reflects the juxtaposition of first- and third-world conditions in the city. Journalist Charles Bowden borrowed this characterization to depict Ciudad Juárez as "The Laboratory of Our Future." Other authors have proposed "border theories" to explain the unclear delineations of the interactions (Michaelsen and Johnson 1997; Welchman 1996). Drawing an even more direct link between this heuristic orientation and the image of the region, literary critic José Saldívar enthusiastically proposes the image of the "borderlands" as an analytical paradigm for multicultural and transnational contacts. In stark contrast, Charles Bowden's account dwells on sordid developments in Ciudad Juárez. He claims that such tragic degrees of pollution, poverty, and crime are bound to emerge in other settings given the rapacious activities of transnational corporations around the world.

Echoes of the frontier underlie these representations of the border. They construct characterizations of the region to decipher changes going on elsewhere. These authors use the image of the region as a space of representation for an unfolding future, much as the colonization of such a frontier is a step toward a given future. For some, such as Gómez-Peña and Anzaldúa, the border is a liberating environment in which new subjectivities are forged and arbitrary rules are transcended. For others, such as Bowden, the border is a disquieting future to be avoided. Within these extremes, other authors highlight the ambiguities of the region as an unclear or uncertain configuration. For all, whether stated or not, the border region is presented as an open space, a taken-over site that, ironically, they also overtake through their descriptive or figurative production of it as a representational space—as an allegory, that is—for the sake of somewhere else.

These representations closely relate to the experience of the border, its representational spaces in Lefebvre's terms. The determining spatial practices of trade and transit, and the use of the border as a space of representation also coincide with its experiential dimension as a step, not only in terms of a progression, but as in a stairway. As a stepping area, as a practical and figurative frontier, the border is, foremost, a site in the function of somewhere else. Local considerations and welfare are pervasively subordinated to the nonlocal. Overwhelmed by the region's linking role for transit and traffic, both legal and illegal, most of the interactions in the region are influenced by this intermediary function. The border's population is disproportionately affected by migration and trade flows. Its welfare and opportunities are overridden by national and international developments and measures. Immigration laws and currency devaluations, for example, have shattering local effects. In addition, much of the economic life of border cities depends on decisions made by companies elsewhere. Finally, transient populations of migrants, tourists, and business agents deeply and extensively affect the border's social life. In turn, the city's residents have little or no significant say in most of these policies, decisions, and migratory flows.

A Crossroad at a Crossroad

Do Mexico and the United States actually blend at the border? If so, to what extent and what are the consequences? Answers to these questions are complicated not only by the asymmetries between the two countries, but by the contradictory developments of globalization. We face contradictory mirages of advances and regressions, or continuity and chasms. For example, within the same contested logics of displacement and breakthroughs, the enhanced operational proximity of the two countries is qualified by cultural, social, and economic distances deeply related to their political asymmetries. These asymmetries, moreover, are not monolithic. Beyond the misleadingly easy characterization of the first world and third world divide, fragmentations and polarizations in each country surpass neat demarcations or simplistic amalgamations (Spener and Staudt 1998; Ruíz and Tiano 1987). Contrary to unexamined generalizations of the United States as a rich country and Mexico as a poor one, severe poverty and inequality pervade the United States, particularly in cities like El Paso. Likewise, not everybody in Mexico is poor. In recent years, both countries have experienced severe polarization in which the gaps between their rich segments and their poor ones have widened. At the same time, the scope of this polarization has become more complex as members of excluded groups (as the case of El Paso shows) have found enhanced opportunities for mobility.

Manifesting the specter of change, along with the interplay of displacements and breakthroughs, the geographical immediacy of cities like Ciudad Juárez and El Paso is disrupted by long delays in crossing through the inspection point of the United States. The disruption of the functional and geographical immediacy of the two cities occurs as the distance from remote places is lessened by technological or legislative breakthroughs. These incongruent or peculiar interconnections only underscore the separations—the "distant proximities"—of the region in the same way that individual breakthroughs underscore polarization.

The pervasive subordination of the local to the nonlocal has exacted a cost that endangers the viability of the border's legendary intermediary function, particularly when the parameters of the integration of the two countries have shifted with NAFTA. At the same time, these new parameters have also offered opportunities that required a new level of integration of the site as a whole. Thus, winners and losers face the common challenge of engaging with a new production of El Paso beyond the spatial practices that subordinate the local to the nonlocal. The corresponding space of representation that is always in the function of somewhere else is becoming too costly to bear in the face of massive displacements in which workers have seen their jobs relocated, as it has looked to them, to maquiladora plants in Ciudad Juárez, only a few miles across the international divide.

The city, which has been a preeminent crossroad throughout its history, faces its own crossroad. In this ethnography, I trace five initiatives advocating for spatial practices that would have secured greater local control over the city's fate through wider participation and more inclusive scopes of collaboration. Based on a generalized recognition of challenges and opportunities, the initiatives shared a sense of urgency and possibility. Their strategies aimed to leverage the integration process to ameliorate the dislocation impacts on the city. Displaced garment workers led one of the initiatives. These workers mobilized under the leadership of La Mujer Obrera, a labor-advocacy group that primarily promotes the rights and opportunities of garment workers, most of whom are women. This group's strategy centered on upgrading the established infrastructure the city had developed in garment production for the national market since the 1950s. Faced with closures and relocations, the labor group sought to position the city as a major center for the international manufacture of women's apparel.

Two of the other four initiatives promoted business strategies that addressed the infrastructure deficit of the region—although with different social priorities. One of these business initiatives was a multimillion-dollar venture that involved investors from different countries. Conceived and coordinated by a real estate agent who had resided in the city since the 1960s, the venture attempted to develop a massive industrial park right along both sides of the border. This megaproject integrated infrastructure elements to prevent mounting transportation, energy, and housing problems that afflicted the existing industrial parks. The second initiative advocated the development of a much wider industrial base that would make the border region the mid-tech manufacturing center of the impending American common market that NAFTA presaged. This strategy was promoted by midsize entrepreneurs under the leadership of a business professor, with support from city and state officials.

The last two initiatives had broader, yet more direct, social goals. One involved a group of Mexican American entrepreneurs who founded the Hispanic Chamber of Commerce in spite of tough opposition from the established business elite, which was overwhelmingly made up of Euro-Americans. The chamber sought to promote Latinos to positions of power in the local hierarchies. The chamber also called for an economic plan for the city that addressed its pauperization process, in which the percentage of Mexican American families living at the poverty level increased from 29 percent in 1979 to 43 percent by 1989. The final initiative was spearheaded by Unite El Paso, a multiethnic group made up of mostly middle- and upper-class professionals in their thirties and forties. Unite El Paso organized several very successful meetings involving people from many different ethnic groups, helping to foster a unified and unifying vision. Members of Unite El Paso eventually played instrumental roles in a legal battle against the state of Texas, demanding a proportionally balanced allocation of funds for public services to the city.

Mobilized as a response to a particular conjuncture, the five initiatives were distinguished by their different constituencies. Each initiative dealt with contrasting conditions that qualified the organizing group's responses and priorities. The desperate apprehension of workers losing their jobs was analogous to, yet not the same as, the concern of entrepreneurs or industrial park owners whose businesses would suffer if maquiladora operations left the region due to infrastructure deficits. The level of resources and the range of options made a significant difference among the diverse groups and individuals regarding the impacts of changes for them and their capacity to respond. Therefore, the possibility of convergence was deeply affected by the asymmetries among the five groups.

The differing scopes and priorities of the five initiatives illustrate the groups' divergent scopes of operation. These divergences reflect complex parameters and delimitations. These parameters are not confined to the local setting, as distant power centers of government and business play overwhelming roles in defining policies that manipulate or reformulate those parameters—seldom with any priority given to the impact on border residents. Equally influential is the aggregate impact of individual migrants, tourists, and other transient visitors, who also "produce" the city as an open space, a frontier to be instrumentally used with little concern for what is already in place. What are the meanings of these changes? How should we assess these complex developments and entanglements swept in the overriding waves of globalization?

Distant Proximities and Local Frontiers: Between Blurs and Overlaps

As multiple parameters and delimitations come to a new and more intense juncture, perplexing and unresolved juxtapositions gain salience. Aside from more expedient flows of capital, merchandise, and people, new demographic and social geometries alter the patterns of interaction in most settings, generating unresolved outcomes and dynamics. David Harvey's recognition of the alteration in our experience of time and space is quite pertinent to our understanding of reconfigured parameters. Addressing the effects of technology and competition to highlight a "new modality of capital accumulation," Harvey coined the notion of "space-time compression" to point to a new experiential and operational relation between these two categories/factors of human existence (Harvey 1989). As communication and transportation technologies have allowed for ever more efficient connections and transactions, our sense of the world and our participation in it have shifted. This alteration, for most observers it seems, is perceived as a shrinking of the world and an enlargement of human reach over it. The Internet, transnational immigration, trade agreements among distant places, and so forth, create the sense that one is inevitably global (Giddens 2000). The representational space of the world as a whole provides an unprecedented sense of proximity. The exhilaration of this proximity, however, remains virtual for many.

Robert Reich also provides another important insight to make sense of the reconfigured parameters. He points out that noneconomic factors, such as ethnicity, gender, age, and nationality, play a lesser role as barriers for access to economic opportunities in a world market reshaped by intensified competition (Reich 1991b). On the one hand, globalization entails reconfigured parameters of access to opportunity. On the other hand, the enhanced access does not benefit everybody equally. On the contrary, in reshaped markets, sharper polarizations ensue as the new parameters of opportunity also work as delimitations in new scenarios of competition. While the success stories in El Paso attest to Reich's insight, the more extensive downside of the development—the losing side of the same coin/city—also attests to the pernicious polarization process that he and other authors warn about as an inherent factor of ongoing developments (Bauman 1998; Gray 1998).

This reconfiguration of the relationship between space and time, on the one hand, and the delineation of inequality in the more abstract form of capitalism on the other, brings up the need to revisit Lefebvre's conceptualization of space. The scope and immediacy of spatial practices have been altered. Expediency has increased and distances have contracted. Yet, they have not changed equally for everybody. Take the cases of David Norris and Alicia Armendariz in the city of El Paso. A former plant manager, Norris is now co-owner and editor of *Twin Plant News*, the main publication of the maquiladora industry, with a distribution of ten thousand issues in seven countries. Initially, the focus of the magazine was limited to the northern border of Mexico because it was the area of operation specified by the Mexican government for maquiladora operations at the onset of the program. This restriction was eliminated in 1972, yet it was not until the early 1980s that offshore manufacturing operations significantly expanded into the interior of that country. The enactment of NAFTA gave this trend additional impetus. Following the industry's expansion, Norris's magazine now dedicates entire issues to states in Mexico's interior.

Norris's expansion of the focus—and market—of his magazine contrasts with Armendariz's readiness to adapt to shifting confines. Armendariz is a displaced garment worker who lost her job in the waves of relocations that the industry has experienced in the city since the early 1980s. Unlike Norris, Armendariz appears less able to contend with the new arrangement, let alone profit from it. She had to depend on welfare, which she resented, and relocate to the outskirts of the city. Even more painfully, she had to give up the custody of her three-year-old to her ex-husband when he relocated to West Virginia to follow a job opportunity after he had also been laid off in El Paso. Though residents of the same city, Norris and Armendariz experience its reconfiguration in dramatically different ways. The intensified integration of the city into global markets displaced Armendariz, who could not relocate because her two children from a previous marriage would be left behind in El Paso, and favored the expansion of Norris's business. At this individual level, their contrasts reflect different social positions and differing abilities to successfully face the changes that will come as globalization intensifies the dislocation of this already dislocated site.

Zygmunt Bauman refers to this divide in terms of vagabonds and tourists, distinguishing their contrasting ability to adapt to the ongoing changes of globalization. Armendariz would be a vagabond, while Norris and the other members of the five initiatives would be tourists. The displaced worker lost her hold on unfolding events. She was disoriented and displaced. Norris and the like, as tourists, were able to ride the waves of change instead of being displaced by them. They could activate sets of privileges that the displaced, the vagabonds, did not have access to because of a lack of money, knowledge, skills, or social capital. As suggested by Reich, the divide is not just one of class, gender, or nationality, but is rather existential. Out of place, in figurative and literal terms, vagabonds exist in time, according to Bauman. They are confined to the outer realms of society through unemployment, poor neighborhoods, inadequate education, and social stigmas. With no place to go, vagabonds have time to waste. They are spatially poor but, because they are unoccupied, they have no restriction of time. Tourists face the inverse situation. They exist in space. They enjoy great mobility due to ample spatial choices. Yet, with many places to go, time is at a premium.

Bauman's characterization points to a widespread divide that is reshaping social arrangements around the world in ways evocative of Reich's description. Beyond the traditional demarcations of race, class, gender, nationality, and age, a new geometry of inequality arises with volatile or unclear delimitations. In this new modality of otherness, the five initiatives of El Paso illustrate that not all "tourists" are rich or Euro-Americans or male. Mexican Americans, displaced workers, and women have taken it upon themselves to mobilize within the new parameters of economic activities to redirect the future of the city. Their venturing into the information age, a dimension driven by symbols, sets them apart from vagabonds, as the case of displaced workers attests. These workers stand in the industrial age, a space and time overtaken by the information age.

The blurring effect of global interconnections does not override the local frontiers, however. In El Paso, these frontiers manifest themselves not only in the discrepant resources of the five initiatives, but also in the incommensurable local and global dimensions. While the initiatives overlap in their analogous efforts to redirect the economic role of the city in its intermediary function, they pursued their goals, generally, in isolation from each other, and, at times, even in competition with each other. The local frontiers entailed, therefore, more than venturing into new realms of economic and social possibilities. Venturing itself took place in a climate of precarious yet almost inevitable autonomy. The precariousness was generated by the pervasive subordination of the local to the nonlocal that undermines the social institutions required for coordinated action to take root. The resulting dislocating condition of the site, on the one hand, allowed the diverse groups to come to a relative agreement on their overlapping strategies. Yet, on the other hand, the strategies did not lead to concerted efforts. Discrepant levels of resources and contrasting priorities reinforced frontierlike autonomies.

This intensified configuration of unresolved blurs and overlaps occurs within the larger context of dramatic divisions between "tourists" and "vagabonds." The widening distance between their operational realms, in terms of time and space, takes place within sites of ever more complicated parameters. The disparities of increasing social distance from increased economic polarization are underscored by the greater levels of residential contiguity brought about by urban gentrification. A conglomeration of "distant proximities" arises: incommensurable differences are compressed into immediate yet abysmal proximity. In global respects, vagabonds' dwellings are confined blocks away from the tourists' home base. At the local level of the border site of El Paso, proponents of the five initiatives described in this ethnography converged in their overall goal yet diverged in their strategies and priorities.

From Space to Hyperspace: Alienated Instrumentalities of the Border

The dramatic overtones of global dislocations fuel the allegorical appeal of the U.S.–Mexican region. The border is conceived as a new sociopolitical entity in which new subjectivities are forged, becoming a paradigm for understanding the changes in other sites. These appealing characterizations, however, fail to acknowledge the prevailing subordination of the local residents to nonlocal developments and interests. In this subordination, most of the benefits accrued from the geographical position of the border have been taken away from the region's residents. In turn, residents contend with a skewed share of the costs of providing the services or resources for the intermediation. This "alienated instrumentality" is pervasive. It shows the wear and tear of transportation networks due to excessive traffic, along with their corresponding environmental and urban impacts. For example, only a fraction of the considerable amounts collected in transit tolls at international crossing points comes back from the federal governments into border cities. Yet, border cities experience heavy traffic of products and materials produced and consumed in cities away from them. The direct and indirect costs of this transit are paid for by the local populations in terms of traffic bottlenecks, pollution, and chaos. Another case of alienated instrumentality shows in the promotion of economic activities that cater to nonlocal markets or visitors at the expense of local needs, autonomy, and stability. A salient example is the case of the maquiladora industry. While companies save large amounts of money in production costs, the already underfunded and precarious local economies are left to cope with the social, and much of the financial, burden of infrastructure deficits. Needless to say, much of this exploitation is borne on the backs of the most vulnerable residents of the cities—such as maquiladora workers, undocumented workers, prostitutes, displaced workers, and the working poor.

The border region is always a function of somewhere else. This pervasive subordination of the local to the nonlocal has given place to the alienated instrumentality of the border for centuries. However, this alienated instrumentality is now occurring at the level of compelling symbols, in hyperspace. Situations of distant proximity generated by the region's overriding intermediary function are being allegorically used to cope with the shock of globalization. Impressionistic accounts are "invoked" as spaces of representation to "paradigmatically" make sense of perplexing configurations—specters of change—in any setting. In turn, the concrete appreciation of the region is occluded along with the people and situations that do not fit the paradigmatic construction.

Claims of hybridity and paradigmatic uses not only replicate the instrumental use of the region for the benefit of somewhere else, but distract from the region's contextual particularities and transformations. More importantly, they erase the local residents while influencing the perceptions and expectations of policymakers, visitors, and company managers of the region, which remains a frontier, an open space for constant takeovers. As with any other instance of exploitation of the region's alienated instrumentalities, the exploitation is occluded in the very erasing of the region. In other words, "paradigmatic" uses are made in terms of very selective allusions to the region and this selectivity precludes the recognition of the very subordination exploited. The implicit erasure of the region also hides its alienated instrumentality, now also made at the level of the hyperreal.

Yet is the border region also a frontier for the millions of people residing in it? Most likely, the way the region is experienced by transient visitors, such as prospective immigrants or tourists, is different from the way it is experienced by border patrol agents, middle-class housewives, or their maids. As the cases of Armendariz and Norris reflect, the border is experienced in contrasting representational spaces: one in space and the other in hyperspace. Spatial practices, representational spaces, and spaces of representation converge at the border, yet they do not merge. Contrary to the seductive claim of hybridity, the proximity of these spaces does not make them blur, but opens deeper distances, even when the delineations of the polarizations are being altered.

Cognitive and experiential parameters, in general, are delimitations often overlooked in the allure of a unified world proclaimed by the marketers of globalization, who range from business promoters to academicians excited by their privileged mobility. These differences are occluded in the blurring image of the border as an allegory. Ironically, in this figurative use, the image is produced and consumed in the same new realm of the information age where Norris's opportunities also occur. Symbols create powerful impacts. They define the parameters of the real in the representational spaces they produce. They influence policies and expectations. For example, laws are formulated or precluded in reference to a given sense of the border, in this case as a frontier. Consequently, other laws and orientations are dismissed or irregularly implemented or observed. In similar fashion, some local residents also have access to this new mobility and expediency of contact. Along with Norris, the five initiatives also had access to wider scopes of knowledge and networks beyond the city. Unlike the case of Armendariz, they operated in this information age, albeit with different proficiencies and with contrasting results. Armendariz was still caught in the industrial society. Her access to resources and employment became obsolete.

The passage from an industrial to an information society contributes to the crisscross of breakthroughs and polarizations that challenge conventional delineations. Lefebvre's conceptualization of space allows us to distinguish the diverse dimensions of interactions that generate the cognitive dissonances or, figuratively, the optic refractions of the specter of revolution. While diverse groups and settings have converged for centuries at the border region between the United States and Mexico, its defining spatial practices of transit and trade have intensified in recent years to unprecedented levels and scopes. The altered relation of space and time recognized by Harvey occurs at this passage from an industrial to an information society. An industrial society is situated in defined spaces and crystallizes in concrete products. An information society is much more defuse. It is articulated in hyperspace, where the imminent replaces the immediate, much as the local is subordinated to the nonlocal in the border.

Hyperspace entails the subordination of spatial practices to representational spaces. It subsumes spatial practices to their representations. In the case of the border region, through the emphasis of transgressions and chaos, the alluring representation of the region sidesteps an analytical engagement with the conditions generating the transgressions and the chaos. At the same time, hyperspace also allows for an expanded space of representations in which an increasing number of accounts coexist, even when their circulation is uneven and they do not interact. The compelling appeal of the image of the border as a hybrid zone par excellence, as alluring as it has proven in academic and artistic circles, does not hold much interest for empirically oriented scholars or residents of the border. It certainly did not inspire the actions of the local residents engaged in the five initiatives described.

Along with these contrasts, another important consideration arises: in the various and elastic interconnections "producing" El Paso, the polarized distinction between local and nonlocal becomes problematic. Are the locals those born in the city? Those who have lived many years in it? Or those who have invested their lifelong savings in it? Who are the locals in this accidental territory of fluxes and displacements? And likewise, who are the nonlocals in this overridden open space? Are the nonlocals the transient visitors, the tourists, the truck drivers transporting products and materials back and forth, or the shoppers from the interior of Mexico during seasonal sprees? Is the maquiladora worker who migrated to Ciudad Juárez and eventually became an undocumented maid in El Paso a nonlocal? Or the maquiladora manager from Ohio temporarily residing in El Paso during an assignment of three years? What about people like my father? He arrived in Ciudad Juárez from Guadalajara to cross without permit into the United States. Instead he settled in Ciudad Juárez and eventually began crossing the border every day with a residence permit to work in El Paso for the past thirty years. What about people like me? Am I a local or a nonlocal, having been born in El Paso, raised in Ciudad Juárez, and then leaving the area twenty years ago, yet still writing about it?

Parameters and delineations are both pervasive and elusive in El Paso. Adjacent to an international boundary, delimitations proliferate in the city, making them at once unavoidable and virtually unsustainable. Permeated by multiple intensified differences, ranging from nationality and class to senses of belonging and social engagement, parameters are challenged and manipulated as much as they are defended and policed. Thus, a maquiladora promoter is outraged by bureaucratic red tape from the Mexican government preventing him from traveling at the spur of the moment to the interior, while oblivious to the human drama of undocumented crossing and the militarization of the border. Discrepancies are overlooked as some "boundaries" are more of a "barrier" for some people than others, and for different reasons. Yet, practically everybody on the border deploys their own manipulations of boundaries. This ambivalent role as a bridge and a barrier is the distinctive characteristic of the city, fostered by the overwhelming subordination of the local to the nonlocal.

The collapse of diverse parameters—and thus of frames of reference—produces the spectral character of the manifestations of ongoing changes. We experience a referential chaos. Our conceptual capacities to make sense of these changes are in shock. This book proposes a case study to ascertain the magnitude of the conceptual challenge at stake, hopefully in a way in which diverse discussions from diverse disciplines can converge. Based on the holistic character of my anthropological approach, philosophical, sociological, and geographical reflections are oriented toward social theory in general or international and border studies in particular.

The approach of this book is both very concrete and very abstract.

In its concrete approach the book documents and analyzes five initiatives in a specific city. It describes the agents, the priorities, the resource levels, and the outcomes of each initiative. It looks at these partial changes and arrested transformations in an effort to highlight human costs and the character of the involvements. Given the distance each initiative has kept from the others, I show how they refract and reflect each other. I ask about the contrasting interpretations and skills setting them into divergent paths, which are oriented toward different ways of being global while inevitably remaining local. In global terms, the book concerns the common ground and general horizon of the initiatives. In local terms, it concerns their standing on a situation of the displacement they try to modify. In this interplay of the global and the local, the account examines the parameters of the revolutionary specter to gain some point of reference in the kaleidoscopic developments of globalization for El Paso and the border region.

From a wider perspective, the focus of the book is not only a city but the decreasing level of autonomy of most cities. Not an allegory but merely a case study, the account reflects widespread contextual changes characterized by displacements and dislocations. Yet, it also presents creative initiatives generated by concrete human beings and the asymmetries and divides that prevail and even widen in spite of the integrative trend of globalization. In this broader light, the spectral character of change is more complex as wider parameters of time and space come into consideration. New insights and questions arise once the overwhelming bearing of global process in the city is recognized in many other cities as a phenomenon of globalization. Through this prism, one can see that specters are more than optical illusions. They reflect a given projection that shocks spectators as they witness a perplexing manifestation that overrides given conceptions.

The book is structured along Lefebvre's conceptualization of space as socially constructed. Chapter 1, "Between an Image and a Hard Place," looks at the city as a space of representation in terms of the image of the U.S.–Mexico border turned into a compelling allegory. The figurative character of the cognitive response reflects the shock of a transition from space to hyperspace. I look at the hyperreal representation of the border region and the connections of the representation with the concrete lives and condition of its residents. I trace the formulation of an intertextual image of the border as a composite of various, incongruent accounts and perceptions that coalesce and influence local conditions and global uses. I argue that most policies, representations, and incursions are greatly influenced by—if not completely restricted to—this stereotyping construction. I point to a persistent and pervasive interplay between recognition and erasure in accounts of, practices in, and engagements with the region. Pointing to the figurative use of the legendary image of the border as a site of transgression, I argue that this usage is another instance of the alienated instrumentalities that perpetuate the region's frontier condition. I look at three pioneers of the heuristic figure, Gloria Anzaldúa, Renato Rosaldo, and Néstor García Canclini. Acknowledging their significant contribution to the recognition of otherness, I point to the cost of emblematic representation of the border for the region, as well as for our understanding of the impacts and modalities of globalization. I question the elucidating value of the allegory at this point in time when it has become a cliché.

Chapter 2, "Undermining Reality," looks at El Paso as a representational space. It describes it as an experiential context overridden by persistent fissures. Residential, class, ethnic, national, and operational boundaries are highlighted to add a more measured perspective to the intensified proximity of otherness in the city. This acute sense of otherness is illustrated in terms of—and to a large extent attributed to—INS operations and the effects of their rampant persecution of undocumented immigrants. Through a handful of poignant cases of alleged violence, I illustrate the effects that such practices have had on most local residents' sense of belonging and entitlement. I show that these practices criminalize many ordinary interactions and thus have torn apart the social fabric of the setting. In this disarray, social aggregates coexist in an estranged setup in which economic connections are fostered while social linkages are thwarted. This perplexing and mobile grid of estrangement and alienated instrumentalities serves as the background for understanding the diverse initiatives for altering the intermediary role of the city—the specter of revolution. These efforts implicitly and explicitly embrace the creation and reinforcement of community in light of the asocial effects of the city's subordination.

Chapter 3, "La Vista Grande: The Common Ground of Displacements and Breakthroughs," is the first of two chapters on spatial practices, the third analytical category proposed by Lefebvre. It looks at three strategies for reshaping the labor market of the city. It contrasts the situation of displaced female garment workers with the prominent new public roles and business successes of other women in the city. Underscoring technical and capital factors, the discussion expands the contrast with two other initiatives. One was a failed project to develop an international industrial zone on the outskirts of El Paso and Ciudad Juárez. The other was an ambitious plan to develop the region into a mid- to high-technology manufacturing zone for the entire hemisphere. The contrasts show that while the convergence and divergence of these three initiatives surpassed rigid ideological delineations, their strategies emphasized different priorities and constituencies. Ultimately, their shared effort to upgrade the economic opportunities in the city was undermined by the site's frontier condition, given overriding imbalances between local and global requirements, on the one hand, and local divisions, on the other.

Chapter 4, "Local Democracy and Global Demography: New Parameters of Community," is the second chapter describing spatial practices. It discusses two additional initiatives in terms of class and ethnicity. The Hispanic Chamber of Commerce promoted a small business strategy to confront worsening poverty in the city. Similar efforts, though greater in scope, were promoted by Unite El Paso, which sought to become a vehicle for innovative and all-inclusive leadership. Both efforts addressed the various fissures disrupting the sense of community in the city discussed in chapter 2. Displaying a remarkable degree of commitment and effectiveness, both groups were able to generate activities that fostered a closer nexus among the diverse constituencies of the city. However, their scope and degree of successes, while still ongoing, have been limited by the severe discrepancies between the local and global levels of resources and decision-making capacities.

The conclusion, "El Paso as an Eternal—Yet Not Final—Frontier," highlights the global dimensions of the dislocations and baffling reconfigurations described in the case studies. While their occurrence relates to the intensification of international competition, they also reflect the reformulation of the parameters of competition itself and thus of community. In the so-called more flexible accumulation process, national and social parameters are becoming more diffuse, posing the challenge of understanding new modalities of otherness. Countering the unrestrained and uncritical use of the border image to address the new modalities of otherness at the expense of the recognition of border situations, I conclude by proposing a different conceptual figure. I propose that the border can be conceived as a sphere upon which surfaces function as a distorting play of reflections. On its inner concave surfaces, the sphere reflects local contrasts between the two contiguous settings of each country. Thus, the two border cities present to each other diametric inversions of their complex spectrum of distances (e.g., animosities and asymmetries) and proximity (e.g., contiguities and similarities). On the outer convex surfaces, each border city reflects the inverse image of its respective country. For example, Mexico's northern border cities have some of the highest per capita incomes in the country, while most U.S. border cities have some of the lowest in the United States. Building on these local and national interpolations, I point to the historical tensions between the ambivalent attitude of Mexico toward its boundary as a *frontera,* both a buffer and a contact zone, and the also ambiguous expansion and containment of the U.S. frontierlike orientation. At the moment, these overlapping nation-making myths implode in the border image. This implosion both reveals and conceals the inherent interplay between the overriding gigantic magnitude of globalization and the multiple reconfigured or redeployed parameters. In these overriding changes, and the asymmetries they reinforce and transform, global integration inherently entails local disintegration and reintegration.

Methodology

I have been exposed and subjected to these complex demarcations throughout my life. I was born in El Paso, but spent most of my childhood in Ciudad Juárez. I learned of the crisscrossed asymmetries while attending third grade at an elementary school in El Paso after two years of schooling in Ciudad Juárez. Contrary to pretenses and stigmas, I grasped at this early age that I was (dis)placed on an inferior education track in the United States, one in which, for example, math was taught at a torturous pace. The subject that had made me look forward to the next school day in the so-called third world became a bore in the supposedly more advanced first world. Because of the frustration of the situation, I sensed the incongruence in generalized assumptions. In recent years, the incongruences have become clearer in terms of winners and losers in the city, but more complex in terms of the backgrounds and gender characteristics of the two. In the thirteen years that I have researched and reflected on the situations described in this book, I have come to learn that the puzzles are not only more dynamic but also heavily dependent on individual engagements and interpretations.

The specific, direct collection of data, notes, and interviews for this study started in 1987, as a preliminary summer research period for my dissertation, when I did an internship with a grassroots organization documenting abuses by the INS. That preliminary research period was followed by seven additional periods of fieldwork. Three of these periods were done as fieldwork for my doctoral dissertation, which I completed in June 1993, five months before NAFTA went into effect. These three phases included a nine-month period from April 1990 to January 1991, a one-month visit in April 1991, and a final one-month visit in April 1993. In September of that year I visited with fourteen of my key informants after they had read my dissertation. I made presentations of my study to a class at the university and to a group of Mexican American professionals. In the summer of 1996, I spent one month in El Paso doing archival newspaper research and visiting with eight of my key informants to ascertain the feasibility of updating my dissertation manuscript according to the new developments brought about by NAFTA. The following year, 1997, three years after the implementation of NAFTA, I spent six months in El Paso reinterviewing many of my previous informants, in addition to interviewing new subjects.

From 1990 to 1997, I conducted 225 interviews with 197 individuals. I conducted 116 open-ended interviews with a total of 102 people for my dissertation and, since July 1993, I have conducted an additional 121 interviews with 87 individuals. I interviewed 26 of these subjects a number of times during various visits, which provided a significant degree of consistency in my ability to follow events and allowed me to examine their insights and perceptions as they evolved. All the interviews were conducted in English with the exception of twelve, in which the informants preferred Spanish. The thrust of these interviews concerned the sociopolitical impact of the integration of the local economy into national and international markets, and more specifically the feasibility of a transition of the city from a low-cost production center to a high-tech production one. I supplemented the information gathered in these interviews with secondary sources, including newspaper clippings and academic works on the history and economy of the city. I also used information from local government offices and the U.S. Census.

I had access to the records and activities of four of the five initiatives described, which serve as the central focus of two of the most ethnographically oriented chapters of the book: the labor advocacy group, the entrepreneurial group, the Mexican American Chamber of Commerce, and the professional group advocating local consensus. I participated in activities organized by three of these groups: (1) demonstrations and workers' meetings organized by the labor advocacy groups; (2) networking and community events organized by the Hispanic Chamber of Commerce; and (3) NAFTA forums organized by or involving members of the entrepreneurial group. Unfortunately, my visits to the city always coincided with moments in which the fourth group experienced low levels of activity.

All names of people, with the exception of nonlocal public officials and the four groups, are pseudonyms selected according to the general ethnic backgrounds of the informants (e.g., Martínez for García and Kelly for Harris). In terms of ethnic labels, my prevalent use of the term *Mexican American* clouds the diverse ethnic labels used by and for the population of Mexican ancestry or origin in the city (Vila 1998, 185). However, I used *Mexican, Mexicano, Chicano, Hispanic,* or *Latino* in agreement with the usage of interviewees. The same clouding effect, unfortunately, occurs with the term

Euro-American. I used this term as an umbrella label to refer to all groups and individuals who are not of Mexican but rather of European ancestry or origin. I use this newer term, *Euro-American,* because it is more inclusive than the often-used *Anglo,* and I have consciously avoided the term *American,* which excludes, or at least effaces, Mexican Americans. I am aware, however, that I am still effacing African Americans, Asian Americans, Native Americans, and even Latin Americans. I apologize for these blurring erasures—an ironic twist to a book that aims to formulate our way out of overshadowing generalizations. On this note, I underscore the tenuousness of the endeavor and the vastness of the delineations to address. The following chapter undertakes the task of highlighting a similar oversight of the border region.

1

Between an Image and a Hard Place

A Persistent Misencounter

I have seen them many times. A middle-aged blonde couple. She was wearing a loose-fitting pair of black nylon pants and a black and white blouse. He was wearing a white shirt and blue jeans. I was eighteen, five blocks away from home, on the main drag of my city, Ciudad Juárez. What were they doing there? I think I know, but I don't. What was I doing there? I was with Winnie, my high-school karate buddy, at the intersection of the main avenue of the city, La Avenida 16 de Septiembre, named in commemoration of Mexico's Independence Day. When I was growing up, that four-lane avenue was colloquially referred to as *la dieciseis* (the sixteenth). By my high school days, it was *la sixtin* for many of us. It was where middle-class teenagers drove around endlessly on Sunday afternoons in a motorized urban reenactment of the plaza courtship rituals of small towns. We called this mating game *sixtinear* (to sixteen). That summer day, a bit after six o'clock, Winnie was waiting for the bus home, and we were chatting about the karate tournament a week away. Somehow, despite my absorption in the conversation, I noticed them, an Anglo couple coming our way, the wrong way, away from the tacitly agreed-upon boundary of the tourist marketplace four blocks away. As tourists, they were supposed to stay in that sheltered zone carved out for the trivial consumption of our Mexicanness, for sale in the form of useless overpriced trinkets, wool blankets and sweaters, sleeping-Mexican ashtrays, and maracas—all merchandised amid mariachis, margaritas, and tequila sours.

Seldom would you see "them" venture beyond their prescribed terrain. "Them" were mostly Euro-Americans, but sometimes "them" included African Americans or Mexican Americans, sporting shorts, cameras, and what appeared to us as a stubborn resistance to speaking Spanish. That resistance was as strong as their casually assumed certainty that we spoke English. Anyway, I kept an alert eye on this straying couple. As Winnie and I went on talking, I discreetly—not wanting to lose my cool or appear servile—tried to figure out how to tell them, in a phrase composed from my four semesters of English, that there were no tourist attractions in that direction. They kept strolling at a leisurely pace, carefree and at ease, into this new (to them) and uncharted territory. I said nothing, playing my part in this unspoken and unexpected scenario, the role of unsolicited and involuntary host. I pretended things were as usual, but I kept watching them from the corner of my eye. As they approached, two local kids, maybe thirteen or fourteen years old, entered my peripheral vision, and everything went into a vertiginous slow motion. One of the kids turned as they passed the couple and grabbed the purse hanging from the woman's wrist. She struggled for an endless second or two to hold onto the black bag, but the other kid gestured threateningly at her to let go of it.

By the time the two kids had run away with her purse, she had managed to call out to her husband. He was still walking and hadn't noticed the incident. Perhaps his attention was centered on us, the two older potential attackers. His shock and her frustration combined into an acknowledged impotence and shared panic. The kids were nowhere to be seen by now. The man turned one way and then the other, making sure he didn't lose sight of us. Perhaps he wanted or expected us to help, or perhaps he feared another attack from us. For a split second I entertained an impulse to run after the kids. Wasn't I ready to fight in the karate tournament in a few days? The impulse was weak and short-lived, overridden by a cascade of conflicting commitments and paralyzing insecurities. My ethical superego was urging on my macho/hero side, but my sense of danger was reinforced by my patriotism and my class identification with the underdog.

But who was the underdog here? Perhaps I did nothing because of an intuitive fear of being mistakenly identified with the attackers in this atmosphere of ethnic mistrust. After some hesitation, the couple turned and walked back to the tourist marketplace. By now I was already torn by a wish to express empathy and offer assistance. At that moment, Winnie's bus arrived and he jumped on it. We never talked about the incident, perhaps not only to safeguard our macho karate self-images.

I see that couple again and again. They often come to mind, particularly when I reflect on the deep connections I have established with Euro-Americans in the two decades I have lived in the United States. Wouldn't I have offered assistance to Beverly, Herb, Frances, Carol, Daniel, or Dwight in a similar attack? What would my response be now, after my deep and prolonged contact with these dear people? Where would my emotional and ethical investments reside now? I think of them as beloved individuals, apart from the complex context of the border, so I have a ready and clear response. However, if I place them in the entangled area of the border, in an artificial and uneven encounter zone of inherent supraordination, the clarity fades. Obviously, my response would be circumstantial, as contingent on the nature and character of the assault as on my own situation. How is the "assault" to be understood, however? Couldn't the two kids who stole the purse be imagined as urban reincarnations of Joaquin Murrieta, the popular California "bandit" who became an outlaw in response to the violent Anglo takeover of the Southwest after the U.S.–Mexican War? To what extent are the consumerist intrusions of tourist exchanges crude reenactments of dehumanizing asymmetries and crippling displacements long established and daily reinforced?

The Elusive Distances between the Private and the Public

The uncertainties and complexities of the border region are often recognized. Awards have been won and careers established chronicling, analyzing, and expounding on its challenged parameters, unsettled interactions, and contradictory meanings (spaces of representation). With different degrees of relevance and studiousness, the list of authors (and of representational spaces) extends from the pioneering works of Don Américo Paredes to the contributions of Oscar J. Martínez, Vicki Ruíz, Mario García, Joel Garreau, Deborah Nathan, Raul Fernández, and Ellwin Stoddard, among others, to the creative explorations of Gloria Anzaldúa and Guillermo Gómez-Peña and the sordid depictions of Robert Bowden. The border, indeed, has gained further notoriety since the 1970s. Diverse factors, ranging from immigration to maquiladora growth to NAFTA discussions contributed to this enhanced focus. Mass media attention to the region's role in these developments facilitated the border's widespread recognition and appeal in academic and artistic circles. The convergence of these accounts, while at times contradictory or unrelated, has resulted in an intertextual construction in which the region operates as a figurative trope, a quintessential "representational space" of dislocations and hybridity, a "no-man's-land" in which anything goes.

This no-man's-land intertextual construction has a long history. As a palimpsest, this construction comprises numerous layers of unrelated and even contradictory accounts and perceptions—some old, some new, but all mixed together. Reaching back to colonial times, Samuel Schmidt notes that the region was perceived as an empty space, and that view still underlies the multilayered image of the region:

> The border region historically has been perceived as empty space. For the Spanish Empire, the border did not have enough resources and labor for tribute. Scattered missions and *presidios* helped create a Spanish presence motivated by a religious interest but never represented economic interests. For the English colonizers, the frontier's Wild West was an area for adventure and expansion. (1995, 187–88)

Tom Barry and Beth Sims also describe a scenario whose evolving perceptions are not exempt from irony:

> [M]any outside the region have customarily viewed the borderlands . . . as wastelands without beauty or life. . . . Until the late 1800s the borderlands were regarded as badlands or *malpais*—the realm of rattlesnakes, *bandidos*, and desert rats. (1994, 19)

By the late 1800s, with the completion of railroad lines and the increased transit of people and goods, the size of the population gradually grew. The area began to be viewed as an intermediary zone. This intermediary role fostered a strong sense of transience, which only added to the underlying sense of an empty space—but a space now conflated with the overtones of frontier lawlessness. This perception gained national notoriety during Prohibition, when liquor manufacturers and gambling establishments relocated from the United States to border towns, reinforcing their longstanding reputation as blank tolerance zones (Martínez 1978; Timmons 1990). From the late 1970s on, the region has attracted increasing attention and has generated different interpretations as the ever-increasing transit and traffic at the border provoke contrasting responses. For most, the presumed inability of each respective government to regulate the flow of people and products is a great concern. Ever stronger measures are advocated to, in Ronald Reagan's words, "regain control of our borders," as well as to win the "War on Drugs." On the opposite extreme, others celebrate the porousness of the border. For them, this porousness makes the region a fertile ground for cross-fertilization and new possibilities (Anzaldúa 1987; Gómez-Peña 1993).

Along with its evolution, the intertextual image of the border encompasses diverse and contrasting accounts. Incongruent descriptions emphasize different aspects or interpretations that arise from contrasting scopes of interactions and goals. For the typical tourist, the border is a long strip of curio shops, bars, discos, restaurants, and tolerance zones. For more engaged observers, it is mostly an overexploited area of great poverty and social chaos (Peña 1997; Schmidt 1995). Still others find it a site of rapid industrialization through the maquiladora industry, which, according to some, spearheaded the economic recovery of Mexico (Stoddard 1987). For other observers, the border is the entire U.S. Southwest, encompassing the bicultural and bilingual accommodations of Mexican Americans and other residents (Velez Ibáñez 1996; Saldívar 1997).

Regardless of varying perceptions of the region, the local population is often overlooked. Local residents disappear in the glare of accounts of cheap thrills, trinkets, or drinks. Local residents are ignored in most mass media coverage of undocumented immigrants, drug traffickers, and maquiladora workers. The same subsumed relevance and recognition of a waiter or a taxi driver is reflected in a complex dynamic of functional interaction and personal invisibility in which the border is at once acknowledged and erased.

This instrumental interplay of recognition and invisibility is implied in Schmidt's elaboration on the exploitive effects of this persistent perception of the border as empty space, which "facilitated the establishment of the highly polluting *maquiladora* industry . . . and is being used as a rationale to install toxic and nuclear waste dumps in the border region" (187–88). Ironically, the relocation of these plants takes place due to the availability of mass labor at a comparatively low wage, yet this explicit motive does not override the underlying sense of the region as vacant. On the contrary, the "empty space" perception is instrumentally implicit, as Schmidt notes, in the leniency of the application of laws or their loopholes. Aside from environmental regulations, labor, housing, and trade laws are often irregularly implemented or unsatisfactorily designed to recognize or address the needs of local residents. This instrumental incongruence, in which the border is regarded as both vacant and populated, is advantageous for certain groups. Only instrumental dimensions are accounted for in narrow agendas. While the locals' lives are directly at stake, they are only partially recognized or addressed—and ultimately erased—in the overarching sense of the region as an empty space. The benefits of the functionality of the region are taken over in this alienated instrumentality. The border remains a frontier, an area open to advancement and takeovers.

Limits to Hybridity and Transgression: The Bounds of Boundlessness

This kaleidoscope-like perception of the border goes unnoticed because no single complete account can match the complexity of the region. Instead, disconnected versions and impressions coexist with little interaction or regard for congruency. Academic attention to the region reflects these contrasting perceptions and interpretations. Highlighting the differences between two salient approaches to the region, David Spener and Kathleen Staudt, editors of an anthology on the border region, talk about "a split discourse." They characterize this split in terms of the scope and emphases of the respective, general focus:

> Version 1 is old style border studies, grounded in history and the empiricism of the social sciences. . . . Much of Version 2 is about literary and critical ideas, rather than observable places or researchable people or things. . . . Version 1, old-style border studies, has a deeper history but a relatively narrow spatial agenda. Version 2 has a shorter history, but its intellectual agenda is extremely broad, considering space, time, and philosophies that challenge modern notions. (1998, 14)

While these two general approaches coexist, the most recent one, Version 2, has a far more compelling appeal to wider audiences. The greater appeal of these works published since the mid-1980s relates to their postmodernist orientations. As evidence of this widespread appeal, Chicano literary critic José Saldívar recently compiled a lengthy overview of works that, in his view, "announce the post-contemporary coming of age of the U.S.–Mexico border as a *paradigm* of crossing, circulation, material mixing, and resistance" (1997, 13, emphasis added). He claims a significant importance for the allegorical trend: "[T]he *invocation* of the U.S.–Mexico border as a paradigm . . . has contributed to the 'worlding' of American studies and further helped to instill a new transnational literacy in the U.S. academy by challenging its traditional insular focus" (1997, xiii, emphasis added).

Pronouncements aside, despite emphasis on crossings and blending, the empirical studies and the paradigmatic versions remain distant from each other (Spener and Staudt 1998, 14). Empirically oriented scholars seldom pay attention to the pronouncements and insights that come from the "borderland paradigm" perspectives. Numerous scholars such as Lawrence Herzog, Timothy Dunn, José Palafox, Ellwyn Stoddard, Duncan Earll, and Josiah McC. Heyman provide invaluable empirical insights and data. Most salient for the purpose of this book are Oscar Martínez's overview of identities along the border (in *Border People*), Velez Ibáñez's suggestive concept of "cultural bumping" (in *Border Visions*), and Socorro Tabuenca's perceptive critique of the borderland's paradigm in her doctoral dissertation, which analyzes texts by two "border" women writers. Finally, Pablo Vila has edited *Ethnography at the Border*, which is based on ethnographic articles and challenges the compelling command of discursive representations of the area.

These empirically oriented works address many of the dimensions overshadowed by the paradigmatic approach. However, until today, the popularity of those works using the latter approach has surpassed the diffusion of the former, partly because of the current vogue of postmodernist trends. Because of their specific focuses and their lack of theoretical emphases, few of the empirical works have enjoyed the wide appeal of the allegorical works. With the exception of Tabuenca and Vila, authors of traditional works have not engaged in the obfuscating allure of the borderland's paradigm. Focused on specific technical or social dimensions and observant of traditional disciplinary boundaries and positivistic orientations, they have seldom engaged in abstract theoretical explorations of the character of the border. In their emphasis on text, in contrast, the paradigmatic approaches celebrated by Saldívar make little direct reference to concrete developments or empirical detail. In Saldívar's own words, the region is merely "invoked." These works display little engagement with traditional approaches, not only because of methodological and conceptual differences, but because they have little use for those particulars of the border that concern empirical studies. As Saldívar clearly states, their interest in the region is mostly paradigmatic. It is not about what the region is, but about what the region represents as an allegory or an emblem.

With little concrete attention paid to the particulars of the region, this figurative transposition of the border image is primarily drawn from the region's commonplaces, those propagandized by the media and reconstructed from fictionalized or anecdotal accounts. Selectively, only certain features of the region are highlighted, while many others are eclipsed, figuratively obliterated. Underlying this lack of attention to specifics is the persistent perception of the border as an empty space. This erasure is even reflected in the intended audience of the paradigm, which is obviously not the region's residents, but those in other areas who find use for and appeal in the allegorical construction. Border residents are left out of both the picture and the discussion.

Enunciative Poverty and the Distribution of Resources

Collective and often incongruent sets of perceptions and events not only arise in the region, but they also give the place its kaleidoscopic, multifaceted realities. My emphasis on intertextual construction aims to highlight the coexistence of numerous processes and accounts. I build from the empiricism of traditional studies while taking advantage of the conceptual insights of newer approaches as recommended by Spener and Staudt. In this chapter, my aim is to carve out a space in the overriding discursive appeal of the use of the border image as a conceptual figure. In the strong allegorical charge of the space of representation of the image, I recognize that the border region, not just its image, crystallizes unconventional situations, and that these situations provide a provocative resemblance to emergent trends in other settings. I contend, however, that to understand these resemblances, our gaze must move beyond the page or the screen, where most of the proponents of the borderlands paradigm remain, to the voices, actions, and situations of local residents. In this ethnographic account, I hope to show that more than being just a hybrid space, the border is a site of distant proximities. More than a site of transgressions, it is a transgressed space. Ultimately, I hope to contribute to the recognition that, after all, the border is not an empty space. I want to bring ordinary local people into the picture, beyond stereotypes, as they have engaged to alter the conditions of displacement that the current allure of the border perpetuates in the overriding tendentiousness toward the bizarre or the extraordinary.

My critique of the allegorical use of the border region is not about whether it is accurate or inaccurate, complete or incomplete. To begin, we need to recognize that any account or representation is inherently incomplete. Michel Foucault uses the notion of "enunciative poverty" to refer to this inevitable incompleteness. In the *Archaeology of Knowledge,* he defines this notion with succinct eloquence: "everything is never said" (1972, 118). No statement, regardless of lucidity or eloquence, can assert the totality of possible meanings or provide an exhaustive description. There is always something or someone excluded in any enunciation or representation.

Foucault's notion of enunciative poverty, the inevitable incapacity of any statement to convey fully any meaning or representation, helps to avoid the pitfall of simpleminded empiricism. He proposed that we examine discursive formations in terms of their appeal at the expense of their omissions, their enunciative poverty. In Foucault's words "to analyze a discursive formation is to seek the law of [enunciative] poverty, it is to weight it up, and to determine its specific form" (120). This analysis entails, in his words again, "to weight the 'value' of statements." Such valorization is not defined by "their truth," or "a secret content." Instead, it is defined by "their place, their capacity for circulation and exchange, their possibility of transformation." Significantly, Foucault emphasizes that such value applies "not only in the economy of discourse, but, more generally, in the administration of scarce resources" (120). So what is the "place" and the "capacity for circulation of exchange" of the blurring allegory of the border? Why is it that the local dimensions are overshadowed by the hyperbolic focus on a handful of given characters and circumstances? What distribution of resources is at stake?

Foucault's formula coincides with Lefebvre's recognition of the impacts of representations in a setting. Over four decades after Lefebvre's conceptualization, the role of representational spaces in the production of space seems to increase with the remarkable instrumental magnitude of symbols in our world today. Jean Baudrillard defines this impact in terms of hyperreality. He uses this term to refer to the confounding effect of signs and symbols (1983, 3, 4). The reproduction or the representation, he says, has a more compelling value or claim to reality than the original piece of art, model, or event; in other words, the hyperreal commands more reality than the real. For example, the cumulative sales of cheap reproductions of famous artworks generate more revenue than the auction of the original. Likewise, just as the curio shop trinket stands for Mexican culture, the selective representation of the border in terms of its allegorical function draws more attention than a more comprehensive, empirical account. Through the massive, larger-than-life, and expedient mythmaking capacities of television, newspapers, film, and now the Internet, symbols have mesmerizing effects.

The compelling representation of the border region is a vivid example of the hyperreal. The region itself matters less than what it represent in its iconic value. In hyperspace, boundaries become a metaphor, a mere emblem of difference in the midst of unexamined amalgamations. Authors using the figurative of the border take the region as a given. Foucault's notion of enunciative poverty allows us to look beyond this partial space of the representation of the border as a blurring allegory. Looking at the economy of discourse as well as the administration of scarce resources, Foucault's insight allows us to understand that the appeal of the image speaks of the pervasiveness of the situation of challenged boundaries and disturbed definitions and delimitations not only in conceptualization, but also in terms of institutional arrangements and social demarcations.

Claims of global integration and pronouncements about the blending of borders highlight only partial dimensions of ongoing changes. In a similar way, the allegory of the border as a site of transgression and hybridity oversimplifies the dynamics and impacts of the integration process, suggesting that asymmetries are resolved or transcended. On the contrary, global integration exploits more than it resolves asymmetries. Companies relocate manufacturing operations to take advantage of "comparative advantages." Products and marketing campaigns are often redesigned or altered to fit local tastes and niches from country to country (Spybey 1996, 6–7; Robertson 1992, 100; Friedman 1992). Likewise, financial speculation is done in terms of geographical alternatives and time zone differences. In short, differences and separations, while perhaps relativized, have not yet become irrelevant. Instead, they remain instrumental, and thus greatly manipulable. These instrumentalities, and their blinding manifestations, give the figure of the border its striking appeal. In the economy of discourse, these claims parallel the neoliberal optic driving globalization in government and corporate quarters. The restricted focus of the NAFTA negotiations presumed a clear demarcation between economic and social terms as commercial concerns were artificially isolated from interrelated social factors. The parallel between neoliberal optics and blurring accounts of ongoing reconfigurations is suggested by the selectivity of their perspectives. Conforming to a given view or set of interests, certain features are recognized or highlighted while others are overlooked or trivialized.

The contradictory roles of the border for the two countries allow for these selective representational spaces. The capacity for circulation of the image of the border draws not only from its legendary repute, but also from its ever more ambiguous function in the administration of scarce resources. At once a bridge and a barrier, the region is also at once familiar and bizarre, one's own and alien, not only for the local residents, but even for the visitors or transient migrants. Thus, curio shops and maquiladoras provide commodified Mexican culture and labor in high demand yet at low prices and with trivialized or paternalistic regards. As often as not, the interactions take place in the midst of mutual mistrust and misunderstanding. Instrumentalized, the region and much of its cross-contacts are partitioned into a fragmented social space of mostly unresolved experiences, such as my anecdote of the Euro-American couple suggests. The distance seems inevitable due to the circumstantial overlaps that seldom merge because of historical, economic, and cultural legacies of incongruencies, conflict, or competition.

As a fetish, the image of the border as a space of representation distracts from key conceptual and political questions. Contextual examination of the conditions and implications for residents is secondary, at most. Space is replaced by hyperspace. The space of representation eclipses the multiplicity of spatial practices as the representational space of this symbolic tourist trap hinders the recognition of mechanics and impact. Caught in representational dimensions, there is little need to engage with the practices and conditions generating the dislocations celebrated or abhorred. In turn, the hyperreal effect of the image provides a fictitious sense of knowing, much as the tourists' impression of the border derived from tourist traps or exoticizing thrills leaves little room for recognizing the social context of the experiences or escapade. Baudrillard refers to this hyperreal effect, this excluding fictive certainty, as simulacra. The "real" is no longer defined by referential accuracy, but by credibility constructed through hyperbolic, self-referential, frantic oversaturation (1983, 3–4).

As with the tourist trap and cheap thrills, the use of the border image as a space of representation presents stark, limited understandings. The allegory, often made as mere pronouncements, describes more than analyzes. Thus the so-called borderland paradigm has very limited, if any, explicative value. To analyze we must take things apart to see how and why they work the way they do. Instead, the figurative accounts do the contrary in a general rush to proclaim rampant hybridities. The conceptual challenge to confront the specter of revolution, the perplexing amalgamations of asymmetries and partial contacts, is sidestepped. If the border is neither Mexico nor the United States, why have U.S. government measures to prevent undocumented immigration become so drastic and disruptive in recent years? Why does the death toll of fatal crossings keep growing? And why are these deaths ignored?

An Overshadowing Allure: Intermittent Highlights and Persistent Obliterations

For the one in transit, the U.S.–Mexican border is always on the way. It is a destination to leave behind (Bartra 1993, 11). Transience, transit, and traffic generate the region's allegorical transmutation, which flares from the gaps of inequality and incongruence as much as from the friction of flows and tensions. The flare momentarily exposes these gaps at the same time that the glare shades the context, which remains unrecognized, even if seen. The recent strong appeal of the discursive formation of the border as an intertextual construction of transgression and chaos can be attributed to three prominent figures. In this section I examine the different uses of the image of the border in the pioneering contributions of Gloria Anzaldúa, Renato Rosaldo, and Néstor García Canclini. Each writer provides a different approach to the region in terms of his or her attention to its particulars. Overall, however, the three coincide in fostering the recognition of the region, or at least of its image, as a conceptual metaphor, or in Lefebvre's terms, as a space of representation.

Anzaldúa, a Chicana poet, pioneered the figurative construction of the border region as a compelling allegory. Her book, *Borderlands/La Frontera: The New Mestiza* (1987), defines the U.S.–Mexican border as an open wound "where the third world grates against the first and bleeds. And before a scab is formed it hemorrhages again, the lifeblood of two worlds merging to form a third country—a border culture" (3). Anzaldúa combines autobiographical snippets, spiritual and feminist statements, Native American concepts, and direct allusions to South Texas. She relies on the notion of *mestizaje*—the term used in Latin America to refer to the biracial offspring of Spanish and Native Americans—to defy racism, homophobia, and sexism in many settings, such as the family and school, and by diverse practitioners, be they redneck Anglo Texans, Tejanos, or Mexicans.

Anzaldúa proclaims a new subjectivity in the form of a new mestiza who is the product and source of the tolerance and creativity demanded by the ambivalence and blending of the "borderlands." Anzaldúa demonstrates the sense of "in-betweenness" in the style of her writing, which mixes poetry with prose and Spanish with English, along with some *Nahuatl* terms and motifs. The figurative use of the border image is clearly stated in the opening paragraph of the preface to her important book:

> The actual physical borderland that I'm dealing with in this book is the Texas–U.S. Southwest/Mexican border. The psychological borderlands, the sexual borderlands and the spiritual borderlands are not particular to the Southwest. In fact, the Borderlands are physically present wherever two or more cultures edge each other, where people of different races occupy the same territory, where under, lower, middle and upper classes touch, where the space between two individuals shrinks with intimacy.

Anzaldúa's figurative use of the image of the border widens the recognition of "otherness." Broadening the scope of variances, she recasts "difference" in a legitimate light through the legendary popularity of the border region as a site of transgression and cultural exchanges. Inadvertently, she replicates the dislocating subordination of the border to the nonlocal: the figure can then be used anywhere else and in practically any context, as her allegorical formulation clearly states. Again, this attention is received at the expense of the region's particulars. By reinforcing an image of the border in terms of legendary characterizations, she elides much of its reality:

> The prohibited and forbidden are its inhabitants. Los "atravezados" live here: the squint-eyed, the perverse, the queer, the troublesome, the mongrel, the mulatto, the half-breed, the half dead—in short, those who cross over, pass over, or go to the confines of the "normal." (3)

Anzaldúa's statement refers to the "inhabitants" of the "borderlands." However, the figurative images overlap (as she states in her opening paragraph) the border region. In fact, her formulation acquires its compelling appeal from the legendary repute of the border as a mecca for vice and lawlessness. Abnormality has been a component of the region's intertextual image since its close association with outlaws. In the late 1800s, the city attracted national attention as much of the vice activities of frontier zones started migrating south of the border, much as maquiladoras started to do in the mid-1960s. By the 1920s, with the Prohibition era, much of the border-concentrated activities such as drinking and gambling were made illegal in the United States. This concentration and the strong pull they had in the public mind consolidated the stigma of the border with rampant tolerance for any vice. For example, the U.S. consul in Ciudad Juárez wrote at the time, "[Ciudad] Juárez is the most immoral, degenerate, and utterly wicked place I have ever seen or heard of in my travels." A few years later, a Euro-American evangelist added detail to this nationwide depiction: "Murder and robbery are everyday occurrences and gambling, dope selling and using, drinking to excess and sexual vices are continuous. It is a Mecca for criminals and degenerates from both sides of the border" (Martínez 1978, 57).

Anzaldúa's characterization of the region, as the "bizarre," dwells on the same perception of the border as a tolerance haven at any cost and consequence. This representational space has been echoed time and again throughout the decades, yet is currently most readily associated with Tijuana. The image, whether stigmatized or celebrated, influences the way local residents of the border are perceived.

Recasting the stigma as a validating reassertion of "abnormality" (e.g., difference), Anzaldúa celebrates a given representation of "border culture" as the locus of new subjectivities that are able to deal with ambivalence. However, shifting the polarity of the claims does not overcome their generalization. On the contrary, plentifully fed by sordid occurrences amply highlighted in media accounts, the stereotypes have acquired new degrees of commonsense certainty in their overriding appeal.

Anzaldúa's contribution is undeniable. Her book formulated a new voice to assert the right of being different against the self-proclaimed right of sexists and racists to legitimize oppression on the grounds of the "abnormality" of the prospective victims. But what are the implications and consequences of the figurative rendition that the border fosters? What is to be gained from the larger-than-life characterizations? And—especially in terms of the frontier condition of the region and its alienated instrumentality—at what cost and to whom?

Anzaldúa's contribution is evident in the work of anthropologist Renato Rosaldo, whose widespread appeal illustrates how indirect evocations still overshadow the border. Rosaldo published *Culture and Truth* in 1989, advocating a semiotic approach to the "remaking of social analysis." It is only in the last chapter that Rosaldo introduces the concept of border zones, ascertaining that "human cultures are neither necessarily coherent nor always homogeneous." Instead, he talks of "border zone pockets and eruptions of all kinds, [that] crisscross our everyday lives" and of "social borders." Some of these "borders" are the conventional divisions of gender, class, race, ethnicity, and nationality. In addition, reflecting the recognition of otherness central to postmodernism, he adds sexual orientation, age, politics, dress, and food to the list (207–8).

Rosaldo's image of border zones evokes Anzaldúa's construction of the U.S.–Mexican border into the borderlands. His broad metaphor seeks to encompass the same extent of difference. Replacing the notion of "divisions" with "borders" to refer to social differentiations softens and expands their contours and interplays. Unlike Anzaldúa, however, he makes no explicit connection to the region in the space of representation he promotes. In this respect, there is more direct influence in the free-floating metaphor offered by Emily Hicks. She uses the figure of the border as a critical paradigm in which even Gabriel García Márquez becomes a "border writer." Still, Rosaldo's evocative transpositions of the intertextual image of the border is suggested by his direct mention of Anzaldúa and Don Américo Paredes, a foremost pioneer in South Texas border studies. Moreover, because of the strong presence of the region in the popular mind, any invocation of the border—particularly if made by a Mexican American—seems to convey a direct association with the region. Saldívar, for example, includes Rosaldo as a prominent figure in his overview of the borderlands paradigm.

An explicit association was also made at the 1993 meeting of the American Anthropological Association by a group of panelists who applied Rosaldo's concept of border zones to the situation of Palestinians in Jerusalem. At the end of the presentation, one of the official commentators warned the panel against equating the situation of the U.S.–Mexican border with the situation in Israel. A scholar of the Middle East and a Palestinian from Jerusalem, she stated that the situation at the border could not compare in severity to the one in Israel. The statement suggests the hyperreal occlusions produced by the alluring use of the border as an allegory. In the discussion period that followed the presentation, I asked the commentator if she had any idea how many people had died the previous year crossing the border—drowned in the river, disappeared in the Arizona desert, or murdered by thieves or border patrol officers. She did not know. At least in terms of casualties, however, her previous assertion had been erroneous. More casualties occurred along the U.S.–Mexican border that year because of undocumented migration than had occurred in Israel because of the Palestinian conflict. Inherent in her erroneous assertion was her fallacious assumption of knowledge, which allowed her to assert something she did not know. This ostensible knowledge/authority was not based on information, as she eventually recognized, but on impressions, the "common sense" generated by media coverage, artistic and academic "invocations," and brief and selective visits to the region. As in the case of tourists, this "sense of knowing" derives from the hyperreality of such experiences and representations and feeds the simulacra of recognition not only of the region, but of the dislocating events of globalization.

The reception of Néstor García Canclini's brief description of Tijuana also reflects this automatic propensity to fit the details into a prefigured picture, rather than using the details to review the overall account. Unlike Rosaldo's book, García Canclini's work refers directly to the Mexican–U.S. border region. This Argentinean anthropologist conducted fieldwork in Tijuana, where, with his research team, he interviewed over four hundred people from the mid- to late 1980s. Out of this extensive and lengthy research, however, he published only a slim photography book with fifty-two pictures and some thirteen pages of text. Coauthored with Patricia Safa and with photographs by Lourdes Grobet, the book was published in 1989 in Mexico and has not yet been translated into English. Its title, appropriately, is *Tijuana: La Casa de Toda la Gente* (Tijuana: The house to all people) and the photographs were selected by diverse groups of residents as representative of the city. As such, the book is presented as a reflection of the way the "city saw itself." Another stated aim, however, was to explore the use of photography as a heuristic medium, a way of apprehending the city through images as opposed to words: "mirar o escribir la ciudad" [to watch or to write the city].

García Canclini and Safa offer insightful observations to contextualize the visual exploration. They highlight the accelerated growth of the city and the consequent inadequacy of the supply of public services. They point to the importance of tourism and maquiladoras to the economy, as well as to Tijuana's social and cultural milieu. Avoiding linear reductionism, they underline ambiguous and contradictory stances toward these influential sources of income from the central government of Mexico, as well as from local residents. They not only acknowledge these contrasting relations, but they try to address them through a representative sample of such dissimilar voices as ushers who work high-profile cultural events, schoolteachers, and students from both rich and poor neighborhoods.

Their inclusive gesture, however, is greatly undermined by the small sampling they published out of such a numerous and inclusive sample. The local voices are restricted to only a handful of quotes. In addition, the study has had a very limited circulation. This brief, mostly visual, overview has not been published in the United States or even translated. A five-page synopsis, including nine pictures, appears in García Canclini's most famous work to this day, *Hybrid Cultures* (originally published in Spanish in 1989 and translated into English in 1995, with a preface by Rosaldo). In this synopsis, García Canclini added a sentence that proved fateful for both the city and the book. Comparing it to New York, he refers to Tijuana as a "laboratory of postmodernity," referring to the chaotic concatenations of social constituencies and cultural manifestations.

While García Canclini does not discuss the conditions generating the comparison, the passing characterization has taken on a life of its own. It has been quoted by many other authors, and it is evoked in other titles related to the border, such as *The Border: The Future of Postmodernity* by Sergio Gómez Montero, and *Juárez: The Laboratory of Our Future* by Charles Bowden. As with Rosaldo's book, García Canclini's explicit allusion to the border has contributed greatly to the fame of the book. Also like Rosaldo, García Canclini did not use the concept of borderlands, though he is cited by Saldívar as a pioneer of borderland studies.

Anzaldúa, Rosaldo, and García Canclini have made significant contributions to our recognition of the dislocating experience of ongoing changes. Unfortunately, their contributions replicate the habitual instrumental use of the border region at a direct cost to its residents. The allegorical, implicit, or direct allusions made by these authors, respectively, distract from the region's concrete complexities. Anzaldúa mentions the region in her title and in other prominent places. Yet, as she makes clear in the first paragraph, the border functions mostly as an allegorical referent through brief and sporadic recollection of memories of her childhood. Rosaldo makes no direct reference. Instead, he evokes the region only in the final chapter of his book in the form of border zones and border crossings. García Canclini is the only one who provides direct observations of the border based on systematic engagement with issues and people. However, the published product of this research is limited to a few quotes from the hundreds of interviews conducted; the limited direct observations are made in reference to his methodological and heuristic method, rather on the city itself. In García Canclini's later work, Tijuana is only an instance of the incongruent concatenations described in the book, as an emblem, a laboratory of postmodernity.

The focus of the work of these three authors is not on the region itself; instead they use the image of the region as a vehicle for expressing their analytical formulations. Though the use of the border image is incidental, however, the reference to the border region by these authors is instrumental in their works. The image of the border for Anzaldúa and Rosaldo is used to embody otherness. For García Canclini, Tijuana illustrates the dramatic juxtaposition of an incomplete modernity project in which the very new and the traditional coalesce with no clear resolution. For the three, the border image is an artifice, an emblematic lens. Yet, the lens is used to explain or understand someplace else. As such it provides a simulacra of the region and a hyperreal understanding of the perplexing effects of ongoing reconfigurations and dislocations.

The Border as a Hyperreal Curio Shop

Tourists, overtaken by the contrast—real and assumed—between the border and their hometowns, experience the border in such stark ways that the exposure creates the simulacra of knowledge. Many such travelers become instant experts after a short visit. The intensity of the experience gives them an immediate expertise based on their very circumscribed forays into the region. Making things even more artificial, these forays are usually confined to tourist traps such as curio shops, bars, and brothels, which cater to and reaffirm the tourists' expectations and demands. These experiences interrelate with the "common sense" representation of space in prominent intertextual images of the border and galvanize its compelling appeal. Because of their very artificiality, the tourist accounts are compelling, given a larger-than-life status, a feeling of the extraordinary or the bizarre. While these experiences and perceptions of the border are not new, this representational space gains new scopes of certainty and circulation with the hyperreal. The hyperreal is, thus, a passage or alteration in the nature of immediacy of the real regarding the social and our experience, conceptualization, and manipulation of it. From the differentially experienced concrete place, the dimensions of representation overtake our direct participation in spatial practices in the predominantly cognitive realm of hyperspace.

In hyperspace, symbols take place as representation—as representational spaces and spaces of representation—overtakes localized practices. Multiple perceptions and conceptions overlap, linking multiple settings and modalities of experience and intervention with contrasting consequences. Thus, the border, as an emblematic figure of these multilocal concurrences, serves again as an intermediary space, now between space and hyperspace. Accordingly, given that it draws from the same production of space of its legendary role, the local is subordinated to the nonlocal as now at the representational moments it is revealed and occluded at once. Baudrillard, talking about the occluding effect of simulacra refers to this interplay of overshadowing recognitions as transparency (1998, 1). This effect is tangible in the metaphorical use of the image of the border by Anzaldúa, Rosaldo, and García Canclini, in which the border becomes a lens for looking somewhere else. The transparency of overshadowing attention is most ironic in the cases of Anzaldúa and Rosaldo. They draw attention to the erased and marginalized people and their situations in any context. Unfortunately, their contributions have been used at the expense of further erasure of the border region. It becomes an image for elucidating dynamics at other places, while the local dimensions are overlooked or stereotyped. For the three authors, finally, their occlusions hide the very condition they tacitly exploit: the subordination of the local by the nonlocal. Now at the symbolic level, the border serves the same function as maquiladoras and tourist traps.

The hyperreal is not false or unreal. It is the new domain of images in our life, in an overlapping dual sense of the word *domain* as context and control. Regarding the border region, the current compelling representations may be artificial to the extent that the seductive attention and exposures of the region are constructed though overshadowing and motifs. The hyperreal effect of these representations is based on the dramatic events of the region. In fact, human lives are lost as people attempt to cross the border and through drug trafficking. Casualties continue to rise with the escalating degrees of poverty, social chaos, and drug-related violence. Sadly, this worsening situation only adds to the allure of the region, given the obsessive and occluding nature of prominent selective representations that render it transparent. The more infamous the events, the more compelling the appeal and the more the region is taken for granted based on rushed impressions. In this common sense, accounts that highlight concrete complexities of the region are pushed aside from the spot shot of hyperreality.

Prevalent attention to the border region is, obviously, also intertwined with concrete developments, interactions, and policies reshaping the region. The blurring of the region is produced not only by discursive figures, but by the momentum of international integration. Along Foucault's insight about the interplay of discursive economies and the economy of scarce resources, the relationship between the alluring representations and on-the-ground events is, however, both symptomatic and problematic. In its selective attention to drama and its consequent insistence on commonplaces, the spaces of representation and the representational spaces miss or fail to acknowledge its transformations. For example, the maquiladora industry is acknowledged in its generalities, but its transformation is unexamined. The selective recognition of given features and the consequent erasure of others is inevitable given the enunciative poverty of any statement. Yet the resulting representation is not inconsequential.

In the connection recognized by Foucault between the economy of discourses and resources, blurring characterizations of the border region reinforce particular practices that perpetuate distinctive situations. Take the following two extreme situations. The representational space of the border at the delineating boundary for the undocumented worker is different from the representational space that the performer or academician also manipulates for his or her particular aims. Accordingly, their spaces of representation are as distant as they are contrasting. For the undocumented worker, the physicality of his engagement is immediate to the tangible experience and conception of the border; it is a delineation, so to speak. For academicians the border is instead a demarcation, a matter of framing contextual parameters through conceptual agility. Significantly, the border zones alluded to by Rosaldo map the conflicting delineations of these breakthroughs for those who have managed to overcome the initial barriers of exclusion. Tellingly, most of the proponents of the allegorical image of the border are either women or Mexican American scholars venturing into new positions of relative power in academic settings. For them, the celebrated image of the border as a "paradigmatic" figure suggested by Saldívar works as a legitimizing motif as much as a cognitive referent in uncertain new parameters of inclusion.

Deeper and wider changes are at stake in the reconfigurations poorly addressed by the notion of "borderlands." David Harvey's claim of the new operational relation between time and space, as well as Robert Reich's insight of a "more abstract form of capitalism," provide greater explicative value. In addition, in more institutional terms, the civil rights movements of the last several decades contribute to the diverse configurations as well as the overlapping spaces of the specter of change. Universities and academic careers are sites and arenas in which new configurations are more than just visible, but are also articulated sites of the production of knowledge. As the representation of women and minority groups gains some visibility and prominence in given disciplines, many of these scholars have found great resonance with the greater epistemological latitude of postmodernism. As heterogeneity is acknowledged and legitimized, the image of the border region provides a space of representation for making sense of the new scopes of intervention for these scholars. As minority scholars, we are a specific sort of tourist, using Bauman's characterizations. We enjoy the relative privilege of mobility, of participation in new markets of symbols and discourses ever more secluded into our own limited self-reference. Most if not everything is seen merely as a text or through texts.

The passage from space to hyperspace implicit in the transition from an industrial to an information society bridges and divides in the same uneven and complex ways that the border region between the United States and Mexico links the two countries. The trendy image of the border region is as artificial as an artifact bought in a curio shop, and it serves a similar purpose. The image is consumed much in the same way that replicas of the Aztec calendar, charro hats, and maracas are bought as souvenirs of Mexican culture. Yet culture is a contextual event made up of more than symbols. The evocative power of trinkets bought at curio shops weakens rapidly once the items are removed from the aura of exotic, romantic, or bizarre Mexico. The curio shop works as the mediated context for the experience. Yet there is more to the trinkets in the perception of the culture they evoke, as there is also more to the curio shop than the site of an exotic trivial experience. The trinkets are traded in places constituted in concrete social relations. These relations are not recognized in the transaction of commodities and services.

Marx refers to this occlusion of social relations as commodity fetishism. The border image, promoted as a paradigm, is a fetish of the border region just as the cheap replica of the Aztec calendar "fetishizes" Mexican culture. This occurs not because of a flaw in the symbol itself, but because of the unexplored conditions of the border as a site of transgression and hybridity. It is precisely these conditions of the production and consumption of the symbol that the fetish at once exploits and conceals. The tourists return to their routines in South Dakota or California after their trip to the border, and the Aztec calendar eventually finds its way to the basement or the attic. The significance of the tourist fantasy soon dissipates: "No, I have not been to t.j. but I have been to Brownsville . . . or was it some other town? I didn't like their nachos, anyway." However, the border is more than tantalizing characters and artificial circumstances. It is the trinkets, but it is also the experience and the setting.

Eclipsed in this simulacra of knowledge, we lose sight of or trivialize the fact that the labor of maquiladora workers is not for local consumption, as the humanity of the prostitute is lost in the degrading "good time" she provides. As the area itself remains a transit zone, so the pervasive instrumentality of the border gives place to its figurative construction as a "paradigm" of incongruent interactions, rushly celebrated as "hybrid." Is it surprising that poverty and social dislocations increase as the prominence and wealth crossing the border increases? What is surprising is that the perverse relationship remains unnoticed and unaddressed and that its effects and manifestations, however sordid, are glamorized—just as the border is exploited. Given the inhabitants' resilience and/or tolerance for dealing with sordid situations, are the sordid situations their choice? What options do they have? What consequences do they face?

These questions may seem inconsequential and overly dramatic to the tourist who is just having fun or the critic who is just making a conceptual or rhetorical point. Under the business-as-usual assumption that the border is there to be taken over again and again, in the intoxication of the hyperreal, it is a nuisance to acknowledge border residents. Their acknowledgment presents a vexing contradiction to the sense of the border as "empty space." Aren't all border residents newcomers? Couldn't they just move somewhere else if they don't like it? Aren't they just waiting for a chance to cross to the United States anyway? In other words, let the good times roll! In any case, wasn't the "local"—the taxi driver, the curio shop attendant, the traffic officer, the prostitute—a willing participant in the mischief—the cheap bargain, the bribe, the getting laid? Didn't he say, "Let's go see the *muchachas*"? Didn't she say, "Pay me whatever you want"? Didn't he say, "I'd let you go"? Didn't she say, "I want you, *papi*"? The context in which the interactions—the alienated instrumentalities—take place is erased not by the "will to know" but by the will to invade and use. When one is getting away with murder, one does not pay much attention to the corpse. What conditions make these engagements so uneven, predictable, and "safe"? Aren't we learning about "them"? Aren't we giving "them" jobs as maids, gardeners, window washers, and maquiladora or nursing home workers? Aren't we spending our money there and thus helping them out by buying their junk and their *margaritas sin sal*? Aren't we bringing national attention to them through our accounts?

Lefebvre and the "Production" of El Paso as an Eternal Frontier

Are we bringing attention to "them" with our accounts? An interplay of disclosure and concealment takes place in the enunciative poverty of any account. Yet, in the instrumental use of the border image there is a manipulated selectivity that further hinders the recognition of social relations constituting the image. The representational space of the region fosters its allegorical use. As a space of representation the image of the border is used to allude to the diverse mergings of experiences and practices of a dislocated world in which new inequalities and opportunities blaze up. The allegory instrumentalizes the region, now in the symbolic realm of hyperspace, as much as its spatial practices displace the local in the diverse flows that take over the place. Conceptually unable to address the displacements and breakthroughs of the specter of change, the image merely overdwells on the unclear meanings of reconfigurated parameters. In turn, allegories pass as analysis in the oversaturating intensity of hyperreality and simulacra.

The allegorical use of the image fictionalizes the border through an overdramatic and selective representation. Yet it fails to perceive the fictive character of border cities all together. It fails to recognize their very restricted capacities to carry out basic administrative capacities to fulfill most residents' needs. As the proliferation of irregular settlements attests, the imbalance between the local and the nonlocal overwhelms these urban centers, which are plagued by problems of excessive transit and traffic (Staudt 1998). Local governments at the border cannot respond to the impacts and demands of these flows because of a lack of resources and autonomy to address ensuing problems, not only because of the magnitude of the flows, but also because of the numerous agencies involved that override local jurisdictions. Not only state and national concerns, but international ones overlap at the border. To make things even worse, the operations of some of these multilayered agencies contradict one another—much as the accounts of the border contradict each other.

Consider immigration and trade, for example. Economic development entities, such as chambers of commerce and city planning departments, promote crossborder commerce. However, their efforts are entangled in the regulatory tentacles of each country's federal customs agencies overseeing trade and the federal immigration agencies regulating entries and exits. Add the Drug Enforcement Agency and the Food and Drug Administration, which are involved in regulating both illicit products and products posing potential health risks. This bureaucratic entanglement is seriously aggravated by infrastructure complications, such as the long lines of cars halted at checkpoints in each direction. Finally, this major source of pollution is ineffectively observed by officers of the Environmental Protection Agency and stoically endured by residents of these administratively fictive cities. A similarly restricted autonomy exists in terms of the economic viability of cities like El Paso. Controlled mainly by nonlocal firms and producing mostly for nonlocal markets, border economies are besieged by low wages and unreliable levels of investment. The lion's share—enormous volumes of trade, manufacturing production, and profits—does not remain in the region. Take the case of the maquiladora industry. While very significant in terms of technological and professional advancements as well as direct employment, the operations of these plants are dangerously contingent on local production costs and nonlocal market fluctuations.

Although border cities may be administrative fictions, their chaos is real. Similarly, much of their economy is fictitious, but their poverty is very real. Aside from the inevitable uncertainties of market fluctuations, the deepening social impacts of accelerated demographic growth and infrastructure deficits make the uncertainty more perilous. Since the 1950s, progressive integration of the local economy of El Paso into national and international markets has generated impressive growth in population, employment, and—significantly—poverty. Local rates surpass those for Texas and the United States, with the only exception being employment growth for the state. The local population grew 315 percent from 1950 to 1990, while the population in the state and the country increased 121 percent and 69 percent, respectively. In the same four decades, the number of workers in El Paso swelled 341 percent, a greater growth than for the population. In contrast, the number of workers in the country increased only 111 percent. The employed population in the state increased 370 percent, 29 percent more than in El Paso. The exceptional growth for the state occurred in the period of economic expansion from 1974 to 1985, closely related to the boom and bust of its oil industry.

Table 1.

El Paso per capita personal income, 1950–1990

Year	Per Capita Personal Income	Percentile of National Averages
1950	$ 1,925	0.99 percent
1960	$ 2,110	0.91 percent
1970	$ 3,009	0.74 percent
1980	$ 6,721	0.68 percent
1990	$11,545	0.62 percent

Source: Data for 1950 and 1960 from Census of Population, Part 45 Texas, Volume 2 and Volume 1, respectively. Data for other years from the Regional Economic Information System (REIS CD-ROM), compiled by the Bureau of Economic Analysis of the U.S. Commerce Department, May 1992, U.S. Census Bureau. Donald Michie and George Tower alerted me to this disturbing trend.

In El Paso, however, the impressive and constant growth rates in population and employment are related to a steady decline in its per capita personal income: from 99 percent of the national average in 1950 to 62 percent in 1990. This steady decline in per capita income is not mentioned in any of the allegorical accounts of the border region. Like the death toll of undocumented crossings, the sordidness of poverty stands only as a backdrop for the allure of the border, overshadowed by the allegorical uses.

Aside from distracting from an engagement with the extents and mechanics of these impacts, the mystification of the region also trivializes the conceptual challenge of dealing with the new heterogeneity. Instead, its multiplicity blurs into easy celebrations or abhorrence, and/or it is sidestepped by a superficial notion of hybridity. Observers are mesmerized by dramatic differences that apparently "merge" or coexist in incongruent juxtapositions. The challenge of accounting for the new complexities of otherness is avoided when the context is obliterated by text. This is particularly clear in the intense attention paid to Tijuana as the quintessential border city. The city's tourist strip, its shanty towns, its maquiladora parks, and the ominous *Linea,* the launching ground for massive undocumented entrances into the United States, stand for the entire region.

What is particular about Tijuana symbolizing the border is that the border is already a symbol. Pronounced "the most visited city in the entire world," Tijuana becomes an emblem for the construction of the border as a metaphor for the dislocations of globalization. The emblem is abbreviated in more intense encapsulated symbolism, but even more is then erased in the abbreviation. Beyond the emblem, the border stretches beyond Tijuana and this extension encompasses dramatic contrasts of great significance and revelatory value: demographic and urban magnitudes, ethnic compositions and interaction patterns, as well as economic and infrastructure particularities among the eighteen main cities along the international divide. To mention only a few contrasts among cities on either side of the border: Nogales has only 37,000 inhabitants, while San Diego has 1,543,000. El Paso is 73 percent Mexican, with a long history of ethnic tension, which contrasts with the far more accommodating interethnic legacy of Laredo, both in the same state (Martínez 1994). Likewise, Ciudad Juárez is home to a fifth of the maquiladora workers in Mexico, producing primarily for U.S. automobile manufacturers. In contrast, Tijuana has 14 percent of the total employment, and most of its production is for Asian electronics companies (Vargas 1998b, 7).

The contrasts are perhaps even more perplexing across the international divide. For example, Mexico's northern border cities have higher per capita incomes than most other cities in Mexico. In contrast, U.S. southern border cities are among the poorest in the country. This poignant contrast stems in part from Mexican cities' considerably higher employment rates compared to their U.S. counterparts. Wages in Mexico, however, are generally lower. In addition, El Paso, with half of Ciudad Juárez's population, uses twice as much water and has double its territory (Staudt 1998). The borderlands paradigm, oblivious to these asymmetries, erases the border as a context. That erasure creates a blur. As a stage of dislocations, the region is an appropriate symbol of the "postmodern condition." Yet this symbolic function appropriates the border by means of a reified and reifying characterization based on stereotypes. Consequently, the transformations in the region are beyond the scope of paradigmatic pronouncements and of the selective gaze that recognizes only what it already has in mind.

A closer look at the extent and nature of contacts at the border sheds light on the distant proximities characterizing the setting, as well as on the varied experiences of otherness in other globalized settings. For the most part, the types and scopes of crossborder contacts remain limited to specific roles and spaces. A clear example of this partial and qualified blending and interaction is the anecdote with which I began this chapter. My friend's nickname was "Winnie," an English name, and we renamed the main avenue of our city *la sixtin* and our urban ritual *sixtinear.* All this shows the influence of the United States on our everyday lives. In addition, many of the cars borrowed from parents for the courtship ritual probably had *placas fonterizas,* and most of us bought our clothes and perfumes *en el otro lado* (on the other side of the border). However, this consumption of symbols and products did not in itself constitute a full embrace of the United States or an obliteration of our attachment and loyalty to Mexico. In spite of these exchanges, as my story went on to demonstrate, the incursion of the Euro-American couple still provoked an alerted sense of invasion in us. The multiple and complex implications and meanings of these exchanges offered the opportunity of the attack to the young thieves and left the "border crossers" with an unsavory memory. This important distinction eludes the advocates of the paradigm because they do not acknowledge these parameters. Yet, these parameters constantly change while the asymmetries they demarcate do not automatically shift. In the many years since the incident, the relation between the two cities is even more complex. On the one hand, you have more companies relocating to Ciudad Juárez and a greater diversity of nationalities among the plant managers and engineers. Yet there are also harsher measures to prevent undocumented immigration, and the levels of pollution, crime, and economic polarization have worsened.

Whose Allegory and Whose Border?

The image of the border region, as currently constructed into an allegory, is conceptually ineffective and politically detrimental. It replicates the instrumentality of the border in which the benefits of its geographical position are alienated from local residents, who are then left to confront most of the costs of the site's instrumentality. At the same time, the elucidating value of the allegory is counterproductive in advancing our comprehension of the extent and nature of the sociopolitical transformations that globalization entails. We are only left with a simile and very few insights for looking deeper beyond the analogy. As with the visit to a curio shop, what we are left with is a cheap thrill and a misrecognition based on very selective representations of the border region. Why is the image of the border so compelling? Or in Foucault's terms, why is its capacity for circulation so strong? In my view, a deeper and more widespread phenomenon is at stake. It involves the shock that the specter of revolution poses to our conventional ways of making sense of the world.

The specter of revolution relates to the obfuscation generated by the fragmented outcomes of polarizations and breakthroughs. Part and parcel of this obfuscation is a collective shock, a profound sense of disorientation. Although global processes alter the confines of interactions in front of our very eyes, most of us refuse to register these changes in their perplexing magnitudes. As T. S. Eliot noted, the human brain can only handle a limited dose of reality. Caught in the comfort of the "known," as Krishnamurti would put it, most of us remain reluctant to face the scale and speed of the transformation inasmuch as they represent a fundamental challenge to the multiple parameters of our sense of self, ranging from our basic concepts, neighborhoods, and countries—and the rights and privileges these cognitive and institutional delimitations entail.

Specters are, greatly, a matter of perspective. They are optical illusions, mirages produced by unexpected and uncommon appearances. They disrupt our sense of the world or what we deem conceivable. Referents and contours seem contradictory and undefined, generating the conceptual challenge to elucidating the specter of revolution derived from partial or individualized breakthroughs in the midst of regressive polarization. Beyond El Paso, in the entire country, new and old rich people of color succeed, while the feminization of poverty escalates at a faster pace and family size among people of color continues to outpace that of the population as a whole. Is this a revolution? Are we winning? Are we losing? Who are we? In short, distinct frames of references collapse and asymmetrical conditions intensify. Contradictorily, divisions at once melt and sharpen.

Perplexed, with different degrees of shock, we strive with functional yet partial certainties. Again and again we struggle to reestablish a sense of coherence or certainty. The image of the border as a space of representation allows us to sidestep this disconcerting complexity, to absorb the shock of difference just as a curio shop distracts from the cultural dissonance of an alien country. Globalization is turning familiar environments into alienated settings of partial recognitions or compromised familiarity. The reconfigured landscapes produce a mixture of thrill and concern, just as a run to the border often does. Yet the conditions of border cities are replicated as other cities become aggregates of contrasting cultural and social interactions of uncertain coherence and disrupted cohesion.

The experiential shock of globalization means that the specter of revolution roams through unsettled boundaries among difference, opportunity, and displacement. These contextual reconfigurations set new parameters for individual maneuvering and group delineations related to perplexing transformations in business practices, technology, and international demarcations. These new parameters and interconnections define precarious balances between human costs and promising innovations as assumptions about the relation between individuals and social groups fade. The ambiguity and contested parameters of the border region make it a handy allegory for this experience, turning it into an alluring space of representation.

Until recently, private and public discourses characterized this relation through distinct demarcations such as black and white, men and women, Mexico and the United States. While these discourses still strongly shape prevailing worldviews, their validity and logic are less automatic. Increasingly, their characterizations appear inadequate in a world challenged by the dynamic interpolations and integrations of multiple sociopolitical processes. Instead, more specific and contingent identities and entities acquire commanding influence, beyond conventional categories of the past. Recently discovered, acknowledged, or asserted self-characterizations have added complexity to our social analyses: the Latino, the white man, the white woman, the woman of color, the gay, the lesbian, and the bisexual.

New modalities of demarcating difference of "otherness" coexist and converge with old delimitations, challenging our established cognitive referents, much as they are put in question by the border region. By otherness I refer to the dynamic yet persistent configurations of identities and positions that constitute the institutional and personal relations of social and private life. The "other" alludes to the multiplicity of social actors different and yet proximate to oneself in their perplexing and partial specificities. It entails the seemingly abyssal distance between a young African American woman and a middle-aged white male implicitly highlighted by the media in the stigmatizing depiction of the welfare mother. Yet it also entails the less recognized differences between a Korean immigrant in Los Angeles and a Chinese American businesswoman in San Francisco. With a different degree of recognition or ascribed significance, each is, well, "the other" to one another. At times the differences can be readily overt or dramatic. At other times, they can be subtle, irrelevant, or polarizing. Increasingly, more specific and even contradictory divisions and fields of difference extend the proliferation of categories into new fields of significance, socially and analytically speaking: the rich woman of color, the poor woman of color, the computer literate, the computer illiterate, the immigrant with documents, the immigrant without documents, the employed, the unemployed, the working poor, the Puerto Rican Latino (Ricky Martin), the Colombian Latina (Shakira), the anti–Mexican American Chicano (Rudy Acuna), the anti-Chicano Mexican American (Richard Rodriguez), the Democrat-like Republican (John McCain), and the Republican-like Democrat (Bill Clinton).

We live in a referential chaos and the figure of the border, as a space of representation, holds a strong allegorical appeal. It provides a simplified glimpse of the changes at hand. It allows us to cognitively digest the shock by reducing its magnitude to a given region. It also distances the sense of proximity of the transformations, keeping it "out there," at the edge. The border region indeed reflects ongoing changes with peculiar clarity. Yet its uncritical depiction as an inherent zone of chaos obstructs a more profound recognition of the magnitude and character of the changes, both for the region and for the country.

Distant Proximities

The paradoxical situation of globalization is vividly manifested in the border, but this new modality of otherness is overshadowed by trivial and repetitive claims of cultural blending. The concept of distant proximity helps to contextualize the new modality of otherness in our globalized social worlds. These limited contacts do not occur only across the border or across ethnic or national lines, as Rosaldo recognizes. Restricted social exchanges also occur along class and social spheres within a city. The internal differences, however, vary from city to city across the two countries. In the border alone, contrary to common perceptions, the differences are more profuse on the U.S. side of the international divide. This greater range of diversity arises from the greater multiethnic and multiracial composition of U.S. southern border cities. The degree of assimilation of different racial constituencies has been far more thorough on the Mexican side, where, in the case of Ciudad Juárez, for example, we find people with ancestors from China. In contrast, degrees of assimilation, disparities, and tensions among diverse groups on the U.S. side, while varied, range from very high to very low. In the case of the recent arrival of Korean people in El Paso, many are now fluent not only in English, but in Spanish, along with their native Korean. By contrast some longtime residents vehemently reject bilingualism. This rejection comes not only from monolingual Euro-Americans, but also from Mexican Americans who speak no Spanish and believe that any connection to Mexico is a stigma or a liability. Between these extremes, bilingual and bicultural Mexican Americans, Mexicans, and Euro-Americans are increasing among certain social groups. These instances lend credence to Anzaldúa's proclamation of new subjectivities at the "borderlands," but there are also instances of chauvinistic intolerance by "Americans," "Mexicanos," and "Chicanos." Lastly, African Americans, Native Americans, Asian Americans, Jews, and other groups—along with a large array of immigrants arriving from all over the world—complicate, enrich, and emphasize the challenge of accounting for the overriding diversity of the region (Ruíz and Tiano 1987; Martínez 1994).

Each of these groups presents distinct yet diverse characteristics among their own members and in their contacts with the other groups. For example, Mexican Americans, who currently make up the majority of the populations of most U.S. border cities, are a very complex group. In terms of their origins alone, they could be the descendants of Mexicans from the period before the U.S. annexation of Texas, the offspring of immigrants from Mexico, or immigrants themselves. In terms of cultural orientations and loyalties, members of the different groups evince contrasting degrees of assimilation and willingness to assimilate to El Paso or to the United States. They also embrace Mexican American and Euro-American practices with different degrees of enthusiasm and success. These divisions among and within the different groups are overlooked, glossed over in the rampant claims of hybridity.

Yet, theirs is not the only discourse, not the only space in the production of the border region as a sociopolitical construction. Maquiladora plant managers, federal and state bureaucrats, visitors, migrants, and other nonlocal agents have their own vision of, and impact on, the region: their own instrumental use for it and their own interpretations and experiences of it. Then you have the border residents, those who stay and seem to count the least—as many seem to be left to believe. Some of the border residents refuse to be left behind, however. Many leave the region, but others take or attempt to take command of local conditions. The five initiatives described for El Paso show particular modalities of these instances in the peculiar circumstances provided by globalization. The initiatives reflect a mixture of opportunity and danger that they perceived in reference to the parameter shifts in the intermediating function of the city.

Much as in the case of the undocumented migrant who chooses to overlook official requirements, a manipulation of the recognition and representation of the region is at stake. In equal respects, just as a corporation cuts its labor and operation costs by relocating its factory to the Mexican side of the divide, a manipulation of the delimitating perceptions of the boundary accrues capital in the diverse arenas involved. Some of these arenas are the prestige for the scholar, the latitude for the policymaker or the implementor, and the access to lower production cost for the maquiladora owner, as well as the border resident who selectively shops on either side, the merchant who caters to those businesses, the Mexican migrant who seeks higher wages coming north, and the U.S. retiree seeking lower property and service values moving south.

The following chapter delves into these divisions and diverse manipulations of the border. It provides a schematic overview of the asymmetries and contrasts in the city of El Paso and in its relation to Ciudad Juárez. The exploration is made in terms of the social disruptions that INS practices have on local interactions and a sense of belonging. This compromised, albeit intensified, sense of belonging is the representational space in which the multiple yet diffuse groupings in the city come together, but do not converge.

In my view, though heterogeneity is finally recognized, we still grapple with the analytical challenge of elucidating the dynamics that its recognition requires, particularly when the logic or conditions of these dynamics challenge established identities and demarcations. The challenge becomes both more compelling and more elusive because of the shock and exhilaration that globalization represents. The following chapter shows that global reconfigurations are, in fact, not ready-made or certain. On the contrary, as with the border region and its intermediary function, they are contested and uneven.

2

Undermining Reality

A Two-Name River

Half of the Mexican–U.S. border is delineated by a river with two names. On the Mexican side, it is "El Rio Bravo." On the U.S. side, it is "The Rio Grande." These names suggest the different historic implications of the river for the two populations it divides. For Mexicans, the river is a scene of tragedy: it is brave, even ferocious. It threatens and kills. Drownings, rapes, shootings, assaults, and murders occur along its banks. Almost always the victims of these incidents are Mexican; the perpetrators are often officers of the U.S. Border Patrol. For the U.S. residents, the river is *big*, a wide canyon of water. It separates their first world from the third world only yards away. So some would like to believe; others see it differently.

Crime and Punishment: Cooperation in El Paso

Justino Samudio is a zestful man in his early forties, probably the most active and enthusiastic reference librarian in the local branch of the University of Texas. He knows the sources you ought to consult for your research, and he eagerly contributes some opinions of his own to your analysis. For his excellent help you must pay with "your ear," as Milan Kundera would put it. Before you know it, you have learned that he is from Colorado; is half Spanish and half Apache; has many sisters; likes expensive bikes, pens, and shirts; is a local patron for unknown local painters; loves Ciudad Juárez's nightlife; and knows the best places to buy antiques. If your consultation is conducted in Spanish, he will explain his heavy "Spaniard" intonations and expressions, alluding to three weeks he spent in Barcelona some years ago. If you will allow it and he is not too busy, he will proudly give you a tour of the new library building. Along the way you will hear a detailed description of the donated collections in the library, which are found in its main conference room, the room where Texas Governor Ann Richards and Chihuahua Governor Fernando Baeza held an official meeting in 1991 to discuss the impending passage of the North American Free Trade Agreement.

Samudio's description of the collection has a great finale. After casually enumerating famous donors and the large financial value of the donations, he will just as casually walk you out onto the room's terrace for a scenic view of Ciudad Juárez's shantytowns. From your vantage point on the fifth floor of the library, you will clearly see—no more than eight hundred yards away, beyond a highway, train rails, and the cement banks of the river—an irregular topographic and residential landscape. The panoramic view is so magnificent and the landscape so dramatic that you will be stunned at the sight of the dusty brown hills dotted with houses dispersed irregularly among paved and unpaved roads. A chill crawls up your spine as you contemplate the sight of air conditioners on the roofs of sturdy houses painted in once-vivid shades of green, brown, and yellow, set among adobe shacks, junk cars and trucks, water tanks, and tin roofs. As your eyes begin to focus on the details, you'll find yourself watching, as if they were scenes in a silent movie, two children walking with their mother to the store, a city transportation van struggling up the steep hills, or a couple of skinny dogs roaming around piles of trash and old tires.

Then Samudio will interrupt your contemplation, saying that he must get back to work. In the elevator he will help you recover by remarking that he likes to show visitors that view. He will grow noticeably less cordial and more rushed, and this sudden change of mood will cloud your memory of the poor areas in El Paso, which, although more hidden and remote, look very much like the view you just saw. Significantly, these areas are called *colonias*, perhaps to suggest the ethnicity of most of their residents or to distance them from the local mainstream. Gradually, however, you will realize that the ironic interplay of physical proximity and institutional (national) distance you observed so vividly from that terrace was real, but misleading and incomplete. That panoramic view concealed the sordid "third world" pockets of El Paso and displayed Ciudad Juárez as a gigantic shantytown, hiding its significant middle-class, upper-class, and even very affluent residential areas.

These binational polarizations are not the only realities that are muted in the all-encompassing flow of Samudio's conversation. An additional piece of information is contained in a newspaper clipping—one that is not included in his well-kept files. It reports his beating and arrest by INS officers (Old 1986). I asked him about this incident at a small gathering at his home. After a tour of his tiny apartment, which overflows with strikingly accomplished paintings and sculptures bought from local artists "to help them out," I inquired about the INS incident.

He was, he told me, walking back from work to his apartment at 5:30 P.M., as he did every day. He heard somebody in a car saying something in Spanish, but he did not turn to look. Gradually, the tone of the voice got louder and angrier: "¿A dónde vas? ¿Tienes papeles?" (Where are you going? Do you have a passport?). Once he understood the questions and realized that they were addressed to him, he turned and said in English: "It is none of your business."

"Yes, it is!" replied the INS officer, jumping out of his car.

Samudio angrily refused to produce identification. "I was speaking in better English than he. Moreover, when have you seen people who have just crossed the river wearing eighty-dollar shirts with expensive pens in their pocket?"

At that point, Samudio noticed that a private car had stopped in the middle of the street. The driver—in plain clothes—stepped out of the car and without warning knocked him to the ground. Once he had been "dragged and pressed to the floor [of the car], [the officers] twisted his arms and put the handcuffs on too tight." Throughout the encounter, Samudio kept yelling that they were "arresting a U.S. citizen." The officer and the other man took him to the officer's car and drove him to the INS detention center at one of the crossing points. "I had bruises on my face and neck. My arm hurt like hell for over a month," Samudio said.

According to the newspaper clipping, Samudio was taken "to [the] Santa Fe Bridge, where they held him for about 45 minutes before *deciding* he was a U.S. citizen and releasing him" (my emphasis). The newspaper clipping quotes the acting chief of the El Paso Border Patrol sector justifying the arrest: "[Samudio] refused to cooperate with the agents who stopped him in an area and time of day that would lead them to believe Samudio was illegally in the United States."

One River, One Country?

How is one to reconcile this disconcerting but not isolated incident, in which the right of a U.S. citizen of Mexican ancestry to walk home from work undisturbed is "decided" in an atmosphere of fear and coercion, with the facile yet overwhelming celebration of the merging of the two countries? Where does the pervasive sense of distance imposed by the INS and reinforced by the ambivalence apparent in Samudio's display of Ciudad Juárez's shantytowns fit with Bill Moyers's claim of "one river, one country"?

Are we talking about a South African or a Palestinian sort of country? In fact, the border region is neither country, in spite of possible parallels or analogies. It is not even a country in itself. It is a sociopolitical landscape of dramatic historic and economic dynamics defined by a pervasive dislocation, a landscape that is experienced very differently by the individuals and institutions involved. Samudio's incident is better described by Anzaldúa's characterization of the region as a "third country":

> The U.S.–Mexican border *es una herida abierta* [an open wound] where the third world grates against the first and bleeds. And before a scab is formed it hemorrhages again, the lifeblood of two worlds merging to form a third country—a border *culture.* (1987, 3; emphasis added)

Anzaldúa's dramatic characterization captures the social costs of pervasive conflicts and inequities on the border, but her notion of the "merging" of a third country is contradicted by Samudio's incident. Her conflation of "country" with "culture," like her notion of hybridity, overlooks the sharp institutional divisions and power asymmetries violently dramatized by such abuse. In her view, border "culture" is characterized by an inherent tolerance for ambivalence. Perhaps *endurance* is a better word than *tolerance* to describe the dislocated situation of the region. Indeed, *intolerance,* as much as *tolerance,* characterizes the ambivalent attitudes of local residents in this frontier atmosphere.

This chapter describes this frontier condition. Along the lines of Lefebvre's notion of representational space, I underscore experiential dimensions that contribute to its persistent subordination in terms of the social divisions among residents of El Paso and, to some extent, between Ciudad Juárez and El Paso. I highlight instances of alienation, in which the recognition—if not the sense—of belonging is always in question. I point out the unclear parameters created by the border's subordination to nonlocal arrangements and interests.

Distant Proximities

The characterization of the border as a single country or culture impedes the recognition of the dramatic differences among the subjects and situations involved (Ruíz and Tiano 1987, 3). At the national level, this mischaracterization trivializes the wide and profound institutional delimitations separating the two countries, delimitations that are dramatically highlighted by the differential access that residents on each side of the border have to the other. Officially, U.S. visitors have unhindered access to Mexican border cities, but Mexican visitors to U.S. border cities need crossing permits. Unofficially, of course, this restricted access to the United States can be bypassed, but this clandestine access does not erase the official barrier. Those who cross "unofficially" run the risk of being caught and deported. However, the demarcation does not stop at the crossing line, nor does it affect only the undocumented immigrant. As Samudio's story shows, the impact of the border asymmetries is pervasive, but it is most directly felt by Mexicans and Mexican Americans.

Along with the national demarcation, dramatic divisions proliferate within El Paso. Its ambiguous function as both a bridge and a barrier underlie the tension between the local and nonlocal and seriously complicate issues of legitimacy and belonging. This inevitably disrupts the social texture of the locality. Because of El Paso's subordinate condition as a transit zone, the nonlocal is bound to displace the local in most practical matters. Belonging is generally externally defined. Local residents attempt to reestablish their own sense of belonging, if not of ownership, through ineffective gestures ranging from naive claims of pride in their identity to a misdirected animosity toward Ciudad Juárez (which is frequently blamed for everything that goes wrong in El Paso). Most often, however, locals respond with a mixture of apathy and frontier individualism that covers up the underlying emotional rawness.

These complex feelings are manifested in the marked contrast between the unbounded generosity directed to acquaintances in private settings and the hostile self-righteousness of public interactions with strangers. For example, I was enthusiastically embraced by almost all of my informants, who generously provided unlimited time and support for my research. Yet such kindness is reserved for "domestic" settings and "kin," that is, for personal relationships. After I left an interview, I often found a significant contrast between the warm personal interactions I had just enjoyed and the impersonal social distrust expressed in petty interactions. One place where this distrust is expressed is on the city's "freeways," the stage for a disproportionate amount of road rage for a city the size of El Paso. These petty expressions of animosity suggest a frustrated desire to maintain some sense of control over one's context. The sharp contrast between behaviors in private and in public reflects a conflicted sense of safety. Local residents maintain a cautious distance at the time of initial contact. Once trust is established, once the "other" is accepted within their boundaries, the aloofness is replaced by gestures of the utmost generosity.

So who is the "other"? It is difficult to define the "other," even more difficult than defining the local or the nonlocal. The "other" is not necessarily the nonlocal. In a dislocated city, some strangers are stranger than others, depending on the individual's real or assumed proximity to the U.S. mainstream in terms of race and wealth. A rich Anglo, even if he or she has just arrived from Detroit to establish a company, is much less an "other" than an undocumented Mexican who grew up a stone's throw away. A rich Mexican, in turn, fares much better than his poor undocumented countryman or woman—especially if he is light-skinned and culturally attuned to the United States. Wealthy or Euro-American newcomers or visitors will probably be more accepted in the city than many Mexican Americans who were born there or Mexicans who have commuted daily to work with the proper permit for many years. Even German soldiers temporarily stationed in El Paso's army base are not singled out to be made to feel as foreign as the long-term residents or employees.

This interplay occurs in the overlapping of the "no-man's-land" space and the living places of local residents, who live or try to live their everyday lives beyond, along, and/or in spite of the dislocating impacts and overriding presence of the nonlocal. These impacts and presences are contained to a large extent by resilient markers that delineate places and spaces. These delineations are indicators of the incompatible—incommensurable?—juxtapositions that the frontier's local residents (long and short term) confront and/or exploit. Some residents can cross or ignore these delineations with ease and fluidity. Indeed, some of them capitalize on this dislocation with little or no difficulty, while others are thrown entirely off balance by it. The latter are more constrained by boundaries of income, skin tone, status, linguistic skills, and technical proficiencies. Such parameters and dynamics of inequality are common to most settings. What distinguishes the border situation is the pervasive presence of nonlocal agendas and actors.

Selective Integration

In the last twenty years, there has been an absolute demographic decline in the number of Euro-Americans in El Paso, coinciding with constant growth in the number of Mexican Americans and Mexicans. Now the city's population is predominantly Mexican American, but this predominance is complicated. It does not translate into ethnic unity or political control, although significant inroads have been made in both directions in recent years. Such inroads so far are mostly made by individuals, and they add to the heterogeneity of Mexican Americans. Internal differences in an ethnic group entail a multiplicity of situations and orientations with respect to class, education, language, social mores, religious belief, political attitudes, and assimilation into U.S. society. This numerical prominence and its complex composition also make for problematic ethnic integration in a city characterized by latent animosities and restricted contact.

A brief overview of the city's residential distribution reflects a complex interplay of ethnicity, nationality, and class. The city's affluent areas are in the north, away from Ciudad Juárez. Wealthy Anglos, an increasing number of Mexican Americans, and well-off Mexican immigrants live in the hills above downtown, overlooking the two cities. Less affluent Anglos are scattered throughout the northern part of the city, with the northeast section occupied by the military personnel of Fort Bliss. The northwest has a concentration of Euro-American professionals, prosperous businesspeople from Ciudad Juárez, and successful Latino professionals and entrepreneurs. Recent urbanization has expanded primarily toward the eastern side of the city, where middle-class European and Mexican Americans reside at a convenient distance from the airport and the industrial parks. Those parks house technical, administrative, and inventory operations for maquiladora production in Ciudad Juárez. Many residences in these housing developments have been constructed by Mexican firms and display a tasteful blend of architectural styles. Increasingly, however, these neighborhoods are dotted with "For Sale" signs and are revealing signs of premature decay and unkempt conditions. This is not surprising, given the occupational instability of the residents and the transience of the business owners. Many people employed in managerial positions in the maquiladora industry have been transferred. Others have been affected by the closure and relocation of plants away from El Paso.

The freeway system cuts the city into northeastern, northwestern, and southern sections. Poor Mexican Americans and recent Mexican arrivals are concentrated in the downtown area and in a wide southern strip bordering the river from the east to the west corners of the city. In general, the poorest segments of this population live closest to the river. Many of the low-paying, labor-intensive factories that produce garments and furniture were located in these neighborhoods and relied almost exclusively on the labor of Mexican and Chicano women. The area also has an oil refinery and a smelting plant, both of which create health and environmental problems directly affecting local residents and the poor neighborhoods of Ciudad Juárez.

The poorest residents of El Paso are concentrated in *colonias.* In 1993 an estimated 68,000 people—about 12 percent of the area's residents—were without running water and lived much like residents of the shantytowns of Ciudad Juárez (Pendleton 1993, 10; Staudt 1998, 91–92). Many inhabitants of these irregular settlements are recent immigrants, but others are long-time residents of the city who have lost their jobs in the restructuring of the local economy or have been pushed to the outskirts of the city by the overall pauperization process. A couple of my informants reported that some displaced workers from El Paso have moved to Ciudad Juárez to live with relatives as a way to save money.

These geographic, ethnic, and class contrasts deepen the distances between different groups. The direct connection between increased percentages of people of Mexican ancestry or origin and increased poverty in the city intensifies latent animosities. On the one hand, significantly larger rates of poverty among Mexicans and Mexican Americans generate feelings of inferiority for some of them, feelings of superiority for some Euro-Americans, and antagonism and resentment for both groups. Wealthy—or at least comfortable—people may see the poor as an unwelcome burden, as incapable of improving their own conditions. As more Mexican Americans join the ranks of the middle class or the wealthy, they may come to share this perception about the poor people of their own ethnic group. On the other hand, the poor contend that those in more favorable economic positions discriminate against them because of ethnic or class prejudice and deprive them of opportunities by manipulating the channels of mobility.

Divisive antagonisms are also related to the high level of transience in the city. Contrary to first impressions, this phenomenon does not affect only Mexican and other Latin American immigrants. It also affects other ethnicities, such as the Germans and the Japanese. El Paso has a large army base with tens of thousands of soldiers from all over the United States, Europe, and Asia. Personnel of the maquiladora industry also live in El Paso while they are employed in plants in Ciudad Juárez. Some higher-paid corporate agents, often from Asia or Europe, remain in the city for a number of years, but each of these constituencies keeps to itself, creating frozen gaps between themselves and other local groups.

Finally, class configures the distinctive spatial arrangements of ethnic and national divisions in reference to undocumented immigration. Poor neighborhoods, made up almost exclusively of working-class Mexicans and Mexican Americans, most directly experience the raw realities of immigration and marginality. They are frequently disrupted by police raids and, until recently, by the border patrol's incursions. These violent raids have collective traumatic effects, subjecting all residents to the constant threat of being victimized by, or witnessing, physical abuse or harassment, or reckless car chases. This violent atmosphere crosses familial and social arrangements. Some families, many of them recent arrivals to the city, have a parent who was—or still is—undocumented. Middle-class and affluent households, and even many poor ones, employ undocumented workers as live-in maids, daily cleaning help, or occasional handymen (Ruíz and Tiano 1987; Romero 1992).

The great diversity among the populations of El Paso and their different relationships to its multiple arrangements attest to the differences in their positions. In this multiplicity, the capacity of individuals to play an active role as agents of transformation or even to contend with dislocating social effects and human costs varies radically. Bauman's distinction between tourists and vagabonds refers to these differences. Their contrasting mobility in the spatial reconfiguration of globalization generates an urban configuration complicated by experientially and operationally sharp contrasts such as Alicia Armendariz, the displaced worker mentioned before, and David Norris, the magazine owner, living in the same city. However, their physical and circumstantial proximity is severed by their contrasting orientations and proficiencies—thus conditions—in this complicated arrangement. As pointed out by Bauman, their relations to time and space have significant differences.

How Far to the First World

Consider the relationship between El Paso and Ciudad Juárez. How one perceives it depends on a number of factors. In El Paso the "one country" image is promoted by local businesses, by government representatives in tourism, and by the maquiladora industry; the two cities are pronounced to be "one," or to be "sister cities." These consolidating representations reflect a Euro-American or business perception that is not necessarily shared by other residents. Even when there is more intense economic integration, most business people in Ciudad Juárez and most Mexican Americans in El Paso are more cautious in describing the relationship of the two cities. These entrepreneurs talk not of one city or of sister cities, but of "one economy." For example, a director in the El Paso office of the Small Business Administration, Ralph Ordonez, described it in the following manner:

> El Paso and [Ciudad] Juárez are two cities. Yet, they are one in economic terms: 55,000 *Juárences* commute daily to work in El Paso. They buy gasoline here, clothes, cars, and so forth. The tourist attraction of El Paso is [Ciudad] Juárez: its bullfights, dog races, dancing halls, golf course. The three bridges are always full. It takes about 30 to 45 minutes to cross over. A lot of merchandise and equipment is bought here: electronic apparatuses, computers. You can take everything to Mexico quite easily. No customs or nothing. As one friend of mine from Mexico put it, "as long as it fits through

> the bridge." People from Mexico and Chihuahua have the money to pay for those items. Devaluations are what hurt all this.

These divergent perceptions mirror to a certain extent the diverse accounts of the intertextual image of the border discussed in chapter 1. Unlike the blurriness of the borderland paradigm, however, local perceptions reflect contrasting demarcations along national and ethnic lines. In very concrete respects, they reflect different degrees of access and limits, or in other words, the contrasting institutional magnitude of boundaries. U.S. citizens and residents, particularly Euro-Americans, have open access to most of Ciudad Juárez, with an especially welcoming reception by its businesses. Given this practically unlimited and unencumbered access to both cities, they perceive them as one. For people of Mexican ancestry or origin residing in or visiting El Paso, the experience is more diverse, complex, and uncertain. As Mr. Samudio learned, even U.S. citizenship does not assure unencumbered access. Even when they constitute over 70 percent of the city's population, Mexican Americans embody the border in their skin or in their last names. Some exclusionary actions, of course, are committed by Mexican Americans and Mexicans themselves. In the most literal striking illustration of the divide, an increasing number of Mexican Americans have become border patrol agents (Heyman 2002). This obviously calls into question Anzaldúa's claim of a "border culture" defined by tolerance and hybridity.

Still, Anzaldúa's characterization applies in other instances. In such cases, non-Mexicans are not exempt from these complexities. Thomas Bernstein, for example, came to the city twenty years ago from Israel and immediately fell in love with the border. He soon created an organization that espouses cross-cultural understanding among children across the international divide through visits to each others' schools once a year. While his initiative is applauded by many, he feels frustrated that the context as a whole does not foster more such efforts. Insightfully, he speculated about broader factors discouraging such efforts. He told me of an overall sense of apprehension some had of being next to Mexico, a misguided perception that saw this contiguity as a drawback rather than an advantage.

> Subliminally we are saying: "we don't like where we are." My answer to those who think that way is that we are getting along. We need to look deeper. We need to become aware of our lack of awareness of our own dissatisfaction. We need to become more positive in the way we appreciate being here. We need to see that we create our own problems.

He illustrated his statement of this subliminal dislike of being next to Mexico with a poignant hypothetical scenario:

> Why doesn't the word *Mexico* appear in any of the highway signs? The only exit sign says: *Juárez*. Put yourself in the situation of someone who is just driving through the city and ends up in *Juárez* because he did not see a sign that wasn't there [a sign that would specify that Ciudad Juárez is in Mexico]. You have your wife, your children, and your dog in the car. You are going to have to unpack everything you have in your car for the customs inspectors both ways and produce the proofs of your dog's shots and birth certificates for all of you. I hope you have them with you. They won't let you in just because you say: "I didn't see the sign." Well, there was no sign. We don't want people to know that Mexico is next door to us.

For Bernstein, no mention of Mexico in the highway signs is another example of the attempt of an unstated policy to gain distance from a stigmatized perception of that country considered to be the source of poverty and chaos for the city.

In these discrepant levels of "otherness," the scope and character of the border are widely manipulated. The manipulation is easier and more beneficial for some than for others. For example, companies with maquiladoras save millions of dollars by acknowledging that Mexico is right across the dividing line. They cross the international divide to take advantage of a lower-wage labor market, simply by relocating the plants a few miles, from El Paso to Ciudad Juárez. At the same time, as mentioned in the previous chapter, local residents fare differently for this manipulation of boundaries. On the one hand, thousands of workers in El Paso lost their jobs in plants that relocated to Ciudad Juárez and other parts of the world. On the other hand, real estate agents, banking officials, accountants, engineers, and practitioners of other professions or skilled trades have benefited from these relocations.

This economic manipulation of boundaries deepens the complexity of social demarcations. Individuals engage in their own manipulation, deciding whom they will relate to as equals and whom they will relate to as "other." The manipulation is not done exclusively by any one group; each individual engages in it to different extents, with different degrees of success, and at different levels of risk. Look at *colonia* residents. As with Mexico in Bernstein's example, the *colonias* in El Paso are also invisible on Samudio's tour of the library. However, both examples, the dramatic "third world" condition of some of El Paso's residents and the staggering saving of maquiladoras in Ciudad Juárez, challenge the generalized perception of monolithic contrasts between Mexico and the United States. The recognition of similarities that reach across international borders is a major contribution of the borderland paradigm. In that innovative emphasis on crisscrossed connections that belie rigid delimitations and monolithic categories, important overlappings and paradoxes are highlighted. This epistemological advantage is insightfully used by Kathleen Staudt in her study of *colonias* in El Paso and Ciudad Juárez. Beyond widespread scarcity of material resources and irregular attention from public officials, *colonia* residents share great resourcefulness in maximizing their options through informal networks that connect the two sides of the border. They might get used products on the U.S. side and sell them in Mexico, then buy basic goods for personal consumption on the Mexican side at a comparatively lower cost. This integrative strategy, however, is carried out against the tide of restrictive policies that hinder the flow of certain people (e.g., the poor) and certain goods (e.g., used products and vegetables). Meanwhile, under NAFTA, conditions for "free trade" are enhanced for corporations (Staudt 1998, 72).

Colonias also illustrate the transborder displacement that the economic integration of Mexico and the United States generates in both cities. They are one of the shadows of the successful expansion of the maquiladora industry. In the dislocating processes and persistent asymmetries that corporations and some residents exploit and reinforce, the social and institutional balances of the two cities are persistently disrupted. While increasingly connected in terms of economic transactions, they remain apart in the restricted contact that their disintegrated social conditions generate. The blurriness of the delimitation and the manipulation of borders increase as the social setting of the city and its connection with Ciudad Juárez are fragmented.

The degree and nature of the economic interdependence of the two cities are uneven and paradoxical. In terms of per capita income, El Paso is one of the ten poorest cities in the United States, and Ciudad Juárez is one of the richest cities in Mexico. Nevertheless, El Paso, with only half the population of its neighboring city, has considerably more public resources. Generally, the imbalance in levels of control in the exchange mechanisms clearly favors El Paso, but in some respects, such control is more complex. Today the maquiladora industry in Ciudad Juárez plays a fundamental role in the regional economy. In addition, as the fifth largest city in Mexico, Ciudad Juárez has more immediate connections with the federal centers of power in both countries than does El Paso, which is the twenty-third largest city in the United States, and one of its poorest. According to Angela Nuñes, an officer at the El Paso Department for Economic Development, local officials appeal to functionaries in Ciudad Juárez, asking Mexico City's intervention in Washington to get the U.S. government to attend to the problems of the Texas city! In this bureaucratic contortion, attention has to be drawn to local problems by turning them into international issues.

There are multiple situations of distinct distant proximities in the city. To begin with, there is the border on the other side, *el otro lado,* which is neither symmetrical nor monolithic. Exchanges and contacts—however transitory, shallow, or restricted—do occur. In both interethnic (Mexican and Euro-American) and intraethnic (Mexican and Mexican American) terms, interaction is restricted largely to the economic sphere. Although many Mexican and Mexican American families in El Paso have relatives in Ciudad Juárez and other parts of Mexico, the maintenance of familial relations wanes for both generational and practical reasons, especially now that cross-border traffic is greatly delayed by INS and customs inspections, and by the increase in the numbers of people and vehicles. Tourist and recreational exchanges in Ciudad Juárez could be considered more social than the primarily commercial and employment contacts in El Paso, but they do not necessarily enhance social cohesiveness. Remember my personal observation of the two tourists and the two teenagers? Such encounters can restrict and even destroy potential cohesiveness.

Language and cultural differences rapidly become intimidating barriers in an alienating context influenced by political and economic asymmetries. However, these fragile balances are experienced in local interactions that contradict third world/first world, poor city/rich city expectations. Residents from Mexico participate in the economy of El Paso not only as documented or undocumented workers, but as coveted customers, investors, and business partners. This statement by Louis Ordonez, a staff member in the city's Department of Economic Development, illustrates these class and national complexities:

> Most upper-class Mexicans shop in [cities like] Houston, Dallas, Los Angeles, New York. They also shop in El Paso sometimes and salespeople in the stores here, Mexican Americans, have trouble understanding how these "tercermundistas" [third world people] can buy so much and drive such nice cars. They come and don't buy just one suit or a pair of shoes, like you and me. They come and buy ten suits, five pairs of shoes, and everything in the store.

While residents of Ciudad Juárez are customers and workers in El Paso, El Paso's residents participate directly in the economy of Ciudad Juárez as customers of tourist shops, restaurants, discotheques, bars, the race track; and as clients of dentists, beauty parlors, auto body shops, and upholstery shops. In the last two decades, especially, they have increasingly participated as managers, engineers, and consultants in the maquiladora industry. Even poor Mexican Americans can afford most of the services and attractions in Ciudad Juárez that cater to the U.S. clientele. The comparatively lower purchasing power of many Mexicans limits their presence to specific commercial and entertainment establishments in El Paso. Again, this limit is difficult to ascertain. Certain segments of poor and lower-middle-class residents of Ciudad Juárez who lack automobiles shop in El Paso's downtown. At the same time, the parking lots of the city's shopping malls contain many cars with plates from Ciudad Juárez, because its residents make up a large percentage of these centers' clientele.

Employment and professional connections offer additional occasions for social contacts between the two cities. Nonetheless, class dimensions are important demarcations of these contacts and articulate different inter- and intraethnic interactions. These interactions are complex and relative. For example, a lower-middle-class Mexican American salesperson in an El Paso furniture store may have to accommodate the arrogant attitude of a rich customer from Ciudad Juárez. At the same time, an undocumented Mexican worker may take care of her children and clean her house for a weekly wage equal to the commission the Mexican American would make from this one sale. These class and technical complexities contribute to the scant social interaction between the cities, centered on and limited to economic exchanges. The cities, therefore, are not as proximate as their geographic and economic immediacies would suggest.

Still, as the integrating strategies of *colonia* residents show, significant efforts and networks bridge the two cities. Neighborhood networks include gangs, high school boards, politically committed college graduates, and dropouts, all with different degrees of interaction with networks in Ciudad Juárez. Religious organizations and individuals, as well as concerned private individuals from El Paso, run shelters and schools in the poorest areas of Ciudad Juárez. Many of these efforts are short-lived, but others have endured overwhelming demand and scarce resources for many years. One such example is Hands Across the Border, an organization created by Thomas Bernstein, which has sponsored an annual exchange of visits by elementary school students from the two cities since the early 1970s. Other residents of both cities also embody the new multicultural subjectivities that Anzaldúa celebrates, but these proponents of multiculturalism are not the rule but the exception in El Paso. To the same extent, perhaps, some Euro-Americans and Mexican Americans vehemently avoid any contact or connection with Mexican culture or language or with the Mexican city of Juárez.

Like NAFTA, official restrictions and biases particularly target the poor. These barriers have not impaired financial and professional interrelations between the affluent circles of both cities. The local folklore of Ciudad Juárez attributes the current wealth of some of its most prominent families to the smuggling of alcohol into El Paso during Prohibition. A better documented example points to an international conglomerate, owned by a multimillionaire family from Ciudad Juárez, that is involved in the distribution of natural gas in Mexico and a number of Central American countries. This conglomerate began as a concession negotiated by the family patriarch with Texas oil companies in the 1940s. Interaction at this economic level expands social contacts more than at any other social stratum. Well-known figures are known to have been on the elite's A-list in both cities. An often-repeated rumor that cropped up during my fieldwork among upper-middle-class men in Ciudad Juárez, for example, concerned one of the sons of a multimillionaire family. This offspring of the pioneer of the maquiladora industry in Mexico was allegedly dating the then Miss U.S.A., a woman from El Paso of Mexican ancestry on her father's side. Visits by international celebrities, such as Senator Edward Kennedy or members of European royalty, are more discreetly celebrated (Hogue and Carol 1983, 63).

At the upper-middle-class level, there is socializing among individuals from both sides of the border. In these situations, the Mexican person is often more affluent and of higher social standing in Ciudad Juárez than the U.S. citizen is in El Paso—especially if he or she is Euro-American. More English than Spanish is likely to be spoken in these interactions, usually over Mexican food. Some contacts are established at high schools or at the university in El Paso, both of which are attended by middle-class youngsters from Ciudad Juárez (many of whom were born in El Paso). With increasing frequency, many members of the middle class are relocating from Ciudad Juárez to El Paso, often for professional reasons. Also the accelerated demographic growth of Ciudad Juárez has had a considerable negative effect on air quality, traffic, and the quality and reliability of utility services. This has brought real estate prices almost to the levels of El Paso. Significantly, many of the sources of income that sustain these relocations are directly and indirectly related to the maquiladora industry and the Free Trade Agreement, and are closely tied to the accelerated demographic expansion of Ciudad Juárez.

Uneasy Contact

These middle-class relocations do not automatically enhance the social or ethnic integration of the two cities. Most relocations are to new areas already predominantly Chicano and Mexican. Intraethnic interaction is still complex and paradoxical. Consider, for example, the case of the Cardona family. Augusto Cardona was born in El Paso and he grew up in Ciudad Juárez. He attended the university at Chihuahua City and earned a double degree in accounting and business management. He worked with the Chihuahua bureaucracy for eight years but in 1986 was offered a management position by the Mexican owners of a recently established construction firm in El Paso. Mr. Cardona's U.S. citizenship facilitated his employment and his family's relocation.

His wife, Edna Cardona, is an energetic and independent woman from a middle-class background with some university education. Edna and Augusto's three sons were nine, seven, and five at the time of the relocation. They excelled in school in El Paso and were already completely bilingual at the time of our second interview, five years later. The relative smoothness of the family's adaptation to El Paso does not mean there has been no uneasiness or uncertainty. For instance, their next-door neighbors were a Mexican American couple with no children. Jim, who was in his mid-thirties, became quite fond of the Cardona children and played long basketball games with them in their driveway after work. On Christmas Eve 1990, right after midnight, Jim knocked at the door of the Cardonas' house loaded with presents for the children, who already had a generous share of them from their own family and relatives. Significantly, Jim was alone. His warm and generous feelings were not shared by his wife, Amy, who maintained an aloof distance from the Cardonas, barely returning their greetings—even when those greetings began to be offered in English.

Edna Cardona likened Amy's attitude to two other examples of the rejection of Mexico and Mexicans in El Paso. Ted, a ten-year-old friend of her boys, lived across the street. His parents, of Mexican ancestry, had explicitly forbidden their only son to learn Spanish, and they frowned on his association with the Cardona children. The second example involved two clients at Ms. Cardona's small childcare center. After two years of classes at the local community college, she had earned a license to operate a childcare center in the remodeled, two-car garage of her house. After about six months of moderate success, a young Mexican American woman named Emily inquired about the care center for her five-month-old daughter. A few days later, her husband, Thomas, a young German soldier in training at the local army base, came with Emily and listened quietly to additional questions and answers. Two weeks later the couple returned with the child. In this visit, the husband carried on the conversation and expressed his willingness to put his daughter in Ms. Cardona's care—on the condition that she would not be exposed to Spanish.

Ms. Cardona told the couple that she would not address their child in Spanish, but that Spanish would be freely spoken, along with English, in both the functioning of the center and the dynamics of her home, which inevitably overlapped. She also mentioned that two of her three other clients had actually insisted on a bilingual environment for their children. Her prospective client shyly explained his request: he and his wife wanted the child to grow up bilingual in English and German, and they were afraid that adding Spanish to the mix would hinder that goal. Again, Ms. Cardona responded that she was most supportive and understanding of their wish, but she could not guarantee an English-only environment. Two years later, Megan, the child in question, was almost three and had spent most of the days of her brief life with Ms. Cardona, to whom she was very attached, and with whom she quietly but eagerly communicated in English only.

Personal boundaries can sometimes be transcended. During a recent visit to the Cardona family, I referred to the next-door neighbors and Mr. Cardona told me that Amy, Jim's aloof and apparently prejudiced wife, is now a good friend of the family. Ms. Cardona believes that Amy's apparent rudeness was actually shyness because her Spanish is not as good as her husband's. She may also have needed time to overcome an ignorant bias against "Juárez people." In the meantime, the Cardona family's accomplishments are reflected in the children's academic successes. The oldest son received his bachelor's degree from a major university in only three years and was accepted into that same school's prestigious MBA program. The childcare center has grown exponentially and has moved from their garage into its own large building with dozens of clients.

The determination of the Cardona family in their incremental incursions into U.S. society highlights the persistence of boundaries in the city. Their accomplishments also reflect their resourcefulness at reconfiguring themselves and their context. Their educational, linguistic, social, professional, and business trajectories suggest a fluid yet focused adaptation that has allowed them to employ the multiple responses and resources at hand. This resourcefulness was necessary when the family relocated to the city in response to the father's job opportunity—which was later lost in the uncertain vagaries of businesses on the border. The family's determination held despite Mr. Cardona's unsuccessful attempts to secure jobs at his skill level, hampered by his initial lack of proficiency in English and the limited value of his formal professional credentials from Mexico. Overall, he and his wife have maneuvered across the given boundaries and made a success of their childcare center. Other people, however, have been less fortunate in their efforts to integrate.

Elusive Crossings: Incongruities and Agencies

Conditions in the city are greatly influenced by immigrants and transient visitors. These two groups represent a wide variety of nations and regions in the United States. People from Mexico are the most noticed because they are the most numerous. Some come with visiting or working permits, while others enter the country without documents. The number of Mexican immigrants and visitors to the city is impossible to accurately ascertain. In spite of the general perception of a constant flow, many "border crossers" do not stay in El Paso. Some relocate, others commute back and forth to Ciudad Juárez, and many proceed to other U.S. cities or return to the interior of Mexico. Regardless of the stream of new arrivals and their diverse destinations, the proportion of nonlocals in the city is imprecise yet determinant. The 1990 census reports 66.9 percent of the population as having been born in the city or at least in Texas (City of El Paso 1992, Table 1). According to the city demographer, undocumented residents may amount to only 1 percent of the total population, or about six thousand people.

Regardless of actual numbers, the flow of immigrants, visitors, and commuters has major impacts. Mexicans bring with them Mexican practices and culture. In economic terms, the immigrants, documented and undocumented, create a dual market economy. One segment of the market employs skilled workers at relatively high salaries. The other employs mostly unskilled or semiskilled workers at very low wages. The low-wage labor market is considerably larger and is overwhelmingly Mexican and Mexican American. These low wages and this ethnic concentration are influenced by the availability of a virtually endless source of new workers from Mexico (Cardenas 1988; Fernández 1989). Low wages and an inextinguishable labor pool are two factors in the subordination of the site to nonlocal interests. A third factor is the social impact of INS operations. We will observe the debilitating effects that rampant and incongruent INS measures create in the city. These measures, while less diffuse since the passage of NAFTA, are still responsible for a climate of hostility and uncertainty. The interconnection between the United States and Mexico is very complex. Central to this connection is the phenomenon of the immigration of Mexicans to the United States. This immigration stream encompasses documented and undocumented workers and sometimes their families. It includes people of both sexes and different ages, places of origin, destinations, degrees of education, amounts of capital, and dispositions to participate in U.S. society.

Locally in El Paso, documented workers are those who have U.S. citizenship by birth or marriage, but choose to reside on the Mexican side. They are also those with "green cards" (permits to work/reside in the United States), who may also choose to commute to El Paso from Ciudad Juárez. These workers are a varied group, but the differences among undocumented workers are more dramatic. Those who cross the boundary without the proper permits may be first-time crossers or they may have been making the crossing for many years. Some get to El Paso in car trunks; some jump the fence at the international bridges; some swim or wade across the river. Some cross at night, others in clear daylight.

Some undocumented migrants were born or live in Juárez and do not want to go beyond El Paso. For others El Paso is just a crossing point on the way to Houston, Dallas, Chicago, Los Angeles, or elsewhere. Of those who stay, some find stable jobs and hold them for a number of years; others look for jobs by going door to door. Some marry U.S. citizens or other documented residents or become parents of U.S. citizens. Some do farm work in the vegetable fields of Texas and New Mexico, four to six hours away from El Paso. Some work in the city as factory operators, gardeners, janitors, domestics, and so forth.

Some undocumented workers make it. For others, venturing to the United States becomes a fatal endeavor: they drown in the river or get run over on the highway or the train tracks. Many are extorted by the Mexican police or robbed on one or both sides of the river. Women are raped and killed on both sides. Sexual exploitation by INS officers has been reported, along with shootings and drownings caused by INS officers' actions or negligence. Some crossers lose fingers, legs, feet, or arms by jumping onto moving trains or over the wire fence.

Institutional Anomalies and Conflicting Agendas

The official crossing points between Ciudad Juárez and El Paso are the inspection centers at the four bridges over the river that divides the cities. The bridges are massive, bow-like concrete structures about a quarter of a mile long and about sixty feet tall at their highest points. At these high points, the two national flags hang from their poles, ten feet apart. Until recently, the fourth bridge, eighty feet long, rose ten feet above the water. In 1991, a considerably larger bridge was built to meet the transportation needs of the maquiladora industry.

The three other bridges have worn out prematurely from the weight of the hundreds of cars and trailers lined up to reach the U.S. checking stations. Hours can be wasted while waiting to cross. The longest lines are usually toward the United States, and traffic congestion is aggravated by the frequent overheating of engines and numerous small collisions. This chaotic wait is often worsened by the apprehension—or the actual occurrence—of rude treatment or denigrating inspections by INS officers, almost exclusively reserved for Mexican and Chicano crossers.

Until 1993 the great inconveniences "legal" crossers underwent were intensified by blatant incongruities in the prevention of "illegal" crossings. While documented crossers had the limits of their exasperation tested in almost constant processions of private and commercial vehicles (including numerous, massive "eighteen-wheel" trailers transporting maquiladora products and components), undocumented workers entered the United States through numerous widely known passages apparently unattended by the INS, whose officers were busy harassing other people of Mexican ancestry or origin in the rest of the city. One habitual unofficial crossing point was at the larger bridge—appropriately though unofficially referred to as the "free bridge" because no toll is paid there.

Picture yourself waiting in the line, irritated and bored, inching your way to the U.S. inspection station, watchful of opportunities to cut into a faster line or to prevent anyone from cutting into yours, desperately deciding whether to tolerate the steam-bath temperature inside your car or to roll down the window and be inundated by exhaust fumes. You cannot help but notice—apparently unlike the officers in the air-conditioned inspection booths—a group of ten to twenty women, children, and men waiting with considerably more anxiety than you, for an opportunity to outrun officers in border patrol vehicles. The peculiar tactics of the INS often go beyond cruel to the truly bizarre. On one occasion, I was trapped in the slow procession of cars through the checkpoint and for about twenty-five minutes I watched a young family. A five- or six-year-old girl held her mother's hand and her even younger brother perched on his father's shoulders. The four of them, along with two other young males, were playing a terrible game of hide-and-seek with two border patrol officers in a van at a break in the wire fence. The olive van would drive toward the little group each time it gathered the courage to move forward. When the family moved back, so did the van. It moved back and forth toward the group every time they attempted to gather enough courage to try a stampede farther into U.S. territory.

Considerably larger groups of undocumented workers daily waded their way through the sixty-foot-wide, six-inch-deep, muddy waters of the international river at different but well-known unofficial crossing points only yards away from a downtown bridge. One well-known passage for undocumented migrants was a little farther removed from the officers' sight, but was only four blocks away from the INS detention center and two hundred feet from one of the downtown bridges. This passage and several crossing scenes were filmed for a television documentary by Bill Moyers in 1983. On January 8, 1987, the *El Paso Times* published a small article accompanied by a photograph of this crossing point:

> A middle-aged woman got into an oversized black inner tube in the Rio Grande Wednesday. She lay face down as Raymundo Péres waded through shoulder-high water, pulling the tube diagonally through the rapid current. On the Juárez side, those waiting their turns bought burritos and sodas from a vendor pushing a shopping cart. "I take maids, carpenters, field workers," Péres said. He charges 50 cents per crossing and takes about 50 people each weekday.
>
> Big inner tubes like Péres's and rubber rafts are floating across the Rio Grande more often these days, carrying illegal aliens on relatively safe, dry, one-minute trips to El Paso. Seven such ferry services were operating Wednesday morning along about eight miles of the river from near the Asarco smelter and the West Side to the south of Azcarate Park. The rafts and inner tubes have been in demand because of unusually high water and an increased number of drownings. More than 40 people drowned in the Rio Grande in 1986.

This well-established avenue for undocumented entries was, ostensibly, not known to the INS. In fact, the route had developed into a well-organized service in which seniority was recognized:

> About 100 people cross every morning at the Chihuahuita raft crossing, said Agustin Belgar Rodríguez, who pulls the raft ropes from the Chihuahuita side. "In the morning, we cross our regular clients. Afterward, whoever comes," Belgar said. Many of the clients are well dressed. Some get on the rafts with their 10-speed bicycles. Antonia Ramirez said she crosses five mornings a week to earn $30 a day as a maid.

I talked with some of these workers during periodic visits I made to this particular spot. Generally, ten or a dozen men and women were gathered by the riverbank on the U.S. side, waiting for the border patrol officers' shift change or watching for the white and green Blazer. Many of them had crossed for many years with varying degrees of luck. A man in his early thirties with a stable job as a welder in a small blacksmith shop told me he had crossed at that point every day for eleven years. He had not been caught by the INS in seven years. A woman in her mid-thirties told me that she was caught just the day before. She was taken to the detention center for about a half hour, then taken to the bridge and ordered to walk back to Ciudad Juárez. Once in Ciudad Juárez, she walked from the bridge to the crossing point and successfully crossed to El Paso.

These well-known crossing points and the relative ease with which, for decades, experienced crossers entered the United States suggest a conscious inefficiency in the implementation of immigration laws by INS officers. A frequent explanation for this is the considerable economic benefits employers gain from the highly exploitable labor of undocumented workers. Mario Barrera makes this point in terms that suggest the same interplay of erasure and acknowledgment:

> The general assumption is that the Border Patrol is intended simply to keep the workers out, given its limited resources. This is not only the attitude of the public at large but often finds expression in the writings of scholars. . . . In my opinion, this is a serious misreading of the situations and there is considerable evidence to support the claim that things are as they are on the border because of the *interplay of some very special interests.* (1979, 126; emphasis added)

Barrera quotes old studies to identify the special interest he has in mind, as well as the longevity of the semiofficial irregularities by the INS. In a 1952 study, George Coalson, then director of the El Paso Immigration District, is quoted as saying:

> Over the years, from the time I came on the job as District Director in March 1929, nearly every year at cotton-chopping or cotton-picking time, the farmers sent a complaint to the Secretary of Labor . . . or to the Commissioner of Immigration, I am certain for no other purpose than to cause an investigation that would result in one of two things: Either, I get word from some higher official to go easy until cotton-chopping time was over, or cotton-picking time was over, or the men who were doing the work would

> be so upset by the investigation that they would go easy on their own. (126)

In this chain of command, it is important to underline the reported latitude officers have in enforcing their official responsibilities. Another study quoted by Barrera suggests the same latitude: "Between the farmers and the Patrol Inspector there exists a considerable amount of informal cooperation from which both benefit" (127). Ellwyn Stoddard found the same collusion twenty-one years later. Writing about the border in 1976 he noted:

> In as much as the INS and its various agencies are sensitive and responsive to political, social, and economic pressures *which may cause them to lose congressional support during budgetary hearings,* their legal operations are frequently curtailed to fit local expectations. For instance, the subtle effect of deploying personnel in those services least likely to interfere with local farm interests has been documented. . . . Although the linewatch activities resulted in the least productive rate of apprehension of illegal aliens, 35 percent of the total officer time was spent in that Border Patrol activity whereas only 9 percent of the officers' hours used for Farm-Ranch checks, the most productive activity in discovering and apprehending [illegal Mexican aliens]. Either the linewatch is mainly a deterrent function . . . or else is the least disruptive but still visible use of control officers without becoming enmeshed in controversies with the politically and economically powerful agribusiness interests in the Borderlands. (Stoddard 1976, 174–75; italics added)

Incongruence is embedded in the operations of the agency, whose budget is determined by the number of apprehensions, not by the prevention of crossings.

Unofficial crossing points were not the only "worst-kept secrets" about unofficial passages. Many holes in fences were used by "coyotes," individuals who lead people illegally into the United States for a fee. Local families participated in similar schemes to help relatives enter the United States for economic, recreational, or familial reasons. The number and the diversity of these unofficial strategies and crossing points, along with the volume of undocumented crossers, are used by INS officials to explain their very limited success in curbing irregular immigration and to increase their agency budget for equipment and agents.

Until 1993 the agency's expressed role of "protecting our borders" was gravely undermined by its irregular and rather incongruent role of regulating the supply of labor. That year, however, a new interdiction policy to prevent undocumented entries went into effect. It required the posting of fixed guards along the urban extensions of the two cities. This stringent measure initially generated intense feelings of support and opposition among local residents. At the moment, its effectiveness in curtailing undocumented entries is unclear, if only because the volume of unregistered people in the city is, obviously, uncertain. However, a sustained watch at these very crossing points seems to have reduced the occurrence of alleged abuses. This relative improvement is contested by some activists, who point out that the severity of the cases has worsened with the militarization of the agency's operations. Others report that the procedure has simply relocated the abuses from Mexican American neighborhoods to official checkpoints.

Increasing waves of undocumented crossings and trafficking, budgetary considerations, bureaucratic factors, political interests, and economic concerns override the implementation of the constitutional mandates of the INS. Its function as the enforcer of immigration laws has been undermined by circumstantial and individual agendas. As a part of the judicial branch of the government, the INS has violated the constitutional mandate to safeguard the civil and human rights of residents and visitors, most of whom are not in violation of any law.

Any simple explanation of INS operations in the complex context of El Paso is bound to fall short. Many interests and individuals with divergent, incongruent, or contradictory agendas and orientations are involved in the unofficial immigration the agency is officially set to prevent. This complexity was first revealed to me years ago by a local Chicano activist. I was requesting sources of funding for a community-based organization that documented human and civil rights abuses by INS officers. He referred me to the officers themselves. He told me about complaints that he had heard from these officers about the detrimental effect of their colleagues' abusive behavior while on professional duty. Nevertheless, these individual concerns seemed not to be supported by the federal agency itself. As evidence of this lack of concern, consider the fact that no officer has ever been penalized or found guilty by the Internal Office of Professional Responsibility. The only official action taken has been to relocate an officer to another city.

The Who's Who in the Costs and Benefits of Abuse and Legal Uncertainty

Obviously, any definition of abuse is circumstantial. It varies with time, place, and the people involved. At the beginning of the 1900s, during massive immigration to El Paso from Mexico's war-torn communities, it may have seemed justifiable to most people on health and political grounds to confine desperate refugees to quarantine camps (García 1981, 41). Later, during the depression, showering Mexican workers with gasoline as they entered the city had considerably less basis on any moral grounds. Sensitivities and priorities change with time and circumstances. The massive and prolonged confinement of hundreds of Cuban immigrants in the 1980s (during the Marielito boatlift) in some ways resembles the situation of Mexican refugees a hundred years ago, but the situation in El Paso and along the border has finally changed. To begin with, the requirements and procedures for entrance have become more specific and rigorous than they were in the last century. Notwithstanding people's persistent need to immigrate on a massive scale, the implementation of imprecise immigration laws is inevitably open to incongruencies and manipulation. During the Mexican Revolution, the massive flow was considered a political phenomenon and was widely seen as a response to life-threatening situations. In recent decades the reasons for the flow are considered economic, and hence optional. In other words, immigrants are seen not as refugees from trouble, but as a cause of trouble. No moral ground is granted to them. Persecution is legitimized.

While the circumstantial dimension of the persecution fades, the context remains, and the persecution has a social cost. In El Paso and along most if not all of the border region, this social cost fosters a pervasive sense of alienation. The social fabric is corroded.

Allegations and Business as Usual

These alleged abuses are expressions and outgrowths of unresolved circumstances, and they remain mostly allegations because the victims seldom pursue legal action. Alleged civil and human rights abuses by INS officers are tangled in the confusion of the legality and illegality imposed on the border. Nevertheless, it is worth looking at some allegations of abuses by INS officers in El Paso. I learned of some of these abuses in the summer of 1988 as an intern for the League of Immigration and Border Rights Education (LIBRE), a small grassroots organization. Additional abuses were reported by the Immigration and Legal Enforcement Monitoring Project for the years 1988 and 1992. By using the term *allegations,* I acknowledge the unclear parameters and the incomplete and sometimes unreliable information. Given the reluctance of the agency to account for and address these allegations and the fact that most incidents of abuse go unreported, it is difficult to be precise about the magnitude of the problem. Central to this difficulty is a problematic overlap between the sovereignty concerns of the INS and the constitutional and human rights of the alleged victims. The agency enforces the right of the federal government to regulate the entrance into, and the actions of foreigners in, U.S. territory. However, the rights and well-being of foreigners, as well as of U.S. citizens and residents, are seriously undermined in the enforcement and pursuit of that sovereignty. In the frontier setting, even the demarcations of human and civil rights are unclear. Are "illegal aliens" deprived of any human consideration because of their violation of immigration law? Do undocumented workers deserve the same persecution as drug traffickers? Can distinctions not be readily established in most cases? Is the distinction between Mexican Americans and undocumented crossers relevant or irrelevant?

In official terms, INS officers can interrogate individuals beyond official crossing points only when there are reasonable grounds for suspicion of unlawful entry. In Justino Samudio's case those grounds left ample room for interpretation and argument. Did walking in the vicinity of the riverbank constitute grounds for interrogation and detention? Did Samudio's ethnicity and appearance automatically legitimize the inquiry in spite of his class, his flawless English, and, eventually, his loud assertions of U.S. citizenship? Was the alleged degree of violence warranted or was it a gesture of dominance and intimidation? Did his "unwillingness to cooperate" warrant the magnitude of the punishment? What was at stake in "cooperation" was his disputed construction of himself. As a U.S. citizen, in his view, he did not need to "cooperate." And what does cooperation mean? Abject compliance? Subordination of dignity and free will? As a Mexican-looking subject refusing to answer the questions posed, he was a potential lawbreaker in the officers' view. Yet, "looking Mexican"—a vague criterion at best—is not only unsatisfactory grounds for interrogation, according to the agency's standards, but unconstitutional because of its discriminatory implications. Ultimately, however, as the eventual outcome of the incident reflects, such distinctions were lost in the agency's sense of its unstated and mostly undisputed prerogatives.

Beyond individual occurrences, do the social costs of these alleged incidents of abuse matter? While collective, the abuses were, indeed, collectively ignored until very recently.

Abuse, Degrees, and a Generalized Climate of Dispossession

I first learned of INS abuses as an adolescent in Ciudad Juárez. My oldest brother, who, from my twelve-year-old perspective, was the definition of cool, came home with his crossing permit torn. The "local passport," as it is inaccurately known, had been torn and thus canceled by an INS inspector at the international bridge. The inspector was reacting to my brother's anger at the way he was being treated. Unlike my brother, I had been born in El Paso. Still, well aware of the relative guarantees that my U.S. citizenship granted me, I would walk away from the inspection site with a sense of relief if there had been no confrontation. If an altercation did occur, I seldom backed down to authoritarian or disrespectful officers. In those instances, I would leave with an adrenaline rush that lasted for an unpleasantly long while.

My infantile revenge aside, it took my brother a number of years to get a crossing card again—and then only after marrying a U.S. citizen and submitting an official apology for the incident with his application. Irony of ironies, I thought at the time, he joined the U.S. Navy a year later. Despite his college education, he had found only dead-end jobs in El Paso, so he followed the path taken by many others feeling the same desperation. He traded his inspired angry tirades against U.S. imperialism for the practical expediencies of border living, in which boundaries are dynamically sorted and interpreted under the raw eloquence of limited options.

Limited options also underline the way people handle abusive attitudes or actual abuse by INS officers. Justified or overlooked as part of border living, such attitudes and abuses are minimized or taken as a given by most people. In an effort to diminish or avoid their unsavory, undignifying, or threatening consequences, impolite and arrogant gestures are ignored. In more severe cases, denigrating or unjustifiable intrusions and penalties are tacitly accepted. Thus, these practices become virtually unnoticeable.

I realized the pervasive nature of this artificial denial of abuses while doing a summer internship with the League for Immigration and Border Rights Education (LIBRE). This small group of concerned residents ran a hotline to document cases of abuse. During my six-week involvement with this group, I learned of some twenty-eight cases of alleged abuse. Three-fourths of these cases concerned documented individuals. A total of 113 people were affected by these cases, which took place between November 1985 and August 1987. These numbers included only cases reported to the LIBRE hotline, reported in the news, and/or witnessed by or reported directly to me. One account involves a group of fifty undocumented workers in a raid. The total number of detected undocumented individuals is eighty. The remaining thirty-three alleged victims were lawfully in this country. In fact, nineteen were U.S. citizens. Of the remaining fourteen, three were legal residents, which means they held permits that allowed them to work and reside in the United States. Nine had crossing cards, a more restricted permit that allowed them only to visit the United States, but not to work in this country. The last two had other specific permits: one was an official refugee and the other was a visitor with a tourist visa.

The severity of the alleged abuses in the sample ranged from eleven cases of altercations or temporary detention to three people wounded and one killed. In only eight instances was a legal procedure started. Most victims were young (in the twenty-to-thirty age group), male (twenty-four of twenty-eight), and poor (only three could be described as affluent). Two were U.S. citizens, though one lived in Ciudad Juárez. The third one only had a crossing card and lived in an exclusive neighborhood of Ciudad Juárez.

Overtones of quasi-orchestrated intimidation are suggested in the two cases described below. In addition, their contrasting responses also suggest the preempted capacity to seek personal redress or institutional change. They reflect particular insights into the abuses and the responses to them. To begin with, the two alleged victims had previously had brief contacts with LIBRE before the abuse took place. Alejandra Lougi, the resident of Ciudad Juárez, made the strongest effort for redress of the two. Ms. Lougi is blonde, an upper-middle-class housewife in her early forties, whose immediate and extended family has been very active in religious events in Ciudad Juárez, where she resides in an affluent neighborhood. At the time of the incident, she and her family were also very active in the electoral challenge that the socially conservative PAN (National Action Party) was posing to Mexico's official party, the PRI, at the local level. Lougi's husband, the grandson of an Italian immigrant, is a prominent local merchant in Ciudad Juárez who owns property in El Paso and has a number of other business connections in that city.

The morning of the incident, after the usual long and uncomfortable wait, Lougi drove to the inspection booth at the "free bridge"" and was instructed to stop at one of the stations for further inspection. These inspections vary from casual searches of the vehicle's interior, trunk, and hood by two officers while they casually chat with each other or with the driver, to rather denigrating searches in which a trained dog sniffs the car for drugs. The character of these searches is unpredictable, as are responses to matter-of-fact requests for officers to clean the dog's saliva and dirty marks from the car's seat and carpet. At the inspection station, Lougi had trouble opening the hood of her husband's pickup, and her trouble abruptly precipitated offensive remarks from the Anglo officer conducting the search. Lougi confronted the officer, who then grabbed her arm, roughly pulled her to the station's office, and ordered the cancellation of her crossing permit. Unlike in the case of my brother years earlier, the office secretary told the agent that there were no grounds for canceling the permit. Still, the angry officer led Lougi to a small detention room near the offices.

After a couple of hours, a Chicano officer came to the small detention room and scolded Lougi for her lack of cooperation. Lougi, who had recently undergone major surgery in a Houston hospital, was feeling sick and requested to call her family and the Mexican consulate. The officer abruptly left the room with no specific response to her request. Later an Anglo officer, in a conciliatory tone, expressed regret about the unfortunate incident and hinted at forgiveness—i.e., the return of her crossing permit—if she would not press charges. Lougi insisted on filing a formal complaint and being allowed to make a phone call. Eventually, she was allowed to call her sons, who came and took her home. Her request for a complaint form was ignored. Lougi knew about the complaint procedure for INS abuses because of her earlier contact with LIBRE. She had attended some of the group's initial meetings after its documentation of a case involving her nephew, a U.S. citizen residing in Ciudad Juárez and attending the University of Texas at El Paso.

A few days after the altercation at the bridge, Lougi contacted the Mexican consulate and LIBRE ("Que Demandarán," 1986). The Mexican consul in El Paso initially offered his institutional support of her request for an official investigation of the case. Members of LIBRE helped her translate her testimony into English. As evidence of the bruises on her arm, Lougi obtained a medical certificate from a hospital in El Paso. Eighteen months later, however, the consulate's support had dwindled and become evasive; the INS investigation had concluded that she had refused to cooperate with INS procedures. When she insisted on contesting the investigation, the consulate's support became weaker, with vague and infrequent responses to Lougi's notarized letters of inquiry. She was still intermittently active with LIBRE and reported painful feelings every time she came to the U.S. inspection booths. To her knowledge, the officer in question was not reprimanded, though he was apparently reassigned to a different bridge.

Lougi's case is of particular relevance because of her insistent, albeit eventually inconclusive, attempts for redress and because of her blonde hair, light skin, expensive clothes, and refined demeanor. It is also significant that she pursued her complaint even when, in official terms, she had only a crossing card. She risked having the permit summarily removed by the INS under any excuse, as the officer had initially attempted or threatened to do. Her determination to request an investigation of her case contrasts with the lack of involvement displayed by Oscar Ramos after his abuse.

Ramos is another alleged victim with an affluent background. Unlike Lougi, he is a U.S. citizen and resides in El Paso. At the time of his incident, Ramos was a recent graduate of an Ivy League university. As part of his undergraduate program in religious studies, he spent six months in Israel, mostly with Palestinian families, comparing the Palestinian and Chicano political situations. Upon his return to El Paso and, with economic support from his family, he established a community-based organization that advocated a hands-on approach to a staggering school dropout problem in a poor Chicano and Mexican community in the downtown area. Previously, and at the time of the abuse, he had been involved with a local labor organization for undocumented and documented farm workers and had attended the initial meeting of LIBRE. These involvements had brought him a measure of notoriety in the community, as well as apparently negative recognition among some INS officers, as the report taken by LIBRE suggests:

> [Ramos] is a labor organizer, a U.S. citizen raised in El Paso, who reports he was in South El Paso at about 1 A.M., corner of Paisano and Oregon, on his way to the shaping up area where farm workers catch buses to the fields at that time of morning. [Ramos] says that a border patrolman named [Anglo last name] alit from a van on the corner of the two streets and asked him his citizenship. Informant answered in English, "I don't have to answer that" [a constitutional fact]. "Why not?" asked [patrolman name]. "Do I look suspicious to you?" [the legal grounds justifying such inquiry] Ramos asked [the patrolman]. "That is not the point," [the patrolman] answered, "I am asking you a question." Ramos insisted that he did not have to answer the border patrolman unless the latter had a reason for asking his citizenship. [Patrolman] said he would detain Ramos for seventy-two hours, then Ramos put out his hands and said, "Go ahead." [The patrolman] then said he would detain Ramos for the remainder of his eight-hour work shift. Thereupon [the patrolman's] partner (unidentified) approached Ramos, lunged at him and put him into a choke hold and dragged him about fifteen feet to a wall, where Ramos was ordered to put his hands up. Ramos says the unidentified partner removed Ramos's wallet from his pocket and checked his I.D. [The first patrolman] removed a book from Ramos's bag and leafed through it. He then asked Ramos, "Do you belong to this group that wants to let all the wets in?" After more talk between the three, [the first patrolman] said, "I am going to let you go but first let me talk to you." Ramos protested that he did not have to listen and said [the patrolman] and his partner could not arrest him. [The patrolman] replied, "We are not arresting you. We are detaining you." He subsequently let Ramos go. Ramos has since contacted the El Paso ACLU and lawyer [name] to explore legal action related to the incident.

This case suggests that the abuse of authority is seen as legitimate by the officers, an assumption that was expressed violently when Ramos asserted his rights and the unconstitutionality of the "detention." Aside from physical violence, the climate of practically absolute control is reasserted by the officers in their intrusive examination of Ramos's book. Stressing his intimidating gesture, the officer then makes an incriminating comment about the young man's involvement with "this group that wants to let all the wets in." Intimidation may have contributed to Ramos's decision not to press legal charges in spite of his initial contact with a progressive lawyer in town. Given his political connection and commitments, as well as his family's resources, Ramos's decision seems even more peculiar. It could be attributed to his relative youth and to his expectations of having little chance of winning.

Denunciations of and solutions to abuses seem to be preempted by the operations of the INS. While it has an internal office to examine the allegations, the functioning of this entity is marred by the frequent reluctance of officers to provide the required "complaint forms" for requesting an investigation. My own lack of success at receiving such forms was frequently corroborated to me by others. An additional corroboration was provided in a local newspaper clipping, along with instances in which the reporter's anonymous requests were ridiculed by the officers (Fried 1994). This apparent institutional collusion at times results in violent expressions of the utmost disregard, as the allegation in the following case suggests:

> [Olivas] says that at about 9:30 A.M. May 16 [1987], she and her sister [her sister's name], age forty-two, were crossing into El Paso . . . with a group of other undocumented workers. Border Patrol agents appeared and a chase ensued. [Her sister] emerged from a culvert and was beaten by a young Anglo male agent, using a billy club. [Olivas] complained that this was improper. All the detained aliens *[sic]* were taken to the Border Patrol downtown office except for [the two sisters], who were taken to the Processing Center on East Montana [some miles away]. [She] says that they both asked to leave, that they wanted to take "voluntary departure" [a habitual proceeding], but that INS official(s) *[sic]* said: "We are keeping you because it wouldn't be good for the INS if this got into the press." Informant insisted that she needed to return to [Ciudad Juárez] as she was breast-feeding an infant child. She was released sometime in the evening May 16 [same day]. According to [informant] and [her translator] [her sister] said she was transferred to the El Paso County Jail at about 11 P.M. May 16. She was held until 10 P.M. May 18, when she was charged with criminal misdemeanor for illegal entry. However, [the sister] says she was never interviewed by an Office of Professional Responsibility agent [the INS internal investigation office on officers' conduct] nor was she brought

> before a U.S. magistrate or INS judge. She has eight children who spent the three days she was in detention without her. She had worked four days a week as a maid in El Paso, but is now afraid of coming back, even to file a complaint with the Mexican Consulate. The Consulate has been apprised of her complaint.

After being struck by the officer, the victim complained, "That was improper." While she was aware that she was breaking the law, she believed that her basic human rights should have prevailed. Not posing or meaning to pose any threat to the officer, she was apprehended and taken into custody. She did not feel that she deserved what she saw as unnecessary violence. Her expectation of respect for her basic human rights suggests the degree of compromise her violation of a civil law—coming to the United States without an official permit—entailed for her. Yet the officer did not share her view of human rights in the context of a civil violation. He struck her, and he took the alleged victim and her sister to different detention centers. Why was the alleged victim kept for three days even when she was willing to follow the standard procedure of voluntary departure? Was it in fact to keep his own abusive behavior from the public eye? Or was it to hide it from a particular supervisor who would be more sympathetic to the victim? Regardless of the explanation, the prolonged detention only increased the human cost of the alleged abuse for the victim and her family—including a nursing child—and worsened the unprofessional behavior of the officer and his associates, who did not intervene to stop him. The aggravated violation, again, subordinated human concerns—and the regard for the alleged victim's humanity—to civil standards, which were not even properly implemented. Yet, the imbalance of power allowed this violation, the attempted cover-up, and, eventually, the lack of official correction for the officer or redress for the alleged victim.

In this power relationship, the overriding position of the INS was not completely unchecked. The victim expressed an outraged exclamation of complaint. Her hurtful reassertion of her human rights was echoed by her sister, the priest translating the call, and the members of LIBRE, who cared enough to attend the hotline. The reestablishment of a sense of community and of human concern was attempted. Whether or not these efforts were successful is uncertain. Apathy and hopelessness are common in the face of the general assumption that the "border patrol is doing its job" or that the abuses are isolated occurrences with little social consequence.

Abuses, alleged or not, have a major social impact. The lack of regard for human rights that they inevitably imply contributes to the atmosphere of desperation with frontier overtones. The degree of tolerance for violence is heightened and regard for social cohesiveness is lowered. Dehumanized, the "alien," the other, becomes prey not only of the INS agent, but of other residents. Sometimes violence rises to extremes, as the following account of a gruesome murder illustrates:

> Six central El Paso teenagers were arrested Saturday morning and charged [the four over sixteen years of age] with capital murder in the slaying of [name of victim], of Veracruz, Mexico. [The victim], who was in his late twenties, was among a group of about eight Mexican nationals who were attacked with bottles and rocks by the El Paso youths a few minutes after they crossed the Rio Grande into El Paso. The attack occurred at 10:45 P.M. Friday. . . . [The police sergeant] said the El Paso youths first tried to rob the Mexican nationals and then chased them, throwing bottles and rocks. Several of the Mexicans were able to flee across the river to [Ciudad] Juárez. Two women from the group, also from the Gulf State of Veracruz, are in police custody as material witnesses of the slaying. When police arrived at the scene, [the sergeant] said, the six youths were chasing the two women as they tried to climb a fence and return across the river to Mexico. . . . The women suffered cuts and bruises, but were not otherwise physically harmed, [the sergeant] said. "They're pretty frightened by what happened. Their companion was beaten to death in front of them." (Hancock 1986)

This specific incident appears exceptional because of the age of the attackers and their gruesome level of violence. However, gruesomeness is not particular to this tragedy. Tragedies of similar magnitude periodically emerge in the form of dismembered, asphyxiated, or drowned crossers, and murdered or wounded victims of the INS. This incident is particularly disturbing because of the intention to harm, but the aberration is made relative by the frequency of its occurrence. With less extreme consequences, this disregard for victims, for the vulnerability of those perceived as powerless, permeates many interactions in the city. As boundaries are defended by drivers with road rage, the self-righteous and simpleminded exclusion of the "other" influences attitudes toward brutality. For some individuals, dehumanizing actions are a matter of pride. With a "wild west" resonance, this dehumanization was expressed with chauvinistic overtones by a Mexican immigrant himself. In 1987 Lucia, a volunteer at LIBRE, and I met with a woman at a Mexican restaurant to talk about the grassroots group and invite her to join. Toward the end of our lunch, the owner of the restaurant, an acquaintance of Lucia's, came to greet her. Lucia mentioned the reason for our meeting but the owner ostensibly misunderstood her. After mechanically uttering a general statement of solidarity, he proceeded to enumerate his complaints about undocumented workers. "I just stopped hiring them; they were lazy and dumb. I beat the shit out of one last week because he ruined a very expensive juice machine in the kitchen. He got a piece of rag stuck in the gears while he was cleaning it. Now the machine is good for shit."

The macho bravado of the statement conveys class and gender overtones: I'm the boss and I'm tough. Perhaps equally significant, his misdirected complaint reflected the knee-jerk response of anti-immigrant feelings in the city. Although an immigrant himself, he was a "legal" immigrant—in his own view, the right type. The delineation between "illegal" and "legal" made all the difference in his eyes, bringing him closer to the mainstream and its entitlements, such as being able to beat the shit out of "them."

Local Impacts of Nonlocal Change

Abuses and excesses of power by the INS or by private citizens are directly related to the overall context of the city. However, they also respond to the global changes of a particular time and space. In this interplay, the context and the abuses change, although not necessarily in a congruent way. Since the 1980s, the INS has expanded its resources and its official mission. Larger budgets and increases in the number of officers correlate with increasing attention by national policymakers to undocumented immigration and drug trafficking. Political sound bites—"gain control over our borders," the "war on drugs"—translate into wider responsibilities for the INS and broaden its arrest authority (AFSC-ILEMP 1992, 8). In other words, with these new attributions and responsibilities, local rights and concerns are more likely to be undermined and "legitimately" subordinated to urgent federal policies. In addition, new agencies have been brought to the task:

> In June of 1986 Operation Alliance was established to interdict drugs, weapons, currency, undocumented immigrants and any other contraband. Operation Alliance's Southwest Regional Command included personnel from the Custom's Office, the Coast Guard, the Federal Bureau of Investigation (FBI), the Drug Enforcement Administration (DEA), the Border Patrol, and police from four U.S. border states. In November of 1989 the U.S. Army established the Joint Task Force Number 6 (JTF6) at Fort Bliss Army Base in El Paso, Texas, marking the formal involvement of the U.S. military in drug interdiction along the U.S. border with Mexico. (AFSC-ILEMP 1992, 8)

Linking undocumented immigration with drug trafficking, the institutional boundaries between the INS, the FBI, the DEA, and the military blur. What's more, the INS has received training and equipment from the military (Dunn 1996). The overtones of these administrative maneuvers are explicitly stated in the militaristic rhetoric of the "war against drugs" and "defending our borders." Noting the implications of these overtones, the American Civil Liberties Union has stated,

> When war is declared on drugs, the implicit message is win at all costs. Basic standards of reasonable force and probable cause become mere luxuries. Wars are the most extreme exercises in us vs. them and necessarily involve the labeling of entire groups of people as enemies whether or not they have individually engaged in any wrongful acts. The result can be tactics and actions that are disturbingly racist. Wars inevitably involve collateral damage on innocent civilians that must be tolerated for the greater cause. (AFSC-ILEMP 1992, 11)

The increasing involvement in INS operations could be explained in terms of the intensified degree of violence related to drug trafficking. A direct effect of this intensification of violence is heightened insecurity for local residents. Another contributing factor may be the officers' escalating frustration in accomplishing their assigned tasks, given that more officers, equipment, and agencies have added up to more bureaucratic layers and, consequently, increased misunderstandings.

> One [Border Patrol] agent told [*Tucson Citizen* reporter Ruben Hernandez] that the military presence has changed an unwritten code of the border and may escalate the violence. "Before, when we met up with drug traffickers who outmanned us and were better armed, we would make a strategic retreat. And usually so would they. We would both back off from having to shoot." This agent criticized the use of a flare in the December 1989 incident as a "Marine tactic." "We never use flares on night patrol," he said. (AFSC-ILEMP 1992, 9–10)

In a warlike scenario, an escalation in surveillance and the use of draconian measures elicit more active responses from concerned citizens, both in El Paso and across the country. In an important effort to coordinate these responses, at least in terms of documenting abuses by officers, the Immigration and Law Enforcement Monitoring Project (ILEMP) has been launched by the American Friends Service Committee. ILEMP collects reports of alleged abuses in five targeted areas of the United States. All but one of the areas are on the U.S.–Mexico border.

In 1990, ILEMP published a report on 380 cases recorded in 1989, citing an estimated total of 814 alleged victims in the five areas covered.

The greatest concentration of abuses reported or detected was in physical abuse (55) and denial of due process (43); 163 of these cases resulted in the seizure of private property. The greatest number of abuses were documented in the San Diego–Tijuana area (209), with the El Paso–Ciudad Juárez area third (27), after the Texas valley area (92).

The abuses detected or reported in El Paso include two cases of inappropriate use of firearms, three arrests of U.S. citizens, two cases of physical abuse, one case of sexual abuse, and one case of illegal search (AFSC-ILEMP 1990). An important observation about these data is that their incompleteness is due to a number of factors. First, until recent years, no attempt had been made to record abuses. Second, the incipient effort to record the incidents confronted the legacy of silence, which discouraged citizens from reporting abuses. The legacy was also based on a lack of information about rights and procedures. The gradual progress of the project was manifested in the increasing thoroughness of the following reports. Unfortunately, no report has been issued since 1995, even though the office still exists.

ILEMP's third report, published in February 1992, included 1,274 alleged cases of abuse identified between May 1989 and May 1991, affecting a total of 392 victims (AFSC-ILEMP 1992, 19). There were more abuses than victims because each report included more than one violation of the victim's rights.

The report included some 360 (28.3 of total) cases concerning "verbal or psychological abuse," 285 (22.4 percent) cases of physical abuse (which included instances of sexual abuse), and 200 (15.7 percent) cases of illegal/inappropriate searches. Percentages aside, the tragedy of the abuses was dramatically expressed in seven deaths resulting from alleged abuses. Of the alleged victims, 56.7 percent were Mexican nationals, 13.6 were Mexican Americans, and 23.2 were Latinos, mostly Central Americans. In total, 94.5 percent of the reports involved Latinos. Also, of the total reported cases, 17.7 percent of the victims were U.S. citizens, while 49.3 percent were undocumented. Of the perpetrators in the allegations, 85.2 percent were INS personnel, with border patrol officers accounting for 49.8 percent of the total. The spatial concentration of the alleged abuses, as reflected in the report, is very uneven. Approximately 31.8 percent of the cases were identified in San Diego. El Paso registered only 12 percent of the total number.

Allegations of Abuse and Action Suit

The militarization of INS operations and greater public recognition of abuses crystallized in a class-action suit against the border patrol in 1992. The suit snowballed after a high-school coach was frisked at gunpoint by a border patrol agent. The coach was driving two of the school's basketball players to a game at another predominantly Mexican American school when he was signaled to pull into a fast food restaurant by a border patrol agent driving behind him.

> "I pulled into a Dairy Queen parking lot, thinking that maybe I had a taillight out," says [Murillo]. "But one of my students said 'Coach, they think you're a wetback.' Then I turned around and saw the muzzle of the officer's revolver pointed at my face." (Plaza 1993, 18)

The officer, according to several witnesses, was holding the gun with his two hands, arms fully extended. The coach, "extremely frightened," told the officer of his position at the school and added, "I have two varsity players with me, and I'd appreciate it if you'd shoulder your gun." The officer responded: "I'd appreciate it if you'd shut up." After "several minutes" of questioning, he explained that he had stopped them because of a report that other officers had spotted an undocumented crosser being picked up by a car similar to his. He then let the coach and players go.

At first, the coach tried to overlook the incident. "I was so angry and humiliated after it happened, but I didn't think that there would be much support for me if I came forward. And also, my religious beliefs told me that I needed to forgive that [agent]." Months later, after he realized that border patrol agents had also abused many students, he decided to file a suit. Six other students and faculty at the school joined the suit. Each of the students had deep-seated reasons for complaining. For example,

> D. R. was also stopped by agents dozens of times, usually while walking home carrying books and backpacks. Even on Sundays on his way to church. But the most humiliating encounter, D. R. remembers, was in June of 1992, while walking home from his school graduation rehearsal. A border patrol car pulled up beside him and his friend, he says, and an officer asked three times what their citizenship was. Each time, the youths replied that they were U.S. citizens. Then, D. R. recalls, "I turned around and left, and [the agent] said, 'Hey, you better stop before I beat you up so bad you're not going to be able to move.'" The teenager cited his rights, and the agent angrily asked the youth whether he was a lawyer. Then, D. R. says, "He started pushing me from the chest and demanding an ID, he kept on asking questions and slammed me up against a fence, smacking me several times to search me." The agent found nothing except a graduation certificate and a seating plan for the graduation ceremony. (Plaza 1993, 20)

A disregard for rights, even when they are invoked by the alleged victim, is not limited by physical size, age, or gender. Another student included in the suit, "Diaz," was only fourteen years old and physically very small when an attack took place:

> She was walking home from track practice, she says, when a Border Patrol agent in a van stopped and asked for her identification. The teenager told the officer she was an American citizen, but recalls that he kept staring behind her, not paying attention. "In my head I was thinking, 'What happened? What am I doing wrong?' [The officer] shoved me, pushed me, and I fell to the ground. He put his foot on my chest and started kicking me." Diaz is small, with doe eyes and a delicate build; hers is not the kind of body that looks as if it could withstand fifteen swift kicks from heavy boots. She said that the beating lasted about thirty seconds. Afterwards, she went home bruised, both physically and emotionally. "As I was trying to pick myself up," Diaz remembers, "the other agent yelled, 'Let's go!' and they just took off. I'm still scared because they'll keep on doing it. Is it because of my skin color, the way I talk? Is it because I'm Hispanic?" (Plaza 1993, 20)

In this swamp of unanswered questions, the judge's ruling in favor of the students and faculty of the high school was seen as a watershed event by many. Even at the national level, Tina Plaza's article published in *The Progressive,* an alternative political magazine, heralded the event as a major landmark. Plaza, born and raised in El Paso but residing in the northern California Bay Area, noted at the beginning of the article that "some Mexican Americans are rewriting the history of this town." In the concluding line, she notes: "No, El Paso is definitely not the same."

The INS Strikes Back

Change, nevertheless, continues. The judge's decision was soon overshadowed by subsequent events—most prominently, NAFTA. To an important extent, the trade agreement was a change in the rules of the game, but the game itself has not changed, at least not yet. Soon after its announcement, NAFTA altered the horizon of possibilities. In El Paso and Ciudad Juárez, a new vision emerged for a "truly international city." Influenced by the trade agreement, the new vision responded to a new sense of possibilities in business fluctuations related to the boom and crisis of the maquiladora industry. This new outlook may also have been related to the high school students' legal victory.

In the emergent vision, El Paso and Ciudad Juárez would interact free of international boundaries, because these would be removed to their northern and southern city perimeters, respectively. The visionary impulse also involved the two cities' mayors, who publicly endorsed a "Good Neighbor Agreement" and stated their desire to find "binational solutions to border problems." The idea was embraced by a reduced yet influential set of business and civic groups in each city. Moving toward that vision, two conferences took place in a single weekend, each organized independently. One, under the title "Redefining the Urban Space toward Binational Metropolis" (Fried 1994, 12), brought together urban planners from both cities in Ciudad Juárez. The other conference was a "community summit" organized by Unite El Paso, one of the groups I discuss in chapter 4. This multiethnic and mostly professional group brought together one hundred and fifty leaders in El Paso to draft a blueprint of strategic goals "interwoven with the concept of a 'borderless region' that would allow El Paso to integrate itself seamlessly into the global market" (Fried 1994, 12). As one organizer stated, "We don't literally mean the elimination of the border but the removal to the periphery of the area of all the federal inspection that clogs up commerce between El Paso and Ciudad Juárez" (Fried 1994, 12). Beyond commerce, the eventual document included a wide range of concerns, from human rights to poverty and from infrastructure to art.

Change is not linear or predictable. One participant, the city's Border Patrol chief, Samuel Aguayo, did not seem to welcome the idea of seamless interactions between the two cities, however. On Sunday morning, September 19, 1993, only hours after the collective pronouncement for "freer" interaction between the two cities, Chief Aguayo oversaw the deployment of Operation Blockade:

> Initially, approximately 400 of the El Paso Sector's 650 agents lined their vehicles up along a twenty-mile stretch of the border, while foot patrols roamed the hills of the northern end of the line. Helicopters went up and down the line in a show of force in the air, sometimes one on top of another. The initial mobilization turned the El Paso side of the border into "a militarized zone, like in Latin America," according to one observer. (Fried 1994, 15)

The harsh measure enjoyed wider support among residents, chilling the binational enthusiasm. Acidly, one editorial stated, "Operation Blockade managed what no other group has managed to do: Unite El Paso." Support for the "blockade" was vividly expressed in numerous gestures and venues.

The media fueled, as much as responded to, the debate. Radio talk shows, editorials, letters to the editor, and ongoing surveys gave full expression to the heightened public sentiment.

Survey calls to radio and newspapers overwhelmingly supported the measure. Some of the statements expressed a greater sense of safety, a diminished fear of local crime committed by "illegal aliens." Operation Blockade was suddenly seen as the solution to annoying problems, ranging from the number of cars stolen to the amount of tax-funded services used by Ciudad Juárez residents in school and hospital services. Among the many pronouncements of support, exaggerated, hasty, or eventually unsubstantiated claims were made. Swayed by public opinion, the recently appointed mayor reversed his initial criticism of the measure. In Washington, D.C., while at the GOP task force on illegal immigration, he claimed that undocumented "aliens" cost the city thirty million dollars, a claim that was never substantiated (Fried 1994).

Support for Operation Blockade was expressed in very direct ways. For example, some residents brought doughnuts and coffee to the border patrol agents stationed along the riverbanks. In addition, many drivers tied olive green ribbons—the color of the border patrol uniforms—to their car antennas. But support for the border patrol measures was not absolute. Angry and shocked voices expressed dismay not only at the measure itself, but at the sense of powerlessness it implied. Critics highlighted the incongruence of seeing Mexican Americans wholeheartedly embracing the measure, and doing so with a blatant bias against "undocumented immigrants." In the midst of the "euphoria," the outnumbered critics of the blockade held their ground. Confronted with simpleminded claims of the right and need of the United States to enforce its laws, critics repeated that the majority of undocumented workers came to this country to work.

Can any actual cause really be served by arguments in which everyone is yelling and no one is listening? Among my interviewees, I sensed a similar eagerness to embrace a cause, to identify, as if the measure or project reasserted their sense of belonging by highlighting their entitlement to belong. Some blockade supporters' statements expressed their frustration over damages they, their relatives, neighbors, or friends had suffered—people whose houses or cars had been burglarized or stolen. At the same time, critics of the blockade also expressed stigmatizing assumptions and prejudices. The degree to which those property crimes could be attributed to undocumented immigrants or to residents of Ciudad Juárez is very imprecise. On the other hand, rumors and long-established perceptions gain widespread credibility. For example, groups of begging children, who had supposedly crossed the river from Ciudad Juárez, had become a common sight in the downtown areas at night. Comments about this nuisance were often accompanied by expressions of fear or accounts of petty shoplifting, general mischief, and irritating or even intimidating requests for money. Rumors of bands of car thieves added to the threat emanating from Ciudad Juárez. And, in fact, levels of car robbery had gone up.

One's own car may have not been stolen, but reports and perceptions of these robberies not only reinforced the sense of danger but also increased car insurance premiums, so that premiums were higher in El Paso than in most other regions of the country. Thus, when accidents occurred, El Paso residents often found themselves without compensation because if the other driver resided in Ciudad Juárez, he or she could evade responsibility simply by not driving the car into the United States. Compounding the problem, the frequent chaotic traffic jams at the highways and crossing points increased the likelihood of accidents. Because of their city's narrower streets, Ciudad Juárez drivers learn to maneuver expertly, and their driving appears daring and even threatening to many of El Paso's drivers, who can identify the visitors by their foreign license plates.

Feelings of being threatened, invaded, and given a bad image may be accentuated by the stigma readily ascribed to anything Mexican, even by Mexican Americans themselves. According to sociologist Pablo Vila, the blockade brought into the open what people only dared to mumble before. He quotes a local resident's letter to the editor of a newspaper: "euphoria: [as if it were] the best of our times; that was the feeling I sensed in El Paso this week as we rallied around the Border Patrol." I add that the animosities and concerns were expressions of the distant proximities I have highlighted throughout this chapter. I do not propose to look at these divisions in terms of such definite characteristics as ethnicity or class, which only lead to ideological perplexities and moralizing dismay: "How can poor Mexican Americans be against their 'brothers and sisters' across the river?" These projected social subjectivities based on monolithic characterizations of "race," "class," or "nationality" deny the personal and practical concerns of individuals. Instead, the dislocation of the setting, its pervasive instrumentality for somewhere else, foster varied adaptive responses to contend with the overwhelming imbalance between the local and the nonlocal. The polarizing effect of the border patrol's operation, for example, brought to the surface competing claims of being "local" and "nonlocal." These claims reflected contrasts in the scope and nature of belonging and entitlement. Adaptive orientations reflect different capacities for adapting to changes and thus in the likely impact of those changes.

These diverse situations reflect different ways that local residents "live" the border, in terms of Lefebvre's category of representational spaces. It is precisely these multiple and contrasting orientations and capacities that get overshadowed in the facile characterization of the border as representing hybridity. The coexistence of these deep separations within the contiguity of difference of the border are not yet resolved or transcended. Conditioned by the overriding dislocation of the setting, the separations are often reinforced by residents. They are not only caused or affected by transient visitors or distant centers of power, but engaged by residents in their everyday struggle to sort, capitalize, and avoid the impacts of the dislocating flows.

This steadfast orientation is pervasive in El Paso given its frontier situation and atmosphere. This chapter highlighted many of the divides and severing conditions of the site. The following two chapters describe local initiatives for addressing the social costs of the divisions by altering the subordinating conditions, the alienated instrumentalities, of the city.

3

La Vista Grande: The Common Ground of Displacements and Breakthroughs

A Mournful Celebration

On April 19, 1990, El Paso mayor Therese Iber proclaimed her city the "Maquila Capital of the World" (Baake 1990)—*maquila* is the colloquial term for maquiladoras. The boast was based on the high concentration of such production plants in Ciudad Juárez and on their economic benefits to the business community of El Paso. The mayor's personal experience directly attested to these benefits: her husband owns a maquiladora plant, and she has long been a successful businesswoman in El Paso. The pronouncement was made at the inauguration of "Maquila: *La Vista Grande*" (The Big Picture), a weeklong series of events aimed at "increasing the level of awareness of the maquila industry and its impact on the local community" ("Maquila: La Vista Grande" 1990). The event was sponsored by the Twin Plant Wives Association with the initiative and help of Marcela Torres, a young entrepreneur involved in the promotion of the maquiladora industry.

The event and the mayor's statement evoked predictably polarized responses, echoing the polemics generated by the maquiladora industry since it began in the 1960s. Advocates of the industry stress the economic benefits of employment and business opportunities (Stoddard 1987), while its critics point to displaced workers in the United States, low wages, limited training, lack of job security, unsafe working conditions, and instances of sexual exploitation of female maquiladora workers in Mexico (Fernández-Kelly 1983; Tiano 1994; Peña 1997).

Both the event and the reactions to it reflected the different effects of global integration on local groups. A local reporter who covered the event contrasted its celebratory mood with the distressing plight of some one hundred workers who picketed the ceremony (Baake 1990). The reporter gave a human face to the contrast by describing the situation of one displaced worker. Forty-five-year-old Leticia Santiesteban was laid off by the largest garment company in the city after twenty-three years of service. Born in El Paso and a lifelong resident of one of its Mexican/Mexican American working-class neighborhoods located a few blocks away from the factory, Ms. Santiesteban dropped out of school at seventeen, only a few months before graduation. She needed to contribute to the financial support of her family: "[W]e had financial problems. My father was a construction worker. Sometimes he had the job, sometimes he didn't." In 1973, she participated in a long and bitter, but eventually successful, strike for union recognition that received national attention through a well-organized boycott of products made by one of the world's largest clothing manufacturers (Coyle, Hershatter, and Honig 1982). Nevertheless, seventeen years later, Ms. Santiesteban was on the streets again—this time fighting not only for her labor rights, but for her very employment. Along with Leticia Santiesteban, a growing number of garment workers (most of whom are Mexican and Mexican American) have seen their jobs relocated to Mexico and other countries. The number of relocations increased after the sharp devaluation of the Mexican currency in 1995, a year after the passage of NAFTA. As a result, El Paso became the U.S. city with the largest number of NAFTA-related layoffs. By 1997, 6,906 of the city's workers were certified as having lost their jobs due to a NAFTA-related relocation. Over half of these laid off workers—4,201—had been employed in the garment industry (Vargas 1998a, 5).

Concurrent with these closures and layoffs, some local women made significant advances in business and politics. For example, in the last ten years women have risen to prominent public positions in El Paso. A county judge, two state senators, a city mayor, three city council members, a university president, a community college president, and two presidents of chambers of commerce have been women. Except for the city council posts, none of these offices had ever before been held by a woman. In addition, five of the eleven women, including the county judge, are Latinas, and several Latina businesswomen have attracted public attention due to their extensive participation in local affairs. One such woman is Marcela Torres, organizer of the La Vista Grande event.

This chapter looks at local efforts to alter the labor market of the city. In addition to the contrasts displayed at La Vista Grande, I highlight the expediency and resourcefulness of four initiatives. Two of these initiatives are illustrated by the cases of Marcela Torres and Carmen Rocha, the director of La Mujer Obrera, the labor advocacy group that organized the demonstration against La Vista Grande. These examples outline alternative developmental paths and show the differing effects of globalization on the condition of women in the city. The other two initiatives were directed primarily by Euro-American men and concern larger business enterprises. Beyond these obvious ethnic, gender, and class differences, I underscore the overriding discrepancy between local and global resources in the persistent frontier condition of the setting. This discrepancy is clearly manifested in the limited control that local workers, entrepreneurs, and public officials have regarding relocation decisions of major global employers, not only in terms of the garment industry, but of the maquiladora industry as well.

Gender, Entrepreneurship, and Change in El Paso

Marcela Torres is a quintessential successful entrepreneur. She was very proactive in her adaptation to the intensified integration of the local economy with globalized flows. In her mid-thirties, Torres, a native of El Paso and of working-class background, holds a B.A. in communications and is fully bilingual and bicultural. In 1987 she started a communications firm in partnership with another prominent Latina businesswoman, Dr. Camille Meras. Their firm catered to the needs of businesses and government offices involved in the direct integration of the region into international markets. The partnership itself arose from their professional contact during the previous year when Meras successfully ran for a seat on the board of trustees of the local community college. Torres was her campaign director and later proposed the communications firm partnership.

Torres is a conscientious citizen with an evident sense of loyalty to El Paso. She is often involved in activities aimed at promoting the advancement of the city. She received the Small Business Administration regional award in 1992 for her advocacy and support of minority-owned small businesses. At that time, she had been in business for only five years but she was already locally recognized as a prominent role model and an accessible mentor for other Latinas contemplating or advancing in business or professional careers. Torres's involvement is influenced by a wider vision, a *vista grande.* She is striving to promote the growth and development of a local entrepreneurial group that could redirect the city's economic growth. In her view, El Paso has been "sold cheap" by city officials without any coherent plan for economic development. She contends that the local economy has been controlled by a couple of powerful business groups that have promoted the city as a "low-wage heaven" for both national and international companies. This shortsighted strategy of "bringing jobs to the city" ignored the developmental and environmental implications of the companies it attracted.

Torres is disappointed with the current orientation of the local economy. She saw propitious opportunities in the maquiladora industry and NAFTA for local development. In her view and based on her own business experience, both economic arrangements offer professional and technical positions with higher skills and better wages. This view underlies her concerned but matter-of-fact attitude toward the workers confronting displacement:

> A worker I met at one of my presentations said, "You are taking my job away and I have been at [company's name] twenty years." We spoke Spanish because she didn't speak English. I said, "Well, you worked [there] twenty years, how much of an increase in wages have you had over that period?" And she had basically [only] wage increases according to what was being increased by law. [She] never had any retraining or learned to speak English because they kept her there for that purpose. They figured, who else is going to hire her? But how do you tell somebody, "It's wrong what they have done to you and now you have to change." Whether this is coming across as being cold-hearted, in fact that's what I have tried to explain to her. She really needs to look at this as a natural change, an evolution that is happening with or without our help.

In Torres's view, the worker mistakenly blamed the industry for the loss of her job. She argued that most of the eliminated garment jobs fell to either automation or relocation, and most of the relocations were not to Ciudad Juárez, but to southeast Asia, interior Mexico, and Central America (in order of magnitude). In fact, disagreeing with workers' complaints, Torres is certain that El Paso would have benefited had the jobs only been moved across the border. In that case, El Paso would have cashed in on the companies' monetary inflow. Their operational expenses would have stimulated other activities such as construction and business services—from janitorial companies to law and customs offices. These multiplier effects would have also produced direct wages and salaries in Ciudad Juárez, most of which would eventually have been spent in El Paso. Instead, relocating the plants to distant regions robbed the city of these potential economic benefits and employment gains.

According to Torres, the workers' demands to keep the low-skill, low-wage production operations in El Paso were neither sound, nor feasible. In an increasingly integrated global economy, companies can inevitably find other cities around the world with lower production costs. She was convinced that the workers and the government should implement training programs to make El Paso competitive in the new global arrangement by upgrading the local labor market, its wage levels, and the overall technological standing of the city. She believed that her business contributed to this upgrading through the activities she fostered and the higher-skill jobs she offered to her employees. In essence, Torres did not see the scarce and rather obsolete developmental contributions of the garment industry as a great loss to El Paso. From her perspective, the workers' situation, while admittedly difficult, will be improved by the *Vista Grande*. The workers' displacement, in this scenario, is part of a series of inevitable developments and transformations that extend beyond any individual or specific place and involves everyone:

> It's going to happen because we, as consumers, want to buy products that are competitive to our pocketbook. We are going to be looking for ways of finding cheaper places to manufacture and it's our own fault. If we had a way of being able to buy American and pay the prices then we could say, "Let's close our borders." But then again, is that smart? I mean, economics tells us it's not smart because that's what Mexico tried to do for so many years. They closed their borders to competition and now you have suppliers that can't even compete in their own country for maquila [contracts].

Torres was enthusiastic not only about the business opportunities at hand, but also about the potential changes ahead: "The beauty of it is that old rules do not apply. Everything is changing and we must make the most of it." This enthusiasm also extends to gender breakthroughs. Years ago, in my first interview with Torres and Meras, they expressed satisfaction at no longer having to confront gender discrimination. Indeed, their decision to start their own business was fueled in part by a desire to be free of gender discrimination. Both recalled instances when professional promotions, recognition, and reward had eluded them. "I saw that women were always teaching men, who would then move on to higher positions, while the women remained in the same position," Meras said. Torres added that when she was the public relations manager of a newspaper, her boss refused her requests for salary raises on the grounds that "she was single and did not need the money." She countered that single male employees received more salary raises and their requests were (to her knowledge) never rejected on personal grounds. In her view, the professional contributions of women were rewarded not in terms of their own value, but in terms of outdated stereotypes that benefited no one but the employer.

Limited Breakthroughs

Torres is not exempt from pressures and vulnerabilities imposed by the demands and insecurities of enterpreneurship and capitalist competition. Significantly, for example, her partnership with Meras dissolved in 1995 due to their different areas of expertise and interest and to the unstable fluctuations of their firm's market. After eight years, they parted on friendly terms to follow their own entrepreneurial paths. Meras focused on expanding a firm she had owned prior to her association with Torres and that she ran independently during their partnership. Torres, who maintained their original firm's name and main product, celebrated the firm's first decade in business in 1997.

I spoke with Torres a day after her celebration party. In our conversation her satisfaction with her accomplishment and success was tangible. However, her enthusiasm about business opportunities was now more measured. Her attitude that "the beauty is that the old rules do not apply" was still present but more restrained. In her earlier enthusiasm about expanding markets, which suggested seemingly endless business opportunities, Torres found herself contending with an avalanche of inquiries about prospective business deals from all around the country. She was caught up in the frenzy generated by pre- and post-NAFTA euphoria. In a 1995 interview, Torres described the great demand for her service as making her "the victim of her own success":

> I go on and I do a presentation to 200 people. Suddenly those 200 people start thinking: "God, the opportunity is so great. I am going to call [Marcela Torres] and I know she can help us." They don't even know what they want to do, but they want to do something. I had a guy call me, "You know, I just sold my sheep ranch and I want to do something in Mexico." He has the money, but I can't think of what I can do to be able to make money as a company and do something for that man. He was going to invest $1 million in Ciudad Juárez. I am not a financial adviser.
>
> You have this type of thing. It has really escalated since this whole media hype on NAFTA. That is our problem right now. I get a lot of calls and I am working, but I am not making a lot of money. I spend the whole day returning people's calls and what's happening is because we love to do work and we know that we are good in

> the information business, we end up taking each one of these calls into consideration and even if you give a half hour of your day to each one, that shifts the whole day for us and one, maybe, out of twenty is a good deal.

The considerable demand on her time and resources and the sheer number of calls led Torres eventually to narrow the scope of her business. However, it took her time to recognize the need for this shift and even longer to implement it, in part because of the alluring potential level of business suggested by a high volume of inquiries and her small firm's initially tenuous position. Some of the inquiries, while often vague and outside her field of expertise, promised generous profit-sharing or commissions that lured her into preliminary explorations. On one occasion, she estimated that she invested close to ten thousand dollars in phone calls, faxes, and time dedicated by her and her staff. This investment produced no return because the business venture did not materialize.

While the ratio between nonprofitable and profitable inquiries was, in Torres's estimate, twenty to one, there was always the potential that the profitable one could not only compensate for the other calls, but could possibly propel the firm along a path of major success. Moreover, because of its recent establishment and its limited capital reserves as a small business, the firm could not afford to blindly shun alternative sources of business. In the meantime, attending to all the calls was a major drain because they seldom yielded profits. On the contrary, most calls resulted in time-consuming initial queries, problematic clients, or aborted ventures.

These complications alerted Torres that her earlier enthusiasm about "old rules" not applying may have been exaggerated. Instead, the apparently favorable market conditions imposed challenging demands on her skills and judgment to sort through nonmarket contingencies derived from her location, her ethnicity, and her gender. For example, Torres said that she often found herself having to negotiate over the price of her directories because of prevailing misconceptions:

> [Some clients] also perceive Mexico as being cheap. This goes back to the way the whole media presented the disparity of wages [between the two countries]. Yeah, you look in the papers: "It is cheap there." No doubt about it. So you have a perception that everything is cheap, including my work: "You charge a hundred dollars for a directory. I can get that information for free." So pretty soon, I am sitting there and negotiating: "What if I sold it to you for eighty dollars?" and I cheapen my own service.

Torres's firm is registered as a U.S. company, it is located in the United States, and most of the companies in her directory are U.S.-based. Nevertheless, the fact that the maquiladora plants are in Mexico, the fact that her firm is on the border, and the fact that she is Mexican American were misconstrued by some clients as part of the bargains to be gained from NAFTA. As a woman, Torres also contended with unprofitable requests and consultations that perhaps would not have been made of a man. Such requests, for example, came from individuals with vague ideas for possible business ventures that they would noncommittally explore with Torres, relying on the reifying perception and unspoken expectation of women as "patient and understanding," i.e., "good listeners."

These unconventional requests may have appeared natural given the image of woman as nurturing. Yet they also suggest the extent to which Torres herself was trapped in this set of traditional expectations. In an endearing tone, Torres characterized her callers as "dreamers" or "opportunists." "Dreamers" were those without capital, but with intense drive for an innovative business idea to take advantage of NAFTA. "Opportunists" were those with capital who would manipulate Torres into doing work for them under the promise of a business deal that would not come into being: "They end up paying me twenty dollars for something I could have probably sold for a thousand dollars," noted Torres. In both instances, these clients took advantage of her good disposition, which without a doubt led her to offer generous advice to the misguided "dreamers" and to trust the manipulative "opportunists."

Aside from gender, Torres's characterization also had a class dimension. Both types of problematic clients took advantage of the firm's weak standing as a new small business. Depending initially on a few temporary contracts, she contended with these different types of contingencies. Once the established market for her product consolidated at a reliable level of sales, Torres could afford to recognize that "a lot of calls does not mean a lot of business." She became less patient with both dreamers and opportunists. She narrowed the scope of her business and became less tempted by vague inquiries and undefined promises. At the time of our interview, the directory's sales had consistently followed the expansion of the industry, increasing in ten years from five hundred to six thousand directories worldwide.

This narrower focus meant a significant restructuring of Torres's firm. The number of employees decreased from sixteen to ten and she moved her business to a smaller office. She expressed regret not only for laying off some workers, but for being unable to create more jobs. Her comment suggested the sacrifice of her social commitments as a citizen and businesswoman to the naked command of the market: "It was difficult laying off employees but I realized that if I didn't do it I was risking my business and then I wouldn't even be able to employ the ones I'm still responsible to for helping bring bread to their homes." In turn, by reducing the overhead costs, the layoffs and the smaller office freed resources to expand and consolidate the quality and circulation of the maquiladora directory. At that time, Torres's main focus was selling the directory on the Internet. Not exempt from hardships and uncertainties, Torres was ready to embark into the unfolding future of the electronic world, while the garment workers seemed to be left behind.

Gender, Change, Layoffs—and Whose City Is This Anyway?

"The garment industry is a thing of the past" was a common statement among local entrepreneurs in El Paso in 1990. Carmen Rocha, the director of La Mujer Obrera (Working Woman), disagreed. For her and the other members of this labor advocacy group, the immediate task at hand was not the potential relocation of maquiladoras, but the ongoing relocations of garment factories.

In the 1950s the number of El Paso garment factories producing for the national market expanded exponentially, often because production operations from factories in other parts of the country relocated to the city (e.g., Levi Strauss, headquartered in San Francisco). These relocations, a national version of what would eventually—in its international phase—create the maquiladora industry, employed primarily Mexican and Mexican American women. In the earlier reconfiguration, many of these workers did not even reside in El Paso, but commuted daily from Ciudad Juárez across the river (Mitchell 1955, 80-81, in Towers 1991, 25). In the later reconfiguration, as major companies increased their geographical dispersion, they also reconfigured their corporate structures, subcontracting many jobs to small businesses that subcontracted in turn, creating a pyramid-like structure.

In El Paso, the fragmentation of larger firms created opportunities for former managers and supervisors to open their own subcontracting firms. In a way analogous to Torres's experience, the change provided business opportunities for new ventures, which were particularly welcomed by entrepreneurial individuals in the face of the ongoing layoffs. On the other hand, the business opportunities were hampered by impending crises that arose from capital and technical challenges that the small contractors were ill-prepared to meet. They had to get by on smaller profit margins due to their lower positions on the pyramid. At the same time, they had to juggle erratic workloads as orders increased or dwindled away in response to the industry's volatile markets (Towers 1991).

The costs and consequences of these problems were often passed on to workers in the form of poor working conditions and subminimum wages. These irregularities sometimes climaxed in overnight closures as owners left, dumping their financial liabilities on the city, the banks, and the workers—who sometimes went unpaid. According to Rocha, some owners would soon reopen, registering their businesses under new names to evade their legal responsibilities. These unfortunate tactics vividly suggest the bottom-line approach dictated by capitalist competition. Yet this was not the only option available. For example, La Mujer Obrera displayed a remarkable degree of resourcefulness and flexibility in adeptly confronting contextual changes and proposing long-range changes.

In 1990, eight years after its founding, La Mujer Obrera had seven permanent staff members and a handful of occasional volunteers. All but one of the staffers were women and, with the exception of two Euro-American women, they were Chicanos, two of whom had immigrated to the United States as adults from Mexico and worked in the garment industry. The group was funded primarily by grants from national and international organizations. Alarmed by the social impact of economic changes—the plant closures and the restructuring of the industry into subcontracting firms—La Mujer Obrera aimed to generate public awareness of what it perceived as the city of El Paso's incongruent economic strategy of promoting the maquiladora industry in Ciudad Juárez. In their view, this strategy was actually inducing plants in El Paso to relocate across the border, thus generating unemployment locally. The incongruity of the city's position was underlined by the disregard shown by many public officials to the aggravating conditions of workers. One evident example of this disregard was the failure of local and state authorities to intervene in the blatantly irregular labor practices of small shops that closed and reopened overnight.

Requests from La Mujer Obrera to protect the workers' rights were met with bureaucratic excuses and claims of insufficient resources and personnel to tackle the backlog of complaints. The initial response of the advocacy group to these bureaucratic dodges was militant confrontation. At first, members demonstrated at City Hall and at the entrances of factories with bad labor practices. When that approach failed, six women—three workers and three members of Mujer Obrera, including Rocha—chained themselves to sewing machines in a small garment shop. This particular shop's owner owed workers back wages, and they saw indications that he might close the factory overnight. The six women were arrested for criminal trespassing, and the three activists spent three days in jail, refusing to post bonds for their release. Their refusal was intended to point out the inconsistency of jailing them for demanding back wages for workers while failing to prosecute the bosses who owed the wages. Given the awkwardness of the situation, the authorities released Rocha and her colleagues (Martínez 1990). Capitalizing on the publicity the event had received, Mujer Obrera began a seven-day hunger strike to pressure the authorities to attend to the workers' problems. During that week they held public meetings with El Paso's congressman, its district attorney, and its city council, asking them all to stand up for workers' rights. In the following weeks, Mujer Obrera also held protests in New York and Los Angeles to bring pressure to bear on the contractors and the retailers of the products manufactured by companies that owed wages. The International Ladies Garment Workers Union supported these activities.

Despite their high visibility, these actions did not produce the results Rocha had hoped for, so she reexamined the issue. In her mid-thirties, college educated, and from a family with a history of involvement in the Chicano movement of the 1960s and 1970s, Rocha was equipped with ample knowledge of both the social effects of the technological and organizational trends reshaping the garment industry and the academic and media discussion of these trends. She stressed that, as plants relocate, cities lose tax revenues at precisely the time when money is most needed to meet increased demands for social services, especially unemployment-related services. Unemployment obviously adds to the need for retraining, but it also increases the rates and incidents of alcoholism, domestic violence, and suicide.

Rocha's direct exposure to the everyday functioning of the industry allowed her to recognize the overwhelming magnitude of the changes and to opt for a concerted solution. Aware of the weak technical and financial position of small contractors, Mujer Obrera looked for a more cooperative approach to the root of the problem: the technical and spatial reconfiguration of the garment industry. This concerted spirit was grounded in a distinction she perceived among entrepreneurs. Displaying a refreshing ideological flexibility, she differentiated between impresarios (entrepreneurs) and *barbajanes* (crooks):

> [*Barbajanes* have] no business plan or ethics. [They are] those who lack a sense of planning, who set up a business just for the quick profit, with no commitment or sense of building anything, just for the quick kill. They don't care about anything, their business, their workers, the community, nothing. As soon as the business stops yielding a huge, easy profit, they fold down and look for some

> other chance to make a lot of money with very little work or risk. They just keep going from one business to another, like hustlers or gamblers.

Rocha recognized the *empresarios,* those business people who, in contrast to the *barbajanes,*

> have a business plan and care about their business and the community. Those who at least pay minimum wages and care about the basic rights of their workers. These are the business people who are committed to the growth of their businesses, who invest with long-term goals in mind. [Those] who understand that they can't just take from the community without putting anything back. Unfortunately, there aren't many of these.

This conciliatory position (which did not mean rejecting the possibility of militant action under certain conditions) took the form of an appeal to the private and public sectors of the city, asking them to formulate a collective plan for revitalizing the garment industry. Rocha's initial idea was well received by a midlevel administrator in the local chamber of commerce who helped her develop and implement the project. The receptiveness of this administrator, Horacio Garrido, arose from his own background. A Latino in his early forties, Garrido had left his native El Paso in his mid-twenties to do graduate work toward a doctorate in political science at an Ivy League school. He returned to his hometown to gather data for his dissertation and found himself involved in a number of community and city projects that have so far prevented him from completing his doctorate. The belief in community empowerment that he had drawn from the works of the Brazilian pedagogue Paolo Freire made him responsive to Rocha's search for creative approaches to revitalizing the garment industry. Garrido served as a liaison between the workers' group and individuals in the industry along with other concerned business people. The tactful Garrido provided contacts and bureaucratic savvy, presenting Rocha's idea as more than simply a "garment industry as a thing of the past" and calming the concerns of business people about working with "militant activists."

Rocha's idea was supported by a handful of garment factory owners, a few public officials, and other *empresarios* (Pérez 1990). However, this cooperative attitude was frequently weakened by practical and ideological factors. Heavy schedules and workloads, as well as a certain amount of mutual distrust among some people involved, delayed the progress of the meetings for some months. Eventually, participants agreed to develop a plan for a concerted effort by the city, the private sector, and workers to capitalize on the long-established assets of El Paso as a garment production center. The plan, which was presented to city officials as a developmental strategy in October 1990, proposed the development of the local infrastructure in accordance with the new technologies and processes of the industry.

The initial part of this strategy was the creation of an industrial incubator, the High Fashion Institute, to foster the stability and growth of small firms in the reconfigured industry. The central component of this initial project was the assistance provided to subcontractors in their environment of intense competition. In Rocha's words, the aim was to help them become "better bosses" through technical training in bookkeeping, marketing, financial programs, and their legal responsibilities to their workers. The success of these small firms, it was hoped, would demonstrate the value of increasing specialization in more sophisticated operations and would assure the garment industry's local stability, as well as higher skill and income levels for workers and the city as a whole.

Limited Breakthroughs II

After the project was presented to city officials, the precarious enthusiasm for this cooperative effort waned. Shortly after the announcement, the promises and uncertainties created by political campaigns for upcoming local elections derailed the project's short-lived momentum. In the meantime, the La Mujer Obrera maintained its efforts to address immediate needs. Its denunciation of bad labor practices finally elicited a two-week Labor Department investigation of local garment factories, which found irregularities—ranging from unpaid wages and wages below the legal minimum to employment of minors—in twenty factories. Working conditions in six of the plants also presented safety or health hazards for the workers, and estimated unpaid wages totaled $85,000 ("Fed Probe Finds Violations" 1990). Despite these findings, no immediate action was taken by any government agency. It took nine months of interrupted debate in the state senate to pass an amendment establishing criminal charges for "willful nonpayment of wages" as a third-degree felony (Scharrer 1991). While the evidence was clear, some legislators opposed the bill on the grounds that it would generate an "antibusiness" image and discourage companies from relocating to Texas.

The militant activities of the labor group were set aside because the growth of the garment industry improved the situation of the workers. In 1993 the group's operations were well under way, but they were undoubtedly affected by Rocha's departure from El Paso to become a board member of a New York City–based national foundation that promotes community-based projects aiming to advance social justice. In 1994, she left that position to become the spokesperson of the Zapatista Army for National Liberation (Ejército Zapatista de Liberación Nacional) in the United States. The high command of this army, which took up arms against the Mexican government in January 1994, selected Rocha as a member of its political team because of her long involvement in the political causes of poor people.

Rocha's departure did not terminate her involvement with La Mujer Obrera, though it certainly reduced her immediate input and the degree of energy she committed to local events. In turn, however, her administrative involvement with the national organization created a whole new level of relationships for La Mujer Obrera, linking it with other groups around the country and giving it access to new resources. Indeed, as many large corporations have benefited from globalization, La Mujer Obrera also gained a broader reach through Rocha's involvement with other networks in her new position.

At the onset of NAFTA, initial developments in the ongoing reconfigurations looked propitious for La Mujer Obrera's plan. The High Fashion Institute opened in 1994 with one full-time staff person, two consultants, and a ten-member advisory board that included owners of garment factories and a representative of the largest garment company in the city. The only direct connection between the institute and La Mujer Obrera, its founder, was the participation of one consultant who worked with both groups. This rather tenuous connection did not seem to concern the members, who stated that they never intended to incorporate or be incorporated by the institute. The institute surpassed its original goals in both of its two first years of operations. It set out to assist thirteen companies per year and to assure employment to a minimum of 39 workers. In fact, the institute assisted fifteen companies each year, and approximately 290 workers benefited.

The institute offers basic bookkeeping and managerial instruction along with help in finding and negotiating contracts with manufacturers. Originally, the institute hoped to promote the diversification of locally manufactured garments, moving from production dominated by denim jeans into other operations, especially those catering to the women's fashion market. This has been a slow process because some subcontractors—given their financial, technical, or marketing limitations—have been reluctant to venture into new operations.

La Mujer Obrera seemed poised and ready to carry on its ambitious plans in 1995. It completed the renovations of a new facility, which would eventually become the child-care center. It acquired an additional large building to use as its training facility. Its attempts to buy a large three-story building to house its offices and classrooms, however, did not materialize in the last phase of the negotiations, and the organization's momentum ebbed from that point on. Significantly, its change of fortune closely followed the employment trend of the garment industry. At the onset of NAFTA, the decline of employment in the local garment industry was temporarily reversed, rising from its lowest point in October 1990 (15,800 workers) to its highest peak ever in September 1995 (21,100 workers). The employment growth was attributed to expansions made by larger companies in specialized operations, particularly in cutting. In addition, there has been significant growth in the business of industrial laundries doing stone and acid treatment of fabric for prewashed jeans. By November 1995 there were only 20,000 workers in the industry, but 20,600 a month later. Local observers attributed these initial fluctuations to the periodic shifts in the industry. However, these fluctuations started a long wave of plant relocations and layoffs.

At the time the trade agreement was approved, money was earmarked for assisting communities that could expect to suffer from employment dislocation. These funds, allocated though the Trade Adjustment Assistance Program, were to provide displaced workers with unemployment benefits, stipends for job training, job placement programs, and relocation assistance. During the first two years after the passage of NAFTA, before the relocations intensified, members of La Mujer Obrera concentrated on influencing the administration of federal funds. However, aside from relocations, NAFTA presented another impending risk, which forced the group to expand its focus beyond the garment industry per se. Stimulated by NAFTA-related commercial and transportation activities, business interests began to encroach on working-class neighborhoods in the downtown areas nearby international crossing points. Thus, workers faced the threat of being displaced not only occupationally, but residentially, as their neighborhoods were at risk for being turned into warehousing and commercial zones.

The labor advocates formulated a plan to promote comprehensive development of these neighborhoods to counter their imminent dislocation. The plan called for the creation of jobs through cultural events, housing renewal, community service projects, and industrial and commercial development. In addition, turning liabilities into assets in an adept fashion, the new plan would give La Mujer Obrera the capacity to operate as a "comprehensive bilingual vocational training center for displaced workers" by administering some of the federal programs. While maintaining its previous functions, La Mujer Obrera would serve as a one-stop training center to meet the multiple needs of the workers, offering classes in citizenship, leadership development, conversational English, and such technical concerns as communication and basic computing skills. The service center aimed to avoid bureaucratic and transportation barriers, since most of these workers have little formal education and very few have cars. The plan also stressed the need for child-care service at the center and for bilingual assistance and training—barriers that could undermine a worker's ability to take advantage of training programs.

The energy and time La Mujer Obrera dedicated to the new plan was soon overtaken by the urgent needs of displaced workers. Ominously, the failure to acquire the new building and consolidate its operations as a one-stop center weakened the group's capacity to apply in the systematic way it had planned for federal funds to address workers' needs.

Bureaucratic Entanglements and Committed Ineptitude

Subsequent plant relocations have indeed made the garment industry in the city "a thing of the past." By 1997 the city had the nation's largest number of NAFTA-related layoffs. In fact, the growth in employment during and after the treaty's negotiations eventually complicated the situation of local workers. In the partial recognitions of alienated instrumentality, the fantasy of growth only distracted from the worsening of local conditions. In this fantasy, first the gradual and then the not-so-gradual wave of dismissals left workers contending with federal, state, and local bureaucracies poorly prepared to assist them in their dislocation.

Overwhelmed by a mounting number of displaced workers, La Mujer Obrera's resources and energies were consumed in day-to-day relief operations and basic guidance for the workers contending with incongruous and callous bureaucratic attitudes. In my interviews with local officers administering the relief funds, I was often struck by their myopic emphasis on the workers' lack of education, timidity, or desperation when they could have been devising strategies for sidestepping the ill-conceived institutional responses designed by their agencies.

Most bureaucrats were unwilling to reformulate their frames of reference to understand the magnitude and urgency of the problems. A factor frequently pointed out by empathetic yet matter-of-fact local bureaucrats was most workers' lack of proficiency in English. Allegations that "they don't want to learn the language" sufficed in their eyes to excuse administrative bottlenecks in which the workers' desperation was increased by unsuccessful visits and long waits to find out that "No han llegado sus papeles" ("Your papers have not arrived yet"). In stark contrast, complaints and pleas about children's school expenses and/or landlords' threats of eviction were met with such definitive answers as, "I'm sorry, but it is not up to me. This is decided in Austin." In other instances, workers who fared better in this bureaucratic loop were caught in the next one—their enrollment in training programs. These ad hoc programs offered training for jobs that did not yet exist, offered lower pay and benefits, or did not consider middle-aged, monolingual, working-class displaced workers to be desirable employees.

La Mujer Obrera had already warned about these chaotic scenarios. Their predictions, however, were dismissed in the glow of the industry's expansion, sometimes even dismissed by explicit statements of company representatives. For example, in 1995, contrary to what I had been told by a staff person at La Mujer Obrera, the community-relations director of a multinational company with numerous plants in El Paso assured me that there were no plans to move operations from the city to Central America. Perhaps the spokesperson did not know about or foresee the relocations that started a few months later. Apparently, in the dynamic scenario of international production, the only guarantee is that there *is* no guarantee. Expect the "unexpected."

These complexities eluded most bureaucrats in El Paso. Single-mindedly, they insisted on stressing the "human capital" factors that perpetuated the culture of poverty and on offering blame-the-victims excuses. At the same time, the cogs and wheels of the bureaucratic machinery squashed the efforts of the displaced workers, augmenting their desperation and their dislocation. In this Kafkaesque scenario, multiple "inadequacies" were invoked but not resolved. In another manifestation of the alienated instrumentalities of the city, the workers' needs were, nevertheless, used to secure funds that were not only poorly used, but that actually worsened the problems. Notwithstanding, bureaucracies increased their public visibility, their budgets, and their "clients." For example, admittance to training programs was conditioned on the completion of a sequence of English courses. Many workers were directed to an old school in a Mexican American neighborhood for these courses. However, many workers I interviewed complained that classes at that school advanced at a tortuous pace and consisted mostly of drills and grammar exercises. In my interview with one of the school administrators, I sensed a greater commitment to "doing things by the book" than to the welfare of the workers. In fact, a number of workers complained that the books they used at school were outdated recycled elementary school texts *(del tiempo de la cachetada)*. Based on the notebooks they showed me, the school officials appeared more concerned with being good administrators than with being good pedagogues. The administrator's concern for guidelines overrode his nevertheless sincere concern for the workers' situation.

Aside from the difficulty most adults have in mastering a foreign language, these students endured outdated and ineffective classes at what they ironically referred to as *la escuelita* (the little school). Resentful and frustrated at being treated like children, the workers half-heartedly applied themselves to acquiring the language. This mixture of hostility and resignation was underlined by tangible desperation over their uncertainty and lack of options. Ethnic resentments worsened the workers' attitudes toward the imposition of English. For some, the requirement was unjustifiable. Repeated pronouncements that "English is the language of business" were ridiculed with bitter retorts about maquiladora workers across the border performing sophisticated operations while being monolingual in Spanish. In the view of a few workers, the precariousness of their situation was being exploited to advance an English-only agenda and to undermine their culture and their sociopolitical position. Certainly, it at least provided a functional smokescreen for ineffective and out-of-touch programs.

Reduced to remedial services, La Mujer Obrera provided a space for many of the displaced workers to discuss their situations and alternatives. It also coordinated activities, such as a food bank, to maximize their scarce resources. At times it mobilized to make collective demands, for example by picketing meetings held to design future training programs. Finally, through endless meetings with Labor Department officials, in 1997 La Mujer Obrera gained a six-month extension in the benefits period for workers whose training opportunities had been impaired by delays or ineffective implementation of assistance programs. This accomplishment, however, did little to revive the dwindling morale of workers and activists. At the time, La Mujer Obrera had only two staff members, down from seven five years before.

Parameters of Capitalist Competition in Its New Modality of Accumulation

In this all-encompassing reconfiguration, the enhanced relocation capacity—which had initially brought a concentration of garment industries to El Paso and had then given rise to the maquiladora industry—signaled danger to promoters and entrepreneurs who benefited from the industry's operations and growth.

A victim of its own accelerated growth from 1982 to 1988, the maquiladora industry had lost its momentum. The industry's rate of growth declined from an average of 25.4 percent between 1982 and 1988 to less than 10 percent in 1989 (Vargas 1990, 28). In its rapid expansion, the industry had outpaced the growth of the local labor force and of infrastructure development. By 1990 these two deficits threatened the maintenance and expansion of the industry in the region. The accelerated growth had drained the labor market. Then, in their frenetic recruitment campaigns to outdo each other in attracting workers, companies cornered themselves, because the campaigns fueled high turnover rates. Workers would quit a job as soon as a relatively better one opened up in another company. This high rate of worker transience increased operating costs for recruitment and training and played havoc with the plants' production schedules.

The accelerated expansion of the industry also overtaxed the technical capabilities of the city's transportation and administrative services. These problems were dramatically illustrated for local promoters and business owners by the closures of maquiladora plants. In local conferences the decline in expansion was attributed to the U.S. recession. Nevertheless, to prevent or defer the decay of the region as an international production site, local entrepreneurs sought solutions for the infrastructure problems caused by, and impairing the growth of, the maquiladora industry. They were aware that, if infrastructure problems worsened, even more companies would search the ever-growing international corporate map for the most advantageous sites: locations where they could cut costs, benefit from technical networks, or gain access to markets without losing profits because of infrastructure or labor market complications.

Business interests responded in different ways to this interplay of closures and new ventures. Some responses were more inventive than others. At the highest level of capitalist competition, five major firms competed to develop industrial real estate, construct industrial parks, and provide services for the day-to-day operations of the maquiladora industry. These services ranged from janitorial and safety contracts to the supply of public utilities. The dominant firm in this market was Grupo Gutiérrez. This Grupo, based in Ciudad Juárez, pioneered the maquiladora arrangement in Mexico in the mid-1960s. Its initial control of this market had been challenged since the early 1980s, when other investors were attracted by the accelerated growth of the industry. By 1990 five other multimillion-dollar firms represented a significant challenge to Grupo Gutiérrez. Two competitors were owned by some of the wealthiest families in Ciudad Juárez. A third, less capital-rich but more innovative, was a construction company that had splintered from Grupo Gutiérrez. Finally, one other company from the state capital, Chihuahua City, operated industrial parks there and in Ciudad Juárez and El Paso.

Only one prospective major competitor in this market was based in the United States, Socorro Enterprise. Although the firm counted on initial support from major local and nonlocal investors and politicians, its project never materialized. A look at this failed enterprise underscores the interplay of local and nonlocal interests within the complex parameters of capitalist competition in global markets. The developmental scope of the enterprise contrasts with an alternative vision proposed by a prominent advocate of regional integration in El Paso, Dr. David Miller. Notwithstanding that both strategies were formulated in direct relation to the challenges and opportunities posed by the expansion of the maquiladora industry, they took divergent routes in promoting local development and, thus, reshaping the labor market.

Socorro Enterprise attempted to develop a large-scale binational industrial zone. It was envisioned, initiated, and mostly controlled by Clifford Crawford, a Euro-American real estate investor and broker in El Paso since the 1960s. The project consisted of the creation of a multimillion-dollar industrial complex for international manufacturing at the scarcely populated west edge of Ciudad Juárez and in the eastern part of New Mexico, right at the Texas border. Crawford planned the project during the period of accelerated growth of the maquiladora industry. Given its magnitude, he gathered financial and political support from a number of major investors in U.S. and Mexican cities at the onset of the venture.

The enterprise included an ambitious plan designed by a Massachusetts Institute of Technology (MIT) consulting team to prevent infrastructure problems. It promised a series of built-in measures to prevent the chronic problems that other industrial parks in Ciudad Juárez had experienced. The project was visualized as an industrial city in which the basic needs of workers ("the main clients of the project") would be assured in terms of preplanned housing, transportation, education, and health facilities. In addition, a water well was under construction that, according to Crawford, would be the largest well in the region. The most salient innovation, however, was the building of a private international entry port between Mexico and the United States.

Socorro Enterprise soon experienced severe difficulties caused by local and nonlocal complications. At the global level, the magnitude of the transformation offered substantial profits and return on investment. However, it also imposed major capital and political requirements. The completion of the ambitious infrastructure projects required a multimillion-dollar investment as well as high-level political negotiations to secure official permits for construction and operations. With such high stakes, in the late 1980s, the end of the accelerated growth of the maquiladora industry together with intense competition from other entrepreneurs brought the success of the project into question. At the local level, negotiations for the official permit for operation of the bridge became a major point of contention between Crawford and other business groups in El Paso and Ciudad Juárez. Crawford's port of entry, while private, still required approval from the federal governments of each country, and such approval relied on intervention by state and local officials.

The eventual unraveling of Socorro Enterprise's plan can be attributed in large part to its fumbled negotiation for this private port of entry. The public process fell prey to private interference from the business groups involved in the development and operations of maquiladora parks. These interests saw their businesses threatened by the state-of-the-art operational advantages and infrastructure capacities envisioned by Socorro Enterprise. Such groups feared that national investors with better financial, political, and technological connections would outpace them in taking advantage of the most profitable business opportunities. According to observers, local competitors pressured officials at different levels in both countries to delay the project through bureaucratic stalling. This maneuver won them additional time to address the infrastructure bottlenecks affecting the competitiveness of their operation and park facilities. Primarily, they aimed to postpone Crawford's operations until renovation of an international bridge closer to their industrial parks had been completed. This renovated bridge would relieve serious transportation bottlenecks that could otherwise motivate companies to relocate to Crawford's industrial zone.

Earlier operation of its port of entry would consolidate the Socorro Enterprise's infrastructure advantage and give it a possible monopoly in the reconstituted local options for maquiladora operations. In addition, official recognition would prove the feasibility and profitability of the enterprise, which were crucial in attracting investors. Nevertheless, rumors proliferated about complications related to personal and political developments in both countries. Allegedly, two state governors, one in Mexico and one in the United States, opposed Crawford's project. Sources claimed that one of these governors, for merely personal reasons, had sworn that Crawford's bridge would not be approved while he was in office. On the U.S. side, a governor was said to have close economic ties to one of Socorro's entrepreneurial rivals—a business group in Mexico. The unofficial consensus was that although the construction of the bridge for Crawford's project was close at hand, its official permit would be delayed—at least until the other bridge was opened.

Crawford minimized these complications at a business meeting held in the conference room of the Ciudad Juárez Country Club. Organized by a U.S. econometrics projection company, the meeting was attended by twenty-three people, including many members of the competing groups. Crawford, the guest speaker at the event, opened his presentation by stating that his project was not going to "siphon off maquiladora operations already in local industrial parks." On the contrary, he proposed that his project would assure the maintenance of the industry in the region by providing relief for infrastructure problems. After a description of the project and its advancement, Crawford closed his presentation with the statement that there was still "room for investors looking for a sound business opportunity."

Crawford's presentation provoked mixed responses that loosely corresponded with the competing entrepreneurial camps. The discussion centered on details of specific infrastructure projects. Crawford maneuvered through the complicated ongoing negotiations over the ports of entry. Sidestepping the delicate issue of the governors' animosity toward his project, Crawford told a story that suggested a close friendship with an ex-president of Mexico, casually suggesting his own powerful political connections. Soon, however, he brought the discussion back to overall infrastructure issues by emphasizing their social aims. Significantly, he referred to workers as the main "clients" of the project. This was a peculiar characterization, given that ultimately the workers would sell their labor. However, in the developer's view, they were the "clients," perhaps because they would buy into his vision of an industrial city in which employment, transportation, housing, and education were all provided.

The comprehensive scope of Socorro Enterprise, meritorious in its social concerns, at the same time evoked images of a "company town." Memories of single employers running entire cities, such as Henry Ford in Detroit or George Pullman in East Chicago recalled the dependency of workers on their employers for their most basic needs. These resonances were underlined by Crawford's control of the ownership and operations of the industrial zone. Indeed, the comprehensive nature of the project ultimately overwhelmed Crawford's efforts. Moreover, according to some observers, his reluctance to relinquish control of the enterprise led some of the main investors to withdraw. By 1993–94 the rumor in business circles in El Paso and Ciudad Juárez was that the major nonlocal investors were losing interest in the project for business, political, and personal reasons. Perhaps the most discouraging factor for these investors was the decline in the maquiladora industry's rate of growth. The end of that accelerated growth meant a reduced demand for industrial buildings and a slower rate of return on their investments. Nonlocal investors were also said to be discouraged by the obstacles posed by politicians and other industrial park developers.

Undercapitalized and weakened by health and legal problems, Crawford has been unable to regain the momentum for his ambitious project. To this day, the projected binational industrial city remains a white elephant. A few preliminary constructions, such as a golf course and a country club, lie underused or incomplete. The future of the project is clouded by a legal dispute in which, according to one source, an investor from Massachusetts owns the majority of the land but has no access to its water mantle because Crawford obtained the legal rights to it when he registered the project's well in the late 1980s.

Rigid Yet Precarious Delimitations of Capitalist Competition

The mixture of political and business interests at the heart of the dispute over official recognition of the crossing points provides insight into the complexity of global competition. Additional complications of competition are evident in David Miller's alternative strategy. Miller was the founding director of the Institute for Manufacturing and Materials Management, a nonprofit institute created in 1989 to promote the technological development of the area. Sponsored by the state government, the institute was based at the local campus of the state university where Miller is a professor. Up-to-date on globalization trends and with a doctorate in management, he displayed great energy in establishing links with business and political groups in the local setting, advocating a "proactive" response to the opportunity offered by the growth of the maquiladora industry and NAFTA. From this vantage point, Miller criticized the Socorro Enterprise as a real estate venture and its binational industrial zone as a "giant maquiladora."

Recognized as a visionary even by people who disagreed with his project, Miller spoke out in a variety of public forums, contending that the region had outgrown its maquiladora phase. His basic premise was that relocation decisions of corporations were decreasingly dependent on wage differentials and increasingly dependent on the "total cost of business." In other words, labor costs represented a diminishing factor in relocation decisions as production processes were increasingly automated. Other costs and considerations, he argued, were more important. Some of these operational costs included location advantages, service costs, access to markets, and technical services. Therefore, El Paso's winning strategy should be based not on low wages, even at Ciudad Juárez's levels, but on its premium location and its already established prominence in international production and trade. In this period of "dynamic comparative advantages," this meant upgrading the region's technical and infrastructure capabilities. Such improvements would make El Paso and its surroundings "the high-tech manufacturing zone for the North American Common Market," for which NAFTA was paving the way. This transformation meant the concentration of a layer of high-tech operations integrating less sophisticated operations initially based in other regions of Mexico and eventually reaching into the rest of Latin America.

Miller envisioned a transition from the region's predominantly low-skilled, low-paid employment to mid-to-high skilled jobs. This technological upgrade would improve the wage scale of the local economies and bring in more public revenues to address infrastructure problems. For this transition to occur, Miller pointed out, a local industrial base was required. This industrial base would attract more sophisticated companies offering better paying jobs. As a logical first step, he recommended seeking greater regional integration. For example, he called for the application of technology developed in military research centers less than four hundred miles away in New Mexico to the manufacturing production of the region. However, Miller did not think that an industrial base could be developed by relying primarily on local resources. He argued that it took decades for the traditional manufacturing centers of the country to develop a trained labor force, one that could meet international standards of quality and reliability. Thus, he recommended inducing well-established firms from other parts of the country to relocate. He was also convinced that the required industrial base could not be constructed by small entrepreneurs. In his view, small business lacked not only capital but also the technical capability to operate on the global level.

In his view, only a few of the wealthiest people in the region had the capital needed to develop the industrial base. He went on to say that this relatively small local elite refused to envision an El Paso in any way different from the city they knew. Entrenched in their traditional endeavors, they saw no need to take risks or to apply themselves to new ventures. Moreover, those wealthy individuals were more interested in maintaining their positions in the community than in reshaping the local economy.

An exception to Miller's characterization of the wealthy business people in the area is Saul Gutiérrez, a son of the one of the pioneers of the maquiladora industry in Ciudad Juárez and Mexico. This entrepreneur in his mid-thirties started a plastic injection molding shop to serve plants in the industrial parks owned by his economic group. I spoke with him after the plastic shop was in business. He pointed out that aside from capital considerations, the vastness of the plastic industry, in terms of products and technical complexities, made venturing into new enterprises in higher levels of industrialization very challenging. In accordance with Miller, Guttiérrez also told me that it was difficult to find technical personnel with an adequate level of knowledge and experience to contend with the specifications and eventualities presented by maquiladora plants.

As part of the challenge, Gutiérrez also mentioned that the proximity of his shop to the local plants did not guarantee that he would obtain business orders from maquiladoras. Those purchasing decisions are most often made at corporate headquarters, which already have well-established supply connections with other firms around the country. In official terms, the established contacts guarantee compliance with rigorous world-class standards of quality control and have proven their capacity to produce the services and volumes required. In less official terms, informal setups between purchasing agents and sales representatives may reinforce the existing arrangement. Gutiérrez mentioned that some business deals were negotiated through casual conversations on golf courses and through similarly informal business interactions.

Other exceptions to Miller's view of local entrepreneurs were business firms that offered "turnkey" operations. These firms would establish manufacturing operations for larger corporations under temporary contracts. At first, such operations were mostly managerial options offered to companies exploring maquiladora arrangements. By 1990 the firms offered a wider range of increasingly sophisticated technical and managerial services. These innovative initiatives—from both established and new entrepreneurs—were increasing in number, yet they still were the exception more than the norm in local business practices.

Miller attributed the scarcity of local efforts to foster significant development to the "small-town mentality" of those who would rather maintain the status quo. Miller's view was corroborated by an innovative entrepreneur, Arthur Gunter, a pioneer in the development of the electronics industry in the area. With a Ph.D. in engineering, extensive bureaucratic and technical experience, and a vast record of international travel, Gunter co-owned a midsize software company that designed visual simulation programs for the Department of Defense and other clients. Discussing the challenges he had faced in establishing his firm, Gunter reiterated Miller's characterization of local business leaders as lacking the vision to understand nontraditional economic activities:

> If you go to a bank with a cowboy hat and boots and ask for five hundred thousand dollars to buy cattle, they might lend it to you. But if you go as an engineer with a project and your business plan and ask for two hundred thousand dollars to buy a more or less sophisticated machine, they won't know what you are talking about and they won't lend any money to you. They have seen a cow and they can relate to you as a cowboy. But they do not have the conceptual image of high technology. They don't understand about that and they won't trust your idea. They can't visualize it.

In spite of this general agreement about local business practices, Gunter did not share Miller's analysis of the situation. Notwithstanding his firm's gradual growth, he doubted that a transition from a low- to a high-skilled labor economy was possible because of serious pervasive problems beyond business practices that he referred to as "factors of social disintegration." These factors included the problems of poverty and the incompetence, disregard, and myopic agendas of public officials at all three levels of government. These problems affected all aspects of life, he contended, so in 1991 he relocated his company to the neighboring New Mexican city of Las Cruces to take advantage of its higher quality of education. He expressed regret that El Paso, a larger city with a bigger university, was behind in the educational programs necessary for the company's development. In a later interview in 1997, however, he reported significant improvements in the range of areas covered by the city's university and community college, as well as in the skill level of their graduates.

Gunter's remarks about "factors of social disintegration" gave me an initial insight into the pervasive effects of the city's dislocated condition. As I looked closer at the dynamics of the city, I noticed that El Paso was constantly subordinated to nonlocal interests, developments, and flows. These linkages were closely related to rampant poverty and official neglect, as pointed out by Gunter. However, I also found that the subordination was fostered by the previous orientation of the economy, by its former leadership (as Miller recognized), and by many of the interactions of ordinary citizens and visitors, as illustrated in the previous chapter. In this perverse interplay between the local and the global, alienated instrumentalities prevailed. For example, the city's mediating role benefited its leaders, but was severely detrimental to most of the local population. El Paso remained a site of inexpensive labor at the cost of its development potential. The industrial base that Miller envisioned had thus been crippled by the preservation of low-wage activities for the many and very profitable ventures for the few.

In Lefebvre's terms, the business elite's promotion of the city as a low-wage market (representation of space) guided their investment portfolios (representational space), their political agendas, and their social policies (spatial practices). This arrangement also generated (e.g., produced), propagated, and reinforced the alienated instrumentality of the site. As a virtual *compradora* class, the elite partook in the exploitation of the site for the benefit of nonlocal development and the entire process revealed quasi-colonial overtones. At the same time, the actions, experiences, and interpretations of other local residents also contributed to the frontier condition of the site. Its "distant proximities," as discussed in the previous chapter, overrode both the cohesion and the coherence of social life.

The Magnitude and Parameters of Competition

The four initiatives described in this chapter strove to generate some degree of local integration to balance or at least counter the overriding impacts of nonlocal developments. With different priorities and focused on different constituencies, these projects mobilized diverse actions to cope with mounting challenges posed by globalization, including the relocation of garment factories and the infrastructure problems of the maquiladora industry. At the same time, they also attempted to capitalize on established global prominence as a garment or maquiladora center. These concurrences of general objectives, however, became virtually immaterial on the concrete level. For example, the dramatic asymmetries between displaced workers and such successful women as Torres cannot be ignored. The city, as the "common ground of displacement and breakthroughs" for different constituencies, is characterized by "social disintegrations" (e.g., distant proximities). This distance is also manifested in the relatively advantageous situations of Crawford and Miller. At the local level, the unevenness of resources among the four groups appears insurmountable.

At the global level, however, the eventual outcomes of these entrepreneurial initiatives add a new perspective to our understanding of the dynamics and interplays of the city's distant proximities. The inequities between the displaced workers and the entrepreneurs—and among the entrepreneurs themselves—acquire new dimensions when compared to the overwhelming discrepancy between local and global resources. The fates of the Socorro Enterprise and the displaced workers, for example, could be seen as analogous. In both instances, economic, technical, and political forces determined their dislocated outcomes. These forces, moreover, were reinforced by the frontier condition of the site. Agendas perpetuating its alienated instrumentalities overrode the integrated strategies proposed by La Mujer Obrera and Crawford. In terms of the Mujer Obrera initiative, shortsighted bureaucrats failed to recognize the condition of workers and the nature of the ongoing change. Trapped in self-promotion or simple ineptitude, officials subordinated local needs to policies dictated by nonlocal functionaries. Stigmatizing preconceptions shattered the design and implementation of the assistance programs. These preconceptions and orientations not only neglected the workers' situation, but they undermined the efforts of La Mujer Obrera to resourcefully and comprehensively respond to the reconfiguration of the labor market. The Socorro Enterprise initiative was derailed, partially at least, by the intervention of established business conglomerates that feared competition. At the end, both possible avenues for addressing the aggravating bottlenecks and social dislocation created by the rapid and unplanned industrialization process were blocked. Thus, the employment of local resources—workers, highways, services, etc.—for nonlocal interests remained practically unchecked.

The parameters of both initiatives, however, are not completely defined. Add, for example, Miller's critique of the Socorro Enterprise. Calling it "a giant maquiladora," the business professor questioned its development potential. Crawford's project could be viewed as an improvement over established ventures, but according to Miller, it still overlooks the opportunity at hand for the region to become a mid- to high-technology manufacturing zone for the entire hemisphere. There is a similar divergence between Torres and Rocha. Like Miller, Torres saw the garment industry as obsolete. Rocha, like Crawford, promoted a comprehensive plan for addressing imminent problems. Ultimately, all four agents had different frames of reference and were sometimes in direct competition. Consequently, coordination was undermined by their different perspectives and positions. In other words, possible confluences or correspondences were prevented by both local and global imbalances.

The current decline of La Mujer Obrera, as well as the relative stagnation of the enterpreneur's ventures, suggest a greater viability for the other two approaches. The outcomes of those initiatives, however, are not necessarily definitive. The high mobility made possible by globalization makes any given outcome uncertain. Increasing the ability of corporations to relocate their production facilities brought the garment industry to El Paso in the 1950s, then it headed south a few decades later. Thus, La Mujer Obrera's concerns about plant closures were related to the concerns behind the other three initiatives, which all focused on the risks of maquiladora relocations away from the region. The interconnection between these related yet different relocations underscores how the city's boundaries are manipulated due to its frontier condition. Yet they also point to the elusive distance between relocations and reconfigurations, as the context is differently experienced, interpreted, and engaged by different local and nonlocal agents.

The four initiatives discussed here reflect agile responses to the impacts of globalization. To different degrees and with different focuses, each initiative altered the overriding subordination of the locality to nonlocal flows and interests. All of them attempted to reshape the labor market and, thus, its global intermediating function. With more passive or less imaginative responses, the traditional business elites, most displaced workers, and many public officials obstructed the initiatives. In general, they were swayed by their own inertia and the overriding subordination of the site. In particular, the elite and the public officials, as direct beneficiaries of the established arrangement, maintained their business-as-usual approach. Workers lacked the means or skills to weather the displacements. Consequently, they remained the most direct victims of the dislocation. All in all, however, the developments, the initiatives, and their arrested successes are framed within the "alienated instrumentalities" of the city's frontier condition.

This chapter illustrated different spatial practices influencing the local labor market and underscored gender and class divisions. The next chapter will look beyond the labor market to two broader initiatives. The two groups described attempted to foster a sense of community, to overcome the "distant proximities" of El Paso and Ciudad Juárez. It looks first at ethnic divisions as they were reflected in the creation of the Hispanic Chamber of Commerce. The second group pursued a wider initiative for bridging pervasive divisions and was led by a multiethnic group of professionals under the name of Unite El Paso.

4

Local Democracy and Global Demography: New Parameters of Community

In March 1991, President George H. W. Bush spoke to the annual meeting of the National Association of Hispanic Chambers of Commerce in Washington, D.C. The president urged the association to support his efforts to get congressional approval for fast-track negotiation of the North American Free Trade Agreement. The fast-track procedure would allow the Bush administration to independently negotiate the treaty because it would restrict the ability of Congress to amend specific aspects of the agreement, thus forcing representatives to vote for either complete approval or complete rejection. Certain groups opposed the fast-track procedure based on specific concerns, mostly regarding labor and environmental issues, which they believed could be sacrificed in the negotiations.

Representing the recently created El Paso Hispanic Chamber of Commerce, Clark Pereira conditioned his support on the president's willingness to attend to problems of Latino entrepreneurs and workers in border areas. For the entrepreneurs, he wanted a loan program that would address capital constraints. For the workers, he wanted assistance, especially for those who had been displaced by plant relocations to Mexico and other countries. Pereira wanted a "level playing field" that would allow border residents to benefit from the opportunities promised by Bush. He argued that support for small businesses should be a matter of policy in the pursuit of national economic recovery, and he concluded his presentation by warning that "with the recession it won't take much effort for labor to convince people." Another entrepreneur, echoing Pereira, noted the difficulty minority business people had in obtaining loans. Two other participants disagreed with his position. A Cuban American entrepreneur trivialized Pereira's demands by inviting the audience to relocate to Miami, alleging that the shortcomings described by Pereira did not exist there. Another Mexican American entrepreneur told Pereira about Mexican government loans designed to promote trade between Mexico and the United States.

The fact that the president of the United States appealed to the members of a minority business organization might suggest an ongoing sociopolitical reconfiguration of the relationship between minority and mainstream institutions. Or it might be merely a symbolic gesture. Such superficiality is reflected in the fact that the meeting did not actually address cultural or business contacts with Mexico (otherwise, why the Cuban presence?). Subtle and not-so-subtle cultural and national distinctions were irrelevant to the political objectives of the president's media campaign, which was geared toward Congress rather than toward the Latino audience. The mostly symbolic nature of the meeting is reinforced by the fact that Bush did not respond to Pereira.

The responses of the other three entrepreneurs, in turn, revealed the lack of unity within the group. Only one of the three entrepreneurs shared Pereira's concern about credit constraints. Frustrated, Pereira referred to his colleagues as *"tíos tacos"*—Uncle Tacos—an adaptation of the term "Uncle Tom," which is used to ridicule individuals who side with people in power to advance themselves at the expense of their ethnic group. He described this opportunism as selfishness *(envidia)*: "Mexican Americans still want to punish their people. When I go and give a talk, it is the Mexican Americans who attack what I say." Other entrepreneurs in El Paso also spoke of "divisiveness" and some saw a contrast with other ethnic groups (e.g., Jews, Arabs, Asian Americans, and African Americans):

> Everybody, every other group, Jews, Arabs, Blacks, helps their own. We are not like that. We don't help our own. On the contrary, if we see someone of our own getting ahead we all pull together then, only then, to pull him [or her] down.

Contrary to a traditional stereotype, these statements were seldom made in a fatalistic vein. For a classic expression of this stereotype as it applies to people of Mexican ancestry in the United States see *The Mexican-Americans of South Texas* by William Madsen. In El Paso, statements made by these emerging leaders underscored a political or an economic subtext of cultural overtones. For Pereira, it was envy: "Envy is the greatest problem of this race." However, he explained this lack of unity in terms of scarcity, not culture: "There is no more unity for fear of losing one's job or business. There is no money." Similar observations were frequently accompanied by a statement about the need to foster unity by attacking the problem of scarce opportunity. For Pereira, however, the solution to fierce competition caused by severe scarcity was cohesion: "The solution is not money but working together." His view was particularly feasible at a time of increasing business opportunities.

An emerging sense of empowerment accompanied new entrepreneurial ventures and expanded the narrowly controlled business environment of previous decades, a time when the local economy and its interconnection with other markets were closely controlled by a handful of Euro-American businessmen. This new sense of opportunity generated a surge of incipient leadership, people eager to "take our destiny into our own hands." A number of Mexican American entrepreneurs echoed Pereira's call for the group to create its own opportunity: "We keep looking for others to do it for us." Pereira contrasted his group to the Cuban Americans who "do it by themselves." The collective expansion of this sense of opportunity created a widespread leadership momentum clearly reflected in the proliferation of diverse organizations formed to foster leadership and cohesiveness. For example, at the high school and university levels, a benefit for a scholarship fund for the local university was named "Unidos! A Latino Student *Leaders* Celebration" (my emphasis) and included nineteen student groups, seven of which had the words "leadership" or "leaders" in their name.

This leadership momentum responded to immediate demographic, political, and economic changes. In 1989 the Hispanic Leadership Institute was created. This group of approximately forty members gathered successful Hispanic individuals from the academic, business, and political communities of the city, as well as from the bureaucratic sectors of the city and state government. The creation of this group was stimulated by the resounding election of a Mexican American woman as county judge, the highest local political position. Justice Ana Chavira's election in 1989 was widely recognized as a landmark in two important respects. First, it marked the consolidation of the Latino vote in local politics, a constituency that in 1990 became for the first time the largest group of registered voters. Second, she was elected in the face of the old Democratic machinery's desperate attempts to prevent it—an effort mounted in spite of Justice Chavira's loyalty to the Democratic Party throughout more than twenty-five years of grassroots organizing. The old Democratic machinery, dominated by Euro-Americans, tried to defeat her by nominating the local party's president at the last minute on the grounds that Justice Chavira was "not electable." In fact, she defeated four opponents, all Euro-American males, without a runoff. Her election demonstrated the possibility of political advancement based on demographic and economic changes. As Mexican Americans became a clear numerical majority—70 percent by 1990—their lack of representation in influential political and business positions became particularly obvious. This absence was addressed by Hispanic entrepreneurs who quickly learned to operate in the dynamic interplay of economic opportunity and political power (Villareal and Mapula 1991).

The previous chapter illustrated different spatial practices influencing the local labor market and underscored gender and class divisions. This chapter looks at additional spatial practices in terms of ethnicity within two efforts to address the debilitating effects of ethnic inequality in the residents' sense of community. It shows that a precarious sense of social cohesiveness intensifies the rawness of contested feelings of belonging and the multiple delineations between self and others.

I look first at ethnic divisions as they were reflected in the creation of the Hispanic Chamber of Commerce. The perceptions, motivations, and class underpinnings that led to the chamber's creation are discussed, with special attention paid to the new ethnic and class dynamics resulting from the reconfigured parameters of competition arising from globalization. These dynamics involve complex attachments of the chamber's founders to the site, attachments that reach beyond business interests into experiential and existential concerns. More than matters of personal comfort, these broader concerns encompass their sense of social contribution and belonging. In other words, the entrepreneurs' sense of community is at stake. The second part of this chapter describes a wider initiative for bridging pervasive divisions. This challenge was taken up by multiethnic groups of professionals, under the name of Unite El Paso, who promoted inclusive and conciliatory activities to foster a unifying leadership. This initiative suggests new, all-encompassing dynamics of class, ethnicity, and race in the city. In so doing, they have offered an unprecedented challenge to the state government, demanding equitable distribution of funds for public services. Both initiatives, like those previously discussed, create new modalities of otherness through attempts to bridge the divide between the local and the global.

The Challenge of Leadership and Ethnic Boundaries

When the boom of the maquiladora industry paved the way for an increase in El Paso's economic activities, new entrepreneurs and entrepreneurial strategies emerged, challenging the leadership of the old business elite. This challenge related not only to business opportunities, but to the capacity to define the direction of local economic development. Members of the old leadership responded to these challenges in a variety of ways:

by relocating, by obstructing change, by including prominent new millionaires or corporate managers, by developing institutional mechanisms to channel new players' demands, and by practicing plain old-fashioned neglect. These diverse responses acknowledged the relative or absolute decline in their capacity to single-handedly control local affairs. The decline derived from various factors. In its most absolute terms, it can be attributed to generational change. Members of the "in-group" were aging, and many of their offspring had moved to other cities to pursue their own business or professional careers. Some others, solidly entrenched in privilege and wealth, overlooked both the opportunities and the demands that emerging arrangements presented. Well-connected to an informal old-boy network, they had thrived during the Texas oil-led boom of the 1970s and collapsed after the oil bust of 1985.

The distance between the traditional business elite and the major economic trends created by the boom in the maquiladora industry was reflected by the decay of the Chamber of Commerce, the elite's foremost public bastion during the most intense period of the boom. The chamber had experienced problems since 1985. According to one of its department directors, membership had declined from about 3,000 in 1988 to 2,000 by 1990. In addition, it had accumulated a $600,000 debt. In response to these problems, the chamber had replaced its director and restructured its organization, although it retained the same board of directors. The two most salient aspects of the reorganization were the central role given to its Economic Development Corporation department and the creation of a Minority Business Council. The combined membership of these two departments generated the greatest revenue for the chamber. The Economic Development Corporation promoted activities to attract national and international corporations to the area. The Minority Business Council was established in response to complaints from young Latino entrepreneurs that the chamber's leadership, composed of Euro-Americans, did not attend to their needs or objectives. Ironically, the few non–Euro-Americans on the board were not Mexican Americans, but prominent Mexican entrepreneurs with close business relations to the chamber's directors. After two years of discussions, some members of the new group opted to leave the existing chamber to create their own.

A new chamber was created in spite of some initial hesitation and distrust among factions. One group was led by Clark Pereira and Roberto Ruiz, who, after initial talks with other possible supporters, learned that a charter for a new chamber had recently been awarded to Mauricio Bencomo. Although he was Mexican American, Bencomo worked for a local bank with strong connections to the Euro-American elite, so Pereira and Ruiz regretfully concluded that he had obtained the charter as a preemptive measure to derail the creation of a genuinely independent chamber. To their surprise, however, Bencomo shared their views and, in fact, asked them to take over. Momentum then built rapidly, beyond Pereira's plans and expectations:

> My hope was to help organize the chamber behind the scenes. I knew that if I were associated too closely with the creation of the chamber my hopes of running for public office would suffer. However, I had to become the first president because nothing was happening. Nobody wanted to do it.

A thirty-eight-year-old real estate broker at the time and a native of El Paso, Pereira explained his involvement through a recollection of his grandfather:

> My mother and my grandfather were migrant farmworkers and I remember listening to my grandfather telling me as a child—he only spoke Spanish so I didn't understand everything—but I remember he told me about the bad things that migrant workers had to put up with and that the worst problem was that we didn't stick together.

Roberto Ruiz, on the other hand, at first spoke impersonally about his pioneering involvement in creating the Hispanic Chamber. A successful stockbroker in his early forties, Ruiz complained of the lack of representation for the majority of the city's population in decision-making positions. His tone changed when he spoke of the late Felix Martínez. In the early 1900s Martínez had been a prominent businessman of the region who held many influential positions. For example, he was chairman of the El Paso Valley Water Users Association at the local level, and president of the Panama–Pacific U.S. Commission at the national/international level. The Water Users Association was at the time a key group that included influential business people. Martínez's former prominence was attested to by the solemnity of his funeral:

> His body was taken to the El Paso Chamber of Commerce to lie in state. The procession was headed by a platoon of mounted police, followed by the Sixth Infantry Band, city and county officers, directors of the Chamber of Commerce and of the El Paso Valley Water Users Association, bank directors, and officials of Martínez's many companies.

As he told me about Martínez, Ruiz's friendly, businesslike demeanor betrayed a pride. This pride, however, turned to sad exasperation as he pointed out that Martínez's prominence had been buried with him:

> Nobody knows about Mr. Felix Martínez. Why? There are streets named after all of his business partners and all other prominent figures of his time. All of those are Anglo. Look at this picture of the foundation of the Chamber of Commerce. He is the only Hispanic, at the center. Why is it that we didn't know about him?

Ruiz's points referred to public statements made by local Euro-American historians in public events in which the Mexican American presence in the development of the city was generally neglected or minimized. A couple of history books on the city, however, mention Martínez and his contributions (see Martínez 1978; García 1981; and Timmons 1990).

Pereira learned about Martínez as he reviewed the Chamber of Commerce archives prior to the creation of the new chamber. The records provided basic information about Martínez's prominent regional roles in business and civic activities, along with his address and names of his family members. The discovery had a strong emotional impact on both entrepreneurs. Ruiz recalled a time when he received a phone call from a sobbing Pereira:

> One afternoon I get a call from Clark, from his cellular phone. He told me: "Can you guess where I am?" "Where are you?" I asked him. "I am standing right in front of what used to be Mr. Felix Martínez's house. The house has been demolished. There is nothing left of it."

Martínez had donated his house to a Catholic school, which was later demolished for renovation and expansion. However, the expansion never occurred. The two entrepreneurs traced Martínez's daughter and learned that she possessed some of her father's records. Soon afterward, they enticed a reporter from Albuquerque to write a profile of Martínez. Ruiz made a copy of that article and, as he handed it to me, pointed out that "many dissertations can be made on this person. This is the guy if you are going to speak of a role model."

Many businesspeople directly involved with the creation of the new chamber were the same age as Pereira and Ruiz. Moreover, their social mobility was related to recently established and rapidly growing businesses, mostly concentrated in the service and professional sectors. Likewise, they were well-informed of the economic basis of the power in the city and the ways in which that power was used to marginalize them as a group. This exclusion became particularly evident through two well-known cases of Mexican American entrepreneurs whose business success was initially hindered by the discriminatory lending practices of local banks controlled by the old elite. Both entrepreneurs had to find loans from banks in other cities. One of these was a local engineer who had created an innovative and highly profitable computer-assisted graphic-design software program. His initial loan came from a Canadian bank and he had used his house as collateral. In the other case, a younger entrepreneur acquired a regional beer dealership.

Uplifted by recent successes yet unsettled by lack of support from local banks, Latino entrepreneurs directed their energies toward increasing their representation in financial organizations in the city. In our interview, a young stockbroker in his late twenties said:

> Eighty-five percent of city employees are Hispanic yet the board of directors managing their retirement programs has only two Hispanics out of ten members. It is the same with the Fire and Police Retirement Boards. There is only one Hispanic. El Paso Community Foundation board also has one Hispanic out of ten members. We have no control over these pools of money.

The entrepreneurs made it their central goal to address this lack of representation on the boards of local banks (Villareal and Mapula 1991). Tactically, their demand for inclusion was made on the grounds of community requirements dictated by the Federal Reserve Bank for private banks. By acquiring the support of functionaries managing public funds, they were able to secure some positions. Their strategy was advanced by the election and appointment of Latino public officials or of Euro-Americans sensitive to Latino concerns. For example, in addition to Justice Chavira, a new mayor was elected, an ex-U.S. diplomat with an Irish father and a Mexican mother who had been a member of the founding board of directors of the Hispanic Chamber of Commerce. The president of the local branch of the state university, a Euro-American woman who had acquired a Latino-sounding last name from her husband, was a strong advocate for its predominantly Mexican American student body. The most recently appointed superintendents of two of the school districts and the president of the city's community college were Latinos. All of these public institutions control considerable amounts of money, and most of their financial operations represent major profits for banks in the city. Therefore, these banks are particularly attentive to these officials' concerns. The entrepreneurs' cause was also aided by national and international financial institutions' acquisition of locally owned banks. With particular symbolic resonance, one of the banks—the one housed in the city's largest downtown building—was bought by a Mexican billionaire.

In this reconfigured context, the founders of the new chapter positioned themselves to channel the ongoing changes toward their specific goals. These goals, however, were broadly defined. Attuned to contextual change, their strategies took into consideration the overall decay of the city. The broader scope of this social awareness was emphasized in public statements about worsening poverty. For example, Pereira's demands to President Bush focused not only on capital constraints, but also on the condition of displaced workers. This concern was also reflected in his response to the Cuban entrepreneur's invitation to relocate to Miami. After ridiculing the invitation with an image of a Miami overflowing with all the Latino entrepreneurs in the country, Pereira's tone grew serious and he asked rhetorically: "What would happen to all the other cities if all the entrepreneurs were to move away?"

Leaders of the new chamber expressed similar concerns in local forums, which traditionally circumvented such topics by either dissociating them from business concerns or trivializing them in the optimistic rhetoric of local boosterism. A lack of public discussion of these topics also shut down discussion of the uneven distribution of the costs and benefits of economic change. The new chamber, in contrast, brought these discrepancies to public attention. Pereira stressed in our first interview that

> [y]ou would never hear discussions about 43 percent of Hispanic families living under the poverty level in the Greater Chamber. That means 192,300 *hispanos bajo el nivel de la pobreza* [Hispanics in poverty]. They only talk about how to bring more companies to the city but not about how those companies are going to benefit or hurt the community, the people in general.

Responses to the New Chamber

The El Paso Hispanic Chamber of Commerce was formed in July 1990 by ex-members of the traditional chamber, which was subsequently renamed the Greater El Paso Chamber of Commerce. Public perception of the new chamber had ethnic overtones in spite of Latino businesspeople's claims to nonethnic motivations. Most Latinos interviewed for this study stated that the new chamber was created because the Greater Chamber placed the needs of big business over those of its other members. They attributed this discrimination to "the old-boys network in the chamber." Only two of my Latino interviewees disagreed. One was an officer of the chamber, instrumental in the creation of the Minority Business Council; he saw the creators of the new chamber as "opportunistic." The other was Ms. Herlinda Lucero, the co-owner of an industrial supply store, who was not involved with the Hispanic Chamber and criticized its creation:

> We are trying to isolate! Why do we isolate if we are trying to belong? *Nosotros mismos nos hacemos menos* [We undermine ourselves]. Am I that handicapped? I have benefited greatly from the Chamber of Commerce. Some Mexicans have complained that it segregates them. I have participated with the Five Points [Business] Association for years and have never thought about segregation. The president of the Greater Chamber is a member of the Five Points Association.

Other Hispanic entrepreneurs' accounts of the creation of the Hispanic Chamber dispute the allegations of opportunism and isolationism. Marcela Torres and Dr. Camille Meras, the entrepreneurs mentioned in the previous chapter, were members of both chambers.

Torres reported a conciliatory and patient attitude among the creators of the new chamber:

> They tried to negotiate with the Greater Chamber before creating their chamber. There was a lot of discussion and many meetings. But it [the old chamber] was afraid of losing control. It was unwilling to make substantive changes. The Minority Business Council was never given real autonomy, only crumbs. It took two years of negotiations and I think that they kept thinking: "Those Mexicans will never do anything: just talk." Now the two chambers are doing work together to have a partnership relation. Yet, even after the split, the Greater Chamber is not giving the [Minority Business] Council full authority. Even when the council is stronger and brings in more money, it is still seen as the stepchild.

Another Mexican American entrepreneur, now a member of the new chamber, also complained about the old chamber's lack of programs for small businesses and the inadequacy of the Minority Business Council in attending to these needs: "The Minority Business Council didn't do it. It didn't want to rock the boat. It wasn't vocal. Yet, there were several factions."

There were complex political dimensions to the creation of the Hispanic Chamber of Commerce, and these also manifested themselves in the responses of non-Latino participants and commentators. Some of these responses were negative. Their tone ranged from paternalistic to resentful and even to outraged (King 1990). Responding to a question I posed to him regarding the polemic, a Euro-American reporter answered with the following succinct account:

> The Chamber of Commerce had financial problems two years ago. It went through some reorganization and the new director was trying to give more power to the Minority Council but a group of Hispanic members formed their own Chamber.

Critiques were frequently aired in letters to the editor of the local newspaper. Personal attacks were made in only one such letter, which was signed "Ortega." The letter addressed the published response of Beatriz Puente, the new chamber's president-elect, to an editorial criticizing it for fostering racism (Letter to the Editor 1990). Ortega argued that the members of the new chamber were rejects from the original chamber. Puente responded to Ortega at the return address given to her by the newspaper, but the address was false and the letter was returned. Significantly, shortly thereafter the newspaper discovered that it was receiving letters to the editor from non-Latino readers using Latino last names (Crowder 1991).

Freed from old entanglements and able to contend with a new environment, leaders of the new chamber responded in a pragmatic and conciliatory manner. They explained their reasons for creating the Hispanic Chamber on technical, rather than ethnic or political grounds. They pointed to the lack of support they had received from the original chamber when they applied for loans or contracts and when they sought general training in the basic mechanics of running a business. Although they firmly stated their dissatisfaction with the old chamber's neglect of small businesses, they maintained a conciliatory tone and called for coordinated efforts between the two chambers.

This strategic approach, translating political and ethnic concerns into technical matters, allowed them to steer clear of ethnic antagonism. Addressing this issue, Pereira pointed out that the new chamber was not restricted to Latinos and that a number of members were non-Latino. He explained that the name had the word *Hispanic* in it because most of the members were Mexican American and many of them required special services because of their limited proficiency in English. Three other members stated adamantly that "it [the creation of the chamber] was not a racial thing." The only ethnic comment was made by one entrepreneur—not an officer of the new chamber—who stated that "the Hispanic chamber is a turnaround." However, she rushed to add that "it is not racist," pointing out that 70 percent of the population was Latino and 75 percent of the small businesses were owned by them, so their lack of representation in the Greater Chamber's Board of Directors was "sticky."

The ethnic overtones of the creation of the new chamber were also underplayed by its leaders' references to the many cities that have Hispanic chambers. Puente, president-elect of the new chamber, who had been membership director of the Albuquerque Chamber of Commerce for eleven years, pointed out that there are more than 250 Hispanic chambers in the country:

> Every major city in the state has a Hispanic chamber. Houston has three: Baytown, the Mexican, and the Hispanic. They [Hispanic chambers] attract more grant money. Moreover, Hispanic chambers can do things that the others couldn't. In some cases the Hispanic chamber has become even bigger than the other chamber.

She noted that "there are ethnic chambers of commerce, like Black or Korean chambers of commerce, in many cities and nobody denounces their existence as racist." In her view the creation of a Hispanic Chamber of Commerce in El Paso was long overdue: "Albuquerque, five [driving] hours away from El Paso, has had a Hispanic chamber for twelve years." She mentioned that 40 percent of its members were Euro-American: "They are there because it is good business: the chamber was packed with people who can make decisions, not like the Greater Chamber, which was just representing corporations, outsiders, bankers, etc."

The two chambers gradually developed a conciliatory attitude. Leaders emphasized their willingness to coordinate activities. Some members were openly pragmatic. Torres and Meras said they participated in the activities of the two chambers according to the needs of their businesses. Yet they spoke enthusiastically about an emerging partnership between the two chambers. This enthusiasm was only partially shared by Pereira, who commented that "there were no problems between the two chambers, at least on the table, but who knows underneath." This statement, made eight months after the creation of the Hispanic chamber, indicated the end of public attacks against it.

Still, animosities against the Hispanic Chamber remained, manifested in more subtle and instrumental ways. For example, the new chamber was invited only at the last minute to an important press conference on NAFTA. This conference, organized by a local newspaper and presided over by the mayor, brought together all the main economic and political groups of the city: city government, the local university, the Greater Chamber of Commerce, and newspapers. The political cost of excluding the new chamber from this conference may have finally forced the delayed invitation. Nevertheless, the invitation was extended the night before the conference, possibly in the hope that it would be declined. Pereira attended the event, though, the first official event with the participation of the two chambers. Significantly, the newspaper photograph accompanying the coverage of the conference shows Pereira addressing the audience under the banner of the Greater Chamber (Jones 1991).

The incident itself symbolized functional inertias handicapping the ongoing changes. The secondary role of the new chamber was emphasized by presenting it in a setting that gave prominence to the older chamber. The marginality of the new chamber can be attributed to its relative newness, but the overwhelming centrality of the older chamber reflected its solid institutional standing, a prominence grounded not only on its longevity, but on its close connection to the established power elite. This close connection was manifested in the older chamber's location in the building that also houses the city's Department of Economic Development, which is part of a larger building complex that includes the city's Civic Center and is right next to City Hall. This was all more than symbolic. It made clear the discrepancy in economic and institutional resources between the two chambers. For example, as president of the Hispanic Chamber, Pereira received no income, while the president of the Greater Chamber had a yearly salary of $120,000. Instead, Pereira's position was costing him money: It took 70 to 80 percent of his time and hurt his business.

Emergency or Emergent Class or Ethnic Dynamics

Pereira's critique of both big business and labor reflected the problems of addressing social concerns with limited private resources. In reference to big business, his critique evoked a Jeffersonian populism. In his address to President Bush, Pereira advocated a national economic strategy based on small businesses. In our interview, he complained that "everything is controlled by big businesses," while "small businesses have no contracts and, if so, no capital":

> I said to the President: "We win with small business." I know that he may not have listened and that most people thought that I was talking *pendejadas* (nonsense). However, you need to put the ideas out. The second or third time they hear it again they are going to be more open to it.

Pereira reformulated the discussion to gain a more solid footing in order to compete with larger businesses. His concerns about organized labor and his rhetorical strategy were even more complex. In his concluding statement to President Bush, Pereira warned of the need to attend to workers' problems before unions capitalized on their discontent. A corollary of this possibility is that business would be affected by labor mobilization against the ongoing economic changes generating local business expansion. Again, however, this public statement could have been a rhetorical strategy based on the assumed antilabor stance of its audience. Accordingly, it underscored the chamber's capacity and readiness to act to head off labor unrest.

This ambiguity points to class complexities intertwined with the ethnic attachments and strategies discussed so far. Pereira's real or apparent antilabor statement drew explicit criticism from Vincente Mendez, a union organizer in El Paso. Mendez described Pereira to me as "a slick guy, who dresses well, speaks well, but doesn't really understand the issues." Mendez saw anything less than strong opposition to NAFTA and the maquiladora industry as, at best, misguided. In his view, his critique was validated by the dramatic evidence of social disruptions caused by the maquiladora industry in Ciudad Juárez and El Paso:

> Nowhere in the world are there more Fortune 500 companies in such proximity as in this area of [Ciudad] Juárez and El Paso. Practically all of the largest companies in the world are next door to each other in these industrial parks. At the same time, this large concentration of wealth and technology only represents increased poverty for the two communities.

While this decay was strongly emphasized in Pereira's public statements, Mendez dismissed those social concerns as public posturing for personal political ambitions. In fact, Pereira did not criticize the maquiladora industry or NAFTA. He referred to the two entities only as business opportunities. In his view, as in Torres's, dimensions are relative. Mendez, in absolute terms, stressed the contrast between the business opportunities enjoyed by a few and the declining living standards of the many. As discussed in chapter 3, the local economy went from being heavily dependent on the garment industry to acquiring a new center of gravity with the arrival and expansion of the maquiladora industry. Even when the plants are located in Ciudad Juárez, the industry presents new professional and business opportunities for those segments of El Paso's population with higher levels of skill and education. While they offer upward mobility to people like Pereira and Torres, these reconfigurations can mean severe pauperization for large segments of society. As chapter 3 indicates, in El Paso the most evident victims of this arrangement are now the workers displaced by plant relocations to Mexico and other parts of the world.

Mendez failed to see beyond this dramatic polarization. However, a broader view would have allowed him to recognize that the entrepreneurs have overlapping roles as both businesspeople and local residents. Beyond their good intentions or what Mendez saw as their narrow personal interests, their broader concerns combined practical, personal, and professional interests. The overlap is obvious in the case of Pereira. As a commercial and industrial real estate agent, he sells the city in the most literal sense, in the form of buildings and land. As a lifelong resident, he also lives in it. For him, as for many other entrepreneurs, the city is not only an operations ground, but also a dwelling place for themselves, their relatives, their friends, and other significant people in their lives. In Pereira's case, given his identification with the Mexican American cause, emotional and political resonances of the past and present also fueled his involvement. In this complex assortment of attachments and investments, the "value" of the city in global markets also includes its social and technical capacities. Both have been gravely undermined by such infrastructure problems as major traffic congestion, environmental pollution, institutional violence, and other social traumas related to widespread poverty and rapid change. This correspondence between social and business concerns was recognized by other businesspeople, even those less emotionally tied to the city. At first there was little agreement as to what route would best lead to a solution to these problems.

Emergent Alliances

The eminent overlap of new possibilities and worsening risks eventually led additional local groups to seek a common ground to bridge the distant proximities that globalization at once deepened and abridged. I first witnessed this conjunction of efforts in late summer 1993. Robert Ruiz, Pereira's co-leader in the creation of the Hispanic Chamber of Commerce, invited me to a public meeting between one of the trustees of the state university and some concerned citizens. The meeting had been called and organized by a handful of local organizations, including both chambers of commerce. Held at the conference room of the old chamber, it drew an audience of about sixty people. The trustee, Dr. Andrew Adams, opened his comments by referring to a ring he had been given by a woman in Mexico four or so decades earlier while he was attending summer school there. In a nostalgic tone, he told the predominantly Latino audience that, while he had not kept his promise to go back, he had always had the ring in his possession.

Once in a while he would be looking for something else in the drawer where he kept it, and he would pause to wonder what had become of the beautiful senorita back in Mexico.

His reminiscences, I am sure, were never the same after that morning. Imprinted in his mind would be the stern looks of most of the audience, people who had little time for irrelevant and manipulative sentiment. Unentertained, the leaders of the groups that organized the event and other members of the audience asked tough questions and demanded concrete answers: Why is there only one Ph.D. program at the local campus? Why do our children need to go somewhere else for graduate education? Do you know that they seldom return? Do you know that we need their talents here? Do you realize that it costs much more to send them away than it would if they could attend graduate programs locally? Why aren't our taxes spent to improve higher education in the city?

Stern, yet not hostile, speaker after speaker requested concrete and rapid solutions. The only exception was a Euro-American man in his forties, short and slim in a three-piece suit. He introduced himself as a lawyer, born in El Paso and trained in Austin. He told trustee Adams that he had enjoyed his graduate experience away from El Paso, but he was very glad he had returned. His concern, he explained, was that his daughter, who would soon graduate from college, would also have to leave the city to pursue a law degree—a proposition that did not appeal to her or to the rest of the family. "I look at this again and again," he said, "and the only reason I can come up with to explain the lack of a law school here in town is racism. I am sure that if the ethnic makeup of the city were not what it is, we would have plenty of graduate programs to choose from."

To my surprise—and maybe everyone else's—the only charge of racism came from a Euro-American. Up to that point, I had never heard a Euro-American in El Paso point out instances of racism—and did not expect it from a man in a three-piece suit—against another Euro-American. I have never seen that man again, but his intervention alerted me to the wider dimensions of the effects of discrimination, effects that are felt beyond ethnic boundaries. This broader view allowed me to understand the all-encompassing conciliatory effort undertaken by the multiethnic group Unite El Paso.

Unite El Paso and a Divided City

Unite El Paso came into being in 1992, born out of a loosely connected group of mostly middle-class Mexican Americans and Euro-Americans who were concerned about social conditions in the city. During its first two years, it consisted of a core group of about twenty individuals energetically committed to fostering collective pragmatic solutions based on the assets of the community. Many members were bilingual and emphasized their strong appreciation for the bicultural dimensions of the city and their equally strong concern about its widespread poverty and ongoing decay. They promoted efforts to generate collective leadership through social cohesiveness.

The initial idea for the group came up in an after-dinner conversation between two members of the local Salvation Army Board of Directors. Nick Herrera recalled that he and Steve Carmichael had talked about the worsening conditions in the city: "Steve and I were having a beer one night at a restaurant. He was the chair of the Salvation Army board and I was co-chair. He and I have a lot in common. We were talking about things in this town, how there are a lot of hurting people in this town. A few doing well."

While Herrera counts himself among the fortunate few, he has direct exposure to the city's poverty through his cousins and their children, who still live in the poor Mexican areas south of downtown. In his mid-thirties at the time, Herrera was in a business whose success was and still is dependent on the maquiladora industry. He has been a headhunter for personnel in these companies since 1978. In this capacity, he has traveled extensively throughout the border region. Through this exposure he discovered an important paradox:

> El Paso and Ciudad Juárez are the most integrated communities along the border but the average local citizen still sees Ciudad Juárez as a distant place. He doesn't know anything about it. There is still phobia about the border yet there are [also] many community efforts.

This perplexing coexistence of integration and segregation, phobia and involvement, makes it difficult for different groups to develop cohesiveness with each other. To contest these distant proximities Herrera points to a whole set of preconceived ideas that need to be challenged. In his experience, outdated attitudes toward the maquiladora industry were a salient example of such limiting preconceptions and of a widespread failure to recognize the industry as an important platform for development and integration:

> The maquiladora industry is not considered a global international industry. It is seen as only a small component of a large corporation's effort to save money. Just a little part of the process. Not a strong partner in the so-called global integration, which is seen as vertically integrated manufacturing. Now they are producing the whole thing. Before [they assembled] just buttons. Now [they

> are manufacturing] the whole keyboard. In the last ten years, the maquiladora plants have graduated into [even] more sophisticated operations.

Caught in the perception of the industry as a "sweatshop," Herrera contends that many observers overlook its transformation. Like Torres, Herrera claimed that developmental opportunities were ignored locally. As a personnel recruiter, he felt that people in the city disregarded eminent professional opportunities. Trapped in their preconception of Ciudad Juárez only as the third world and maquiladoras as sweatshops, they looked for chances to relocate away from the area. Instead, people from other regions pursued the local opportunities:

> I get Harvard and Yale MBA graduates saying: do you have something in the international arena? [They see it] just like Japan and other manufacturing hubs. Before I was looking for engineers, now for executives to run the whole company or design engineers to create the blueprints.

Herrera said that the evolution of the industry and the opportunities that NAFTA offers are clouded by extreme emotions. Some saw these developments only in terms of plant relocations and job losses. Others saw them as only beneficial. In his view, both these extreme opinions are misguided. He pointed out that, while it was true that thousands of jobs had been lost since the passage of NAFTA, it was also true that previous records of dismissals did not attract public attention. Thus, the dramatic numbers were misleading.

Herrera insisted that a more accurate understanding of local conditions requires setting aside preconceived impressions. To overcome the sweatshop image of the maquiladora industry, he proposed a new term—"international companies"—to foster and capitalize on the alluring glow of globalization and thus to entice local graduates to seek employment in the maquiladora industry. At the same time, he also believed that exaggerated claims about opportunities related to NAFTA were counterproductive. Such claims, in his view, inhibited local entrepreneurs, who thought that only large companies could enter the emergent markets. He suggested that new leadership was needed, leadership that could put a stop to the misguided bickering that only clouds the issues and divides the community.

Herrera's vision of leadership would foster the social integration of the two border cities. Contrary to the perceptions described in chapter 3, he said the lowest level of integration in the two cities was in their business worlds, as demonstrated by the scarcity of local initiatives to take advantage of maquiladora opportunities. The new leadership would channel the synergy of the two communities in a new direction. It would go beyond business or professional interests to reinforce and increase existing linkages at community levels as well.

Steve Carmichael explained the creation of the group as a response to opportunities missed because of a lack of coherence and cohesion. He expressed his concern in more local and immediate terms than Herrera:

> A number of movements like Unite El Paso were trying to address needs because El Paso in 1991 was not reaching its potential. Distant elements were pulling it in different directions. There were five communities in El Paso: a sophisticated West Side, focused on international trade and outlooks, with a lot of money. Central El Paso was a matriarchy, a bunch of broken families led by strong women. Northeast had the military, either retired or active. East is a commuter's community. Its residents work in other parts of the city. The Lower Valley was something else, more like the South Valley of Texas. To seize the future a vehicle was needed. How can we take the different elements and get them to work together?

Like Herrera, Carmichael was a native of the city and in his mid-thirties. While perhaps more locally focused, he was not provincial. He also had extensive knowledge of conditions in other cities along the border and elsewhere. At the same time, he was more critical of maquiladoras and of the overriding impact of nonlocal interests:

> The multinationals were not paying benefits. The bankers weren't doing it either. What brings us together? How can we maximize our resources? How does the other interest override the interests of the community? That is what's happening all over in the U.S. and Mexico. Here it was even worse. We wanted the maximum return for the community, not for the maquila [or] for the bank. How to keep the maximum amount of resources here.

As a lawyer and the chief of staff for the first female state senator in El Paso's history, Carmichael's exposure to the particulars of the city differed from Herrera's, whose job kept him abreast of developments in the maquiladora industry.

Passionate in their concern for their city, both professionals used different talents and exposures to understand the complexity of El Paso. Carmichael, from his involvement in politics, noticed with particular clarity the city's administrative complexity:

> If you look at Omaha, Nebraska, and you say, bring all the decision makers to the table, four people show up. The mayor, the county judge, someone connected to the state governor, and the school superintendent. If you had the same situation in El Paso, thirty-seven people show up: the international boundary and water commission, the customs, the border patrol, the county judge, the state senator, the congressman, the mayor, the commander of Fort Bliss has a lot to say with what happens here, the mayor of Las Cruces, who determines what happens with our electric business here, the mayor of [Ciudad] Juárez because of what happens on the bridges everyday and what happens with commerce, he has to do with that. All those people show up at the table. So they need to say, how can we work together? The need is so much greater here than in any other community because of the dividing lines, the multiple overlapping jurisdictions.

The multiple entities involved in the functioning of the city (which I pointed out in chapter 2, discussing its fictive administration) parallel the multiple identities and agendas on the site. Carmichael himself embodies this multiplicity with particular clarity. Extremely proficient, Carmichael speaks a Spanish with the flavor of rural towns in Chihuahua. Given that a significant number of blonde rural people are dispersed throughout these towns dating from the *Porfiriato,* when many Europeans and Euro-Americans came to the area as landowners or railroad, mining, or lumber company personnel, at first I thought he was Mexican. Carmichael's connection to El Paso, however, dates back even further. His mother's great-grandfather came as part of the invading U.S. Army in the late 1840s. His linguistic heritage, moreover, even predates the invasion: his ancestor had acquired the language as a merchant in Chihuahua and then served as a translator for the army. This connection to the language has prevailed through generations in Carmichael's matrilineal family, where children learn Spanish before English.

Carmichael's cosmopolitan background has been expanded by his own experiences. He has lived in Mexico City, and in Mexicali, Baja California. In addition, he was a Peace Corps volunteer in West Africa for two and a half years. These experiences broadened his understanding of the situation in El Paso and Ciudad Juárez:

> We were looking for likeminded people, who believe in tolerance and diversity, and who describe themselves as being a *paseño.* We are *paseños de aquí y de alla* (from here and there). We can't talk about transportation, health, water, and environment in El Paso

> without including Ciudad Juárez. [We] can talk [about] how [to] work in concert with Fortune 500 companies that are coming here and are using a large part of our tax base through [tax] abatement programs. [They] would move to either side [of the border] to take advantage of whatever situation without putting their share of the improvement of this community like they would if they were in St. Paul, Minnesota.

After their initial conversation, Herrera and Carmichael started to talk with their respective circles of friends about forming a group to try to reconcile the needs and the potentials of the city. Early in these discussions, a parallel was suggested with the city of San Antonio, which a decade earlier had overcome longstanding ethnic and political divisions through a political movement centered on the figure of Henry Cisneros. Inspired by that precedent, Carmichael arranged a conference call with one of Cisneros's early advisors, Chuck Ford. The first meeting was held at Carmichael's house, where eight of the eventual members of Unite El Paso's core group listened to Ford's recollections and recommendations by speakerphone. After the call, the small group, greatly inspired, agreed to form Unite El Paso.

The group's meetings rapidly grew in both frequency and attendance. The founding members' circle of friends and professional acquaintances consisted of a wide array of people involved in other civic or political groups with their respective networks and expertise. For example, John Oliver, a former city editor of a local newspaper, became the secretary of the organization and kept remarkably well-maintained records.

As a first step, members of the group sought to involve established leaders in the city. Sometimes their invitations were accepted. For example, the CEO of the city's general hospital became actively involved, and the president of the local campus of the state university made public statements in support of their efforts. In addition, the group had access to the university's facilities for events and meetings. Similar support was provided by the new leadership of the old chamber of commerce. Sometimes, on the other hand, the group's invitations were rejected. Some established leaders questioned the members' motives or doubted the feasibility of the project. Others attacked even the desirability of the project on ethnic grounds. One member of the old elite blatantly stated that the group had "too many brown faces." Ethnic fears were occasionally invoked in undertones, as when a member of a younger Euro-American group (allegedly hoping to become the next elite) warned a core-group member of Unite El Paso that they were provoking a "race riot" in which many Euro-American "heads would fall." Ethnic concerns were also expressed by Latino critics. A woman entrepreneur took issue with the name of the group: "How come now that we Latinos are coming together they, who are mostly an Anglo group, come talking about uniting El Paso? Is it that only they can unite the city? Couldn't they join our groups?" Another Latino professional ridiculed it as a "feel good, cheerleading" group, referring to its emphasis on finding common ground and to its efforts to highlight the strengths of the community.

The members of Unite El Paso paid little attention to these criticisms. They were busy using their professional expertise and contacts to consolidate the group and define a mission around which multiple groups could coalesce. It was quickly chartered as a nonprofit organization, and meetings were conducted to formulate plans and to define the character of the group. Heavily influenced by the heightened sensitivities regarding the city's frontier status, the members paid careful attention to agreeing on and publicizing the group's "fundamental principles." These principles were summarized in a small brochure that was issued after a couple of months of activities. The first paragraph clearly stated the integral and integrative nature of the effort:

> We have arrived at the fundamental belief that the goal ultimately is the process. This means that the most important thing we can produce is a process by which different segments of our community can synthesize their differences and turn them from community weaknesses into community strengths.

The core group aimed to steer Unite El Paso along democratic and all-inclusive guidelines that would serve as an example and a vehicle for advancing the participatory leadership that the group wanted to promote for the entire city. Oliver referred to the phrase "the goal is the process" as the group's mantra. That wisdom translated, however, into some very long meetings at which all decisions were reached by consensus. Because of this instrumental emphasis on inclusiveness, the meetings and the records of the organization were open to the public, and active recruitment of new members was ongoing. While they were an ethnic mix of Mexican Americans and Euro-Americans, the core group members were well aware that they lacked representation from working-class constituencies. Therefore, to maintain the group's commitment to an all-inclusive participatory process, community meetings were organized in different areas of the city. For example, one took place in the Segundo Barrio, a predominantly Mexican American and immigrant working-class neighborhood. During its formative phase, despite conscious efforts to strengthen community ties, their success in attracting working-class members was limited.

The growth of the group rapidly surpassed its founding members' expectations, nevertheless. An editorial published in January 1993 reported that "Saturday's meeting, by the way, was expected to draw only 15 to 20 people, and when 60 showed up it was a big but pleasant surprise to the organizers." That meeting's featured speaker was Chuck Ford, the San Antonio citizen who had spoken by phone with the founding members when Unite El Paso was begun. This time, assessing the result of the community-building efforts in San Antonio, he expresed regret that "[w]e were not bold enough." In his view, paraphrased in the newspaper clipping, "community building . . . is always painful and never easy." The editorial closes by quoting the activist:

> You got to practice together. You learn to work as a community by practicing working together. It's not fun. It's not easy. It's just sweaty gritty work. Just keep doing what you are doing. Trust in each other. Make the leap of faith. After all, all we're put here to do on the Earth is to do good and forgive.

Similar spiritual overtones, but without relation to any religious creed, influenced the group's public statements and the private attitudes of its members. One of its "fundamental principles" stated: "Part of our working method has been to ask participants to 'check your egos at the door'" (Old 1993b, 4). The final paragraph of the brochure stating these principles closed with the following call: "With broad enough community support, we can create a moral force that will bring the community together, heal divisive differences and allow us to move forward" (3). To foster unity, the group explicitly stated its respect for differing commitments and priorities: "We have not asked any group to set its own agenda aside but to help us conceive a process that will recognize the multiplicity of agendas in our community and let various groups work toward their goals with the least friction and the fewest obstacles" (2).

A fact sheet about Unite El Paso stated that as of April 1993 it had "a roster of 480 individuals" and "a Board of Community Trustees of 31 individuals from the diverse areas of our community to guide its functions." The group consisted by then of "14 committees with over 3,100 volunteer hours to date." It listed as its ongoing involvements assisting in a pilot project to advocate for two new federal judicial positions, the creation of two new neighborhood councils, in South and Central El Paso (which were mostly Mexican American and Mexican working class), and the development of an education task force. The roster listed people who had attended meetings, not all of whom had become members of Unite El Paso. Typically, even among the group's membership, the brunt of the organizational work fell on a handful of individuals. The core members—a circle that grew at a slower pace than the overall membership because it entailed a greater commitment of time—looked for concrete ways to channel the expanding collective enthusiasm the group had generated.

The first major event organized by Unite El Paso was a "goal-setting conference." The event was open, free of charge, to the entire city population. In addition, guests from Ciudad Juárez and Las Cruces, a neighboring city in New Mexico, were invited. Presented as the first in a series of conferences to be held during the year, this event was announced as a community congress. It was initially conceived as a "large meeting where representatives from as many community organizations as possible join together in a day-long meeting at the Civic Center, to agree to set goals for our community." The announcement of the event mentioned plans for a follow-up community summit and other subsequent meetings at which participants would join neighborhood councils and focus groups. Significantly, the Spanish words *tu comunidad* (your community) became a part of the Unite El Paso logo. The community congress became the central focus for the following three months. Innumerable hours went into the multiple tasks involved: discussing the ideas, gathering the funds, advertising the event, and managing all the other logistical details. Grant proposals were written and public relation activities were begun. Tapping the wealth of contacts and expertise in the group, organizers soon obtained a couple of grants to partially fund both the congress and the community summit. These accomplishments added to the momentum of the group and to its public credibility. All this good fortune, however, had some unwanted side effects. Internally, the group engaged in a long discussion over the hiring of a professional moderator for the community congress. Some saw it as unnecessary and expensive. Others felt that, in light of the importance of the congress as an opportunity for substantial dialogue, a professional was needed to mediate potential misunderstandings and conflicts and to keep the focus on the central goal of the event—the formulation of a community vision. The group advocating the professional approach managed to win consent from their opponents, but that discussion foreshadowed a deeper division that arose later regarding distinct differences in the scope of change some members desired and in the degree of responsibility they were willing to take. Externally, critics pointed to the group's success in securing funding as proof of their middle-class status and thus of the shallowness of their commitment to the poor constituencies. "How could they, in their privileged situation, understand or represent the poor?" was a question that a La Mujer Obrera staff member posed to me.

The community congress took place at the city's Civic Center on June 19, 1993, bringing together nearly 1,500 residents and a handful of participants from Ciudad Juárez and Las Cruces. Throughout the day, a collective dialogue took place, and everyone was encouraged to add his or her own concerns and hopes to the formulation of a common vision for the entire city. According to a couple of its organizers, the meeting was a resounding success. As proof of this they pointed to the resulting momentum that led to the community summit only two months later.

For the summit, a committee made up of ten widely regarded leaders selected 150 individuals from among the congress participants. These people were brought together for an entire weekend to work on the recommendations developed by the community congress. Participants ranged from elderly individuals to high school students and encompassed all the residential, professional, and ethnic groups in the city. According to the "vision statement" produced from these discussions, these 150 participants were requested to follow specific instructions:

> The chief task of summit participants was to think "not-traditionally" about the future. They were told not to think of "incremental change" and to avoid the crippling M-word, assuming that "the money"—and other resources—needed to pay for it all would come from doing more effective things instead of doing the old things more efficiently. It would come, as many a participant said, echoing [the moderator], from "collapsing the time it takes to create knowledge out of information." This, they were told to assume, could help them achieve anything the community reached consensus on. Participants were organized into eleven discussion groups which periodically reconvened for general discussion.

Symbolic dimensions were not overlooked in the organization of the event. For example, each group was given the name of a plant of the Chihuahua desert—Prickly Pear, Lechugilla, Agave, Golden Barrel, Sotol, Maguey, Ocotillo, and so on. Significantly, the list included English, Spanish, and Native American words. At the end, the event closed with a collective rendition of a song in Spanish led by a Euro-American woman who had been active in a number of civic groups and a Mexican American man who had been a lifelong activist in the city. The song, "De Colores" (Of many colors), was first introduced to wide Euro-American audiences in the 1960s during the farmworkers' movement led by Cesar Chavez and Dolores Huerta. Although perhaps less widely known as a political/spiritual anthem, it has public resonances similar to those associated with "We Shall Overcome."

The inclusive sensitivities and bold imagination of the summit participants were also evident in the document issued to report on the summit proceedings. This press release, entitled "Dreaming the Future and Living the Unity: El Paso Makes Strategic Choices" (Old 1993a), opens with a "vision statement":

> Imagine this scene: It's the year 2011. Your oldest child is 18 this weekend. You work at the Spaceport recently finished at McGregor Range on Fort Bliss. Your spouse—one of the nation's leading experts in Latin American trade—has just returned from Minneapolis where the Rio Bravo Port Authority has opened a new "embassy" designed to give competitive advantage to Minnesota companies wanting to do business in South America. They approached El Paso for a reason. There is full employment here. No graffiti adorns any wall in any neighborhood in the city. Every school is a neighborhood center where people can go for information on public health, nutrition, child care and entertainment after classes end at 3:30 every afternoon. Graduation is nearly a hundred percent, and there are literature classes for senior citizens offered in the same building after school's out.
>
> Your children, fluent in both English and Spanish, are completely bicultural, and one is planning to earn a doctorate at El Paso University, which has become an internationally recognized center for the transfer of technology and applied research. Delegations from countries all over Latin America visit the university campus with such frequency that you don't even try to keep track of them.
>
> Your second-oldest will pursue a graduate degree in fine arts and hopes one day to become curator of the Southwestern Art Institute here, which made museum history last year by putting together a traveling art exhibit that created enormous lines and stunning reviews in Paris, Madrid, Rome, Berlin, and Moscow.
>
> The "baby" of the family, born in 1995, has just finished helping connect a neighborhood computer network, part of a Bowie High School class project sponsored by the region's largest computer distributor, to finish "wiring" the Segundo Barrio. That makes residents there the first in the region to have a computer terminal online in every home.
>
> The accounts in the local news media—available to you in complete text and interactively in your home, your automobile and now even on the Border Transit Authority monorail—are be-

> ginning to bore you. Yet another city from "back east" is coming to attend yet another seminar on "Intergovernmental Collaboration in a Multi-Cultural Environment."
>
> "What's wrong with those people?" you say to yourself. "Can't they get it together?"
>
> "Oh well," you think, "I might as well enjoy myself tonight at the San Juan de Oñate Festival." Over the past fifteen years this festival has become one of the nation's hottest historical celebrations. "What are they celebrating tonight anyway?" you wonder.
>
> You go to your computer terminal and check the Rio Grande Free Net—noticing from an announcement on the screen that its participation has just expanded to three new states via the Max-Tel Communications Satellite the region has leased space on—and learn that a no longer existing organization called Unite El Paso is being honored. You note that it held something called a Community Summit from September 17 to September 19, 1993, the same weekend your oldest child was born. (Old 1993a, 1–2)

This projected scene was then contrasted with the problems enumerated by participants at the beginning of the summit:

> From the early sessions, issues poured out: Political leadership was fragmented; economic development was lagging; voter apathy was intolerable; crime statistics, drug use and gang participation were at unacceptable levels. Education was everyone's concern: there was insufficient parental involvement; preschool preparation was minimal; the quality of public education was too low; laborers didn't have the necessary skills to succeed in the work place. The issues seemed interminable.
>
> On the economic development front, reports were just as troubling: skilled jobs in El Paso were far too few; there was too little capital; wages were abysmally low and unemployment unacceptably high; and there was no incubation of small business.
>
> To make matters worse our young people were leaving and not coming back; housing was inadequate; there was little sense of community—much less the feeling that El Paso was part of an integrated region; the place was seen to be running out of water; and environmental practices were far from the ideal. (Old 1993a, 4–5)

In terms of assets, the enumeration was more succinct:

> All was not bleak, however, and many participants noted that our location seemed to be excellent in terms of trade with Mexico and the rest of Latin America; that we have an enormous asset in

> the military in *El Paso* itself and other governmental assets *in the region*—White Sands Missile Range in New Mexico as well as the government laboratories of Los Alamos and Sandia.
>
> Beyond that and in spite of our historic inability to deal with it fully, was our diversity and our rich multicultural heritage here at the Pass of the North. The number and quality of our institutions of higher learning on both sides of the border was noted, as was the presence of a young, able workforce. (Old 1993a, 5; italics in original)

The second day of the event, the participants were asked to imagine a detailed vision of human resources and economic development. As reflected in the brief descriptions, the subgroups' visions mostly coincided, with each spokesperson generally reiterating or refining the preceding statements. The general areas of coincidence related to education, trade, and unity. In terms of education, the discussants emphasized education as an ongoing venture for any person (e.g., lifelong learning). In addition, they also emphasized the need to catch up and keep up with technological developments as well as to upgrade the skill level of the labor force. In terms of trade, a general consensus emerged on the ideal geographical position of the city and region to become "an international trade mecca" (Old 1993a, 7). One intervention suggested the wide scope and the social character of the projected prominence:

> We are going to become the Latin American economic development center. We are focusing on Latin America to define our market better. But if they want information on how to get water to their towns, on how to create affordable housing—by the year 2011, El Paso will have solved its housing shortage and water problems—we are going to take that knowledge and make it available to the rest of the world. (Old 1993a, 6)

Consensus also arose about the need for unity to accomplish these goals. Greater integration was advocated, in terms not only of ethnic diversity, but also of the optimal integration of regional resources, including Ciudad Juárez and Las Cruces. The same participant articulated this integrative goal with particular clarity: "We're going to become a model for cooperation among state governments working together. What we are going to do is get rid of all the barriers to trade in their states and two nations" (Old 1993a, 6). The idea of removing "barriers" to trade was based on a seemingly general agreement about the desirability of making El Paso an "open border city." The delimitation of this "open border" concept was introduced by David Miller, the university professor whose vision of regional economic development was described in chapter 3. He suggested the relocation of customs and immigration inspections for both countries to checkpoints at the outskirts of the cities, forty miles from the dividing line. This relocation would remove the obstructions created by the inspection operations. The removal of this pervasive divider would enhance the cohesion and coherence of the city and the region.

The INS Strikes Back—Take 2: Beam Me Up, Scottie

The community summit generated intense enthusiasm among many of its participants, not just the members of Unite El Paso. That enthusiasm, however, was abruptly quenched a few hours later by the deployment of the border patrol's Operation Blockade. As mentioned in chapter 3, border patrol district chief Samuel Aguallo had participated in the summit. During those two and a half days, he sat through the discussion aware of the imminent blockade in which border patrol officers were posted, perhaps permanently, along the dividing line of the two cities.

The public response to this border patrol operation overshadowed discussion of any other local event for months. The propagandized outpouring of public support for the operation shocked and paralyzed most of its critics. Members of Unite El Paso were also dumbfounded, not only by the severity of the action, but by its overwhelming effect on the call for transborder cooperation. The impact of the measure, moreover, had a chilling and eventually grave effect on the structure of Unite El Paso itself.

A few days after the blockade went into effect, some members of Unite El Paso proposed an activity to counter the strong expression of animosity provoked by the border patrol's action toward Ciudad Juárez residents. At one meeting, possible responses were discussed. Some members visualized a massive gesture of contact between the two cities: They would organize two chains of people holding hands on each side of the riverbank along the downtown areas of both cities and coming together at the international bridges. Other members of the group questioned the logistics of such a project, given the short time they had to put it together. Oliver stated that it would take thousands of people to reach along the proposed distance. He reminded the group that a recent march in memory of the deceased Cesar Chavez had brought out only three hundred participants, and it seemed unlikely that Unite El Paso could recruit even a thousand demonstrators in the short time available. Another member mentioned protests against the blockade in Ciudad Juárez, where the U.S. flag had been burned, and expressed concern that things might get out of hand in the intense emotion of the moment because anti–United States gestures would backfire and become major setbacks to Unite El Paso's unifying goals. Oliver warned against sacrificing the long-term goal of the group for the short-term satisfaction of a public protest.

As the discussion proceeded, the projected activity shrank. Eventually, the meeting ended with a plan to organize marches in both cities to the dividing line, where presents would be exchanged to symbolize the cooperation of both cities. It was planned for December 12, after La Virgen de Guadalupe, an important religious/cultural day in Mexico, as well as for both Mexican Americans and some Euro-Americans in the city. Some weeks later, Oliver recalled in an interview that he had left the meeting exhausted, but feeling that a general agreement had been reached. To his surprise and evident despair, he soon heard rumors that after the meeting some proponents of the massive demonstration had made statements calling him and Carmichael racists and sexists. Oliver had tears in his eyes as he reported these comments and explained that his disagreement with the idea was on purely logistical grounds. His deep frustration was obvious as his tears increased. After a second or two, he apologized for his expression of emotion and asserted that there was no reason to be upset. To stress this point, he told me about a statement made by a member of Unite El Paso at a retreat they had while organizing the community congress. A lifelong resident of the city, Marcos Sierra had served in the Korean War only to return to El Paso and be harassed again and again by the border patrol because of his ethnicity. Now, weeping openly, Oliver told me that his distress at being called a racist and a sexist could not compare to the harassment Sierra had suffered at the hands of the INS—especially after risking his life in a war. Regaining his composure, he said: "We Anglos don't know how to ache."

Oliver and Carmichael dismissed the rumors and continued their involvement in Unite El Paso, but efforts to restart its arrested momentum were stalled even by the weather. On December 12, the day scheduled for the activity to counter animosities generated by the blockade, strong, cold winds swept through the city, threatening to turn into a storm. The event was postponed until March. However, like the storm, which never progressed to more than the sound of thunder, the celebration never took place. Meetings of Unite El Paso continued, but less regularly. Eventually, the momentum dissipated and the group went virtually dormant for the next year.

The group was partially reactivated in 1995 by the hiring of Magdalena Sotelo as full-time executive director. Sotelo patiently undertook the task of reestablishing the functional structure for the group. She had limited success in bringing previous key members back to their initial levels of involvement. Though they were supportive, people like Oliver and Carmichael could not offer the same degree of leadership. By then, both men were involved in other ventures that also advanced the agenda originally established by Unite El Paso. Some ex-members, in addition to feeling continued disappointment over Operation Blockade, felt uninspired by the direct approach the new leaders proposed. These new leaders intended to implement the global vision generated at the summit through specific projects. For example, they obtained a grant to promote preventive health practices in one poor area of the city. This accorded with the inclusive and participatory spirit of the initial Unite El Paso. Since it had to operate with fewer members, however, the group concentrated solely on this single project for the following year. Some ex-members dismissed the group as a single-issue entity, like a number of other valuable groups. It seemed to them that Unite El Paso had lost its distinctive desire to foster unifying leadership for the entire city. As months passed, however, the new Unite El Paso expanded into other areas. Sotelo's commitment to day-by-day engagement, even though the group often lacked the funds to pay her salary, sustained much of this expansion, as did the recommendation and support of former members like Carmichael, who had been recently elected to the state senate.

The "new" Unite El Paso has gradually brought to fruition some of the recommendations made at the community summit. Ironically, it has had relatively less public visibility, partly because it is no longer a novelty and also because its direct engagement in specific tasks has fractured its image as a coalescing force. In May 1997, the program for its "First Annual El Paso Unites Dinner: A celebration of our 'UNITY,'" lists nineteen members on its executive board, thirty-seven members on its steering committee, and thirty-three on its advisory board. At the time, the group had twelve ongoing projects. For example, in education, it was involved in promoting free access to the Internet throughout the city. In addition, it advocated the use of school facilities as community centers to maximize their social contributions in terms of health education, parental involvement in education, closer attention to school desertion (dropout) rates and to gang activities, and other matters. A related project, the Family Preservation Council, was promoting "a mutually beneficial marriage between targeted neighborhoods and approximately forty different agencies in El Paso." According to the group's assessment, in its year of operation "over 10,000 persons" were served. In certain schools, self-improvement classes and counseling services were being conducted with the aim of strengthening families.

In the area of economic development, the group joined in sponsoring youth services as part of the Enterprise Zone Project obtained by the city government in a national competition. It also promoted meetings to develop a community action plan, and in support of this effort Unite El Paso developed the El Paso del Norte Public Policy Institute in partnership with the two main college institutions in the city. Both initiatives have striven to process and circulate comprehensive yet accessible information to the public as a whole, as well as to people in decision-making positions. In terms of health, Unite El Paso entered its second year of a five-year grant for community clinics to encourage preventive practices and self-management among poor and undereducated constituencies at the outskirts of the city. In social terms, Unite El Paso's Celebrating Our Outstanding Legacy committee aimed to "increase pride within the community" through two projected events to enhance residents' self-image and their image of their city. One project was a "diversity day," a citywide festival with booths and entertainment from the various ethnic and racial groups in the city. The second was the recognition of four hundred individuals, one for every year of the city's history.

The Court of Inquiry

Unite El Paso has solidified its reputation as a serious and committed channel for creative, organic community programs. Its ambitious initial project, however, has been complicated by the local fractures described in chapter 3, as vividly exemplified by the responses to Operation Blockade. However, Sotelo's difficulty in recruiting the active involvement of Carmichael, Oliver, and other members was due partly to their involvement at the time with a major project directly connected to the aim of Unite El Paso. In the broadest sense, the project continued the group's efforts to maximize local resources, as well as to emphasize local concerns over nonlocal agendas. The project created a court of inquiry, a legal resource through which a federal judge, Antonio Mendoza, requested information on the funding formulas used by the state of Texas to allocate resources to the city. Implicit in this request was the tacit assertion that El Paso was not receiving its "fair share." For the next two years, while the case was actively pursued by a cadre of local lawyers, some politicians, and a number of local residents, "fair share" was the mobilizing cry in their demand for better services from the state.

The court of inquiry was the brainchild of Alfredo Contreras. Contreras, a native lawyer with a master's degree in public policy from Harvard, approached the members of Unite El Paso when the group was entering its dormant phase. Contreras told me that he had not joined Unite El Paso because he had found its agenda too broad to be effective. His strategy was to look at the "flow of moneys" to find out why El Paso was poor. He enumerated the sequence of deductions that led him to think about the court of inquiry in the following manner:

> Always try to go to the most basic things. First of all, who are you? Demographics. Look at this area and you find out that not just now but for decades we have been the youngest in the United States. If you look at our workforce, only about 42 percent of the people here are in the workforce. Why? We have a huge number of children. . . . If you go down to Star County, which is one of the poorest counties in Texas, it is about the same. If you go up around the suburbs of Dallas, their labor force participation is about 60 percent. Right away, before you know anything else, you can tell which community is going to be at an advantage and at a disadvantage. . . . [With about 12 percent unemployment, only] 35 percent of the people [actually] go to work. . . . These 35 percent need to support the other 65 percent. If you are a policymaker sitting in Austin, you think these people are in big trouble. [Yet] on top of that you strap these people with the lowest wage structure, not in Texas but in the United States.
>
> Now the state comes in with its policies. The state of Texas decides that the way it's going to raise its money for the most part is with the sales tax. That means, the poorer you are the higher your rate of taxation as of the percentage of your income. What do [poor] people do? They also make a lot of babies. What are the most expensive things we have? Schools. The way we finance our schools and local government is through property tax. That means that these people who make all the babies basically have to make their own schools. Here you start with the people who are the poorest anyway. Then you hit them with the highest state tax for general revenue purposes. And then, for local revenue purposes we overtax them again because we let them bear the brunt of those costs that are so high for them by themselves.
>
> [Poor communities] have the lowest tax bases. Austin, for example, a city about our size, has twice as large a tax base on the value of property. If we want to raise one dollar, we need to make twice the effort. We need to tax twice as hard. But it doesn't stop there. People think that it is inexpensive to live here but it is not. As a matter of fact, we are more expensive than Dallas, much more expensive than Lubbock. . . . [El Paso has the] highest electrical rates, highest gasoline prices, high food prices. You make very little money, then you have all these costs. The detrimental impact of

> this uneven distribution of funds spreads into the private sector, augmenting the poverty of El Paso and deepening its problems.
>
> Much of the movement of private initiative money is based on public infrastructure: educational facilities, crime, arts, tax bases, recreational facilities, all sorts of things. Many things that are within the control of the government and we can work with those. Embedded in a complex array of discrepancies and inequalities, the problems are perpetuated in the overlapping of agendas and self-interests.

In Contreras's view, these inequalities extend beyond racism:

> Texas is really two worlds. You have the world that exists in Austin, Dallas, and Houston, and so forth, where people make very good money. Their standards of living, their educational institutions are on a par with what they are in the wealthy areas in the country. Then you have South Texas and the Border. You can't compare them with other parts of the United States, unless you go to the Mississippi Delta, some pockets of poverty that exist in the Appalachia and others.
>
> Policymakers know this. They have always known this and yet when it comes to making policies . . . to assist with those who need more development consistently what they do is [one of] . . . two things. They either ignore that, and keep the status quo, or . . . they want to punish it even more to benefit the wealthy areas of the state. In fact, we are subsidizing the wealthy areas of the state. If you only wanted to look at [transportation] institutions, for example. . . . Just a rough estimate [from 1990 to 1995], in highway money, we got one third of the money our population should have gotten. Here is the thing and [it] is kind of dreadful. . . . Of those funds, I'd say 45 percent were federal funds. [We gave them] one quarter of our federal taxes and got not one cent of our state gasoline tax in this community.
>
> Policymakers know but do nothing about it. It is not that they look at Mexicans and say, "I don't like you," although in essence that's what happens. But what happens is that policymakers are basically running commissions, and are not elected people. They are wealthy people generally, contributors to the conservative system, contributors to the pyramid, politically, [who] are put on these commissions. We have no control over them, and they go in with their own agendas. From Dallas, from Houston. Do you know what that means in terms of dollars? That is not any coincidence. They give preference to their own areas. These people are always getting more than their share.

According to Contreras, whose successful law practice allowed him to retire in his mid-forties to pursue multiple interests—including research on these matters—the solution started with information:

> It happens for two reasons. One is, we let it happen. We are ignorant and we don't have an inclination to move the status quo. The second reason is that if we don't tend to protect ourselves they are not going to. It is a Darwinian system in which those who have more get more.

Contreras's analysis found a welcoming ear among some original members of Unite El Paso. Together, they approached Judge Mendoza, who agreed to proceed with the court of inquiry. Since its onset, Contreras saw Unite El Paso as a political tool to foster local development: "You don't have a lot of immediate control over private capital. Private capital is perfectly free to move and leave any basis. But what you can do is try to move public capital—with that [public capital] you have more control over, politically."

The court of inquiry electrified the community. With an unprecedented degree of local assertiveness, numerous individuals and groups supported the measure. Judge Mendoza deputized a handful of lawyers who volunteered to work on the legal action. After examining the funding history of different services, four areas were targeted for initial attention because of their significance or dramatic irregularities. These four areas were the allocation of public moneys for the construction and maintenance of highways, provision of services for the elderly, provision of services for children with special needs, and provision of psychiatric care. A rapid succession of developments, along with the evident discrepancy in funding, suggested that a favorable decision for the city was at hand. In its most dramatic moment, state's attorney Matt Murillo was summoned to testify. Contreras displayed both his trial skills and his intimate knowledge of the case as the prosecuting attorney. Symbolically, the most prominent characters in this shoot-out were Mexican Americans at opposite ends of the case, if not necessarily of the issue.

In spite of, or because of, this show of power, the court of inquiry was derailed. To this day, there has been no decision reached and the proceedings have been swamped with appeals and technical manipulations by state officials. In one instance, Oliver told me, box after box was delivered to Carmichael's office from the state's attorney's office. The boxes contained information on highway funding that Carmichael, who was handling the case against the transportation department, had requested. The innumerable reams of computer printouts in those boxes, however, did not include the key for the coding system that would make sense of the data. In bitter bemusement, Oliver put it this way: "They buried us with data." In formal compliance with Carmichael's request, state officials had managed to follow the letter of the law by supplying information and to mock the spirit of the law by failing to make that information usable.

The gap in influence and resources between advocates of the court of inquiry and state officials was widened by local critics in El Paso. The establishment, apparently including the mayor, called for restraint so as not to further alienate the authorities. Some found the legal match between Contreras and state attorney Murillo particularly disturbing. Ironically, in their calls for reason, they ignored a paramount incongruity: the state's attorney, who is supposed to guarantee due process, was defending the state's own improprieties.

Like Unite El Paso and, even earlier, La Mujer Obrera, the court of inquiry represented a significant effort to alter the subordinated or marginal position of the city by presenting a collective, conciliatory local front. However, like the other two efforts, it was eventually overwhelmed by the striking discrepancy between local and nonlocal resources. Underscoring and magnifying this discrepancy, endemic divisions eventually eroded the initial successes of the three efforts. These setbacks, however, did not completely override or eliminate the accomplishments or destroy the initiatives. While little mention is made of the court of inquiry—except by cynics to justify their apathy—some of its main promoters expressed great satisfaction with their involvement and with the partial results. For Contreras, its architect, the court was, and could only have been, no more than a political statement that dramatized inequity and moved people to respond. Consequently, while it still doesn't get its "fair share," the city has seen funding increases from the state government. Oliver put it more passionately: "The court of inquiry told them, you won't f—— with us again." In more circumspect terms, reflecting the etiquette and bicultural character of the city, Carmichael said it had conveyed to Austin a powerful message: "¡Basta! No more!"

Competition, Coincidences, and Potential Confluence on the Eternal Frontier

The exchange between Clark Pereira and President Bush during the NAFTA negotiations illustrates the limits faced by individual members of underrepresented groups as they achieve new levels of participation. Similarly, the legal showdown between Contreras and Murillo attests to the new public prominence of Mexican Americans in the state. As described in chapter 3 in the contrast between Torres and the displaced workers, breakthroughs mostly have occurred on an individual basis among the members of this group. Efforts to broaden the limited extent of the breakthroughs are greatly influenced by discrepancies between global and local levels of resources, as well as by imbalances in the local setting itself. The two initiatives discussed in this chapter, the Hispanic Chamber of Commerce and Unite El Paso, addressed these discrepancies and inequities. As spatial practices related to the frontier condition of the city, these initiatives fostered institutional reconfigurations that pointed out the divisions and also served as vehicles to overcome them.

Like the initiatives in chapter 3, these two initiatives also espoused different parameters of involvement. The Hispanic Chamber of Commerce had a narrower scope, primarily focused on ethnic and business dimensions. Unite El Paso, in contrast, advocated broader and more inclusive agendas and constituencies. Initially, there was little interaction between the two. Eventually, however, contacts were established. Most significantly, the third president of the chamber was the Unite El Paso chairman when Sotelo, its first executive director, joined the effort. In 1997, the director of the Economic Development department of the chamber also headed the Economic and Work Force Development committee of Unite El Paso. From denunciations of "divisiveness and racism" raised against the founders of the Hispanic Chamber to the suspicion and trivialization of Unite El Paso's calls for cohesion, the consolidation of the two initiatives offers new roles and opens new avenues for those who want to bridge the distant proximities of the city.

The frontier condition of the city and its pervasive subordination to nonlocal interests and flows challenge and limit the five local initiatives described in this chapter and chapter 3. In other words, the persistent alienated instrumentalities characteristic of the border region undermine the initiatives. These responses, nevertheless, took hold of overwhelming changes and channeled them into paths that altered the frontier condition of the site. Still, the monumental discrepancies between local and nonlocal forces, as well as disruptive local contrasts, continue to deepen. NAFTA and the consequently enhanced mobility of production arrangements translate into worsening poverty and sharpened polarizations—posing urgent challenges and providing unprecedented opportunities. In the conclusion, I continue the discussion of these interrelated yet disparate possibilities. I also elaborate on proposed approaches to contending with the conceptual challenges presented at the beginning of the book.

Conclusion

El Paso as an Eternal—Yet Not Final—Frontier

Globalization and International Boundaries

In the mid-1980s, the premiere of a television movie about an atomic attack on the United States by the Soviet Union was followed by a discussion among a panel of commentators. Astronomer Carl Sagan made the statement, "There has always been the same amount of evil in the world. Today, however, it is better armed." I don't know about evil, but I find his formulation applicable to international boundaries: there have always been borders, but today they are both more numerous and more proximate. Ironically, in the relatively short time since the movie premiere, the Soviet Union has disappeared, eliminated not by an external nuclear attack (though seriously weakened by the threat of one), but by the hammering at its eroding internal walls. In fact, the disintegration of the Soviet bloc contributed to the increase of international boundaries, as its former republics became independent countries.

As in the former Soviet Union, global integration has not reduced, but has multiplied the number of international boundaries. Likewise, qualifying claims of cultural merging, national identities, and idiosyncrasies persist (*Economist* 1998). Meanwhile, in polar contrast to the implosion of the former Soviet Union, trading blocs have been exploding in Europe, East Asia, and the American hemisphere. Country after country is being linked by the capitalistic domino effect of free trade agreements. In the European Union, integration aims to overcome asymmetries among its members. There, international borders have been functionally transcended, while being symbolically recognized. The relative poverty of countries such as Spain, Greece, and the former East Germany have received special assistance (Velde and van Houtum 2000). Here in this hemisphere, the integration proceeds differently: transnational contrasts are not harmonized but exploited. Borders are to be transcended economically, while being reinforced socially. This contrast was clearly expressed in the parameters of negotiation of the North American Free Trade Agreement (NAFTA) among Canada, Mexico, and the United States in the early 1990s: immigration issues were left off the agenda, while environmental and labor issues were reluctantly addressed (Rothstein 1993).

While it is a global process, closely related to the baffling specter of change, international integration proceeds differently within countries and produces varying impacts from region to region. Within these regions, moreover, differences are not absolute, but relative to their internal confines. These differences are vividly manifested along the U.S. southern border, as well as between this border region and the rest of the United States. These contrasting impacts are shown in Table 2, which compares per capita income levels of border cities from 1970 to 1997 and shows how they correspond to national totals.

Table 2.

Annual per capita income (net earnings) for main border cities, in percentage of national figures

City	1970	1980	1990	1997
San Diego	105.14	100.24	103.60	95.03
Nogales	78.80	74.97	56.89	51.21
El Paso	74.24	63.21	61.00	58.47
Laredo	55.83	54.74	49.02	53.08
McAllen	50.66	53.88	46.03	44.08
Brownsville	44.80	48.41	42.84	41.24

Note: Figures calculated by author, based on information provided by REIS (Regional Economic Information System, 1969–97); RCN-0230 U.S. Department of Commerce, Economics and Statistics Administration, Bureau of Economic Analysis.

Aside from the sharp unevenness in the overall declining trend of the region and national income levels, as revealed in its border cities, internal contrasts within the region are also striking. San Diego's figures were above the rest of the country, while the other border cities have been well below. Yet, in recent years, even San Diego has seen its income levels decline, though still not at the drastic rates of the other cities. The disturbing character of these declining income levels is underscored by employment growth in all of these cities.

Table 3.

Wage and salary employment growth in main border cities

Location	Number of Workers 1970	1997	Total Growth 1970 to 1997
United States	91,281,600	156,410,400	71 %
San Diego	577,697	1,243,195	115 %
Nogales	5,055	12,288	143 %
El Paso	135,444	266,577	96 %
Laredo	24,008	65,249	171 %
McAllen	40,694	105,323	158 %
Brownsville	43,871	150,294	242 %

Note: Figures calculated by author, based on information provided by REIS (Regional Economic Information System, 1969–97); RCN-0230 U.S. Department of Commerce, Economics and Statistics Administration, Bureau of Economic Analysis.

How is one to explain this perverse relationship between employment and poverty? Contrary to developmental claims, more jobs and more international economic activity have not translated into wealth, but into poverty. This perverse outcome characterizes the dramatic effects of industrialization in the third world (Halebsky 1995). Thus, how is one to explain the fact that U.S. cities along the international divide experience this "third world" effect? Part of the answer is in the dislocating effects of globalization. These effects are not only felt in the "third world" or in the border region. Most U.S. cities have also seen their situations greatly altered by the reconfiguration of their economic activities (Bluestone and Harrison 1982). However, most of these cities have seen progressive overall improvements through the decades (Sassen 1994; Wilson 1997). Within these cities, Latinos, African Americans, and women have seen contrasting, yet uneven impacts. Some segments have amply benefited, while most have suffered decay in their social and economic conditions (Carnoy, Daley, and Ojeda 1993; Reich 1991b).

The unevenness of these processes is particularly manifested along the border. I look at this particular manifestation and to the significant, yet limited insight that the region provides for understanding other settings. I contend that, beyond the globalization process itself, the unevenness derives, in part, from contrasting social approaches between the international integration process of the European Union and that promoted by the United States in the American hemisphere. This contrast entails the socioeconomic orientations apparent in this hemispheric "gap" between "difference" and "inequity." In Europe, international divides are seen as "borders of difference." They are to be transcended with special programs in which transnational inequities are softened (Houtum 2000). In America, international boundaries are seen as "borders of inequity." Beyond difference, inequities are to be exploited through socially blinded economic policies driven by ideological dogmas about "comparative advantages" and "market laws." Without a social focus, promised "trickle down" benefits instead yield dramatically uneven costs for diverse groups.

The international boundary between the United States and Mexico is particularly affected by the exploitation of inequities because of its sociopolitical relation to both countries. The thesis of this book is that this border region remains a frontier. I use the notion of frontier to emphasize that local concerns are persistently and pervasively subordinated to nonlocal interests. In other words, the region remains open to subsequent takeovers. I use the phrase "alienated instrumentality" for the dynamic and impacts of these takeovers. With this term, I underscore the persistent and multiple exploitation of the region's resources and geographical position for interests and concerns primarily related to nonlocal constituencies. In turn, local constituencies are not only deprived of or outcompeted for these resources, but are left behind to contend with the detrimental effects of the takeovers: ecological disruptions, social chaos, border animosities, and so forth. It is this subordination that has translated greater employment into worsened poverty as the city has "enjoyed" greater participation in international activities.

The alienated instrumentalities of the site are differently confronted by local residents. In relation and in response to the distant proximities of the city, some residents engage more "proactively" with the takeovers than do others. These different engagements were illustrated in terms of the five initiatives that came about in direct relation to the challenges and opportunities that globalization has presented to the region since the 1980s. These efforts took place in the U.S. border city of El Paso as residents attempted to overcome its frontier condition by altering the economic orientation of the city in relation to global markets.

Being an international link has seriously undermined the city's coherence and cohesiveness, perpetuating its social fragmentation and frontier individualism. Faced with externally imposed regulations designed for nonlocal priorities, local residents and transient visitors often cope by side-stepping these alienating regulations for reasons of expediency, desperation, or illegal gain. Incongruous bureaucratic requirements, scarce employment opportunities, or profitable (albeit risky) smuggling schemes lead to irregular observance of laws such as those outlawing undocumented crossings or drug trafficking. All of these infringement activities, in different degrees and with diverse consequences, undermine the cohesion of the community and render a constellation of "distant proximities."

Distant Proximities and Alienated Instrumentalities

Globalization has widened El Paso's geographical scope of interaction and has intensified its intermediary function. Since the 1960s, it has facilitated connections between the local and the nonlocal at the same time that it has underscored the discrepancy between local and global options and levels of resources. Likewise, it has deepened the distances among various groups within the city at the same time that it has made it mandatory for local efforts to find innovative solutions and foster collaboration among the diverse constituencies of this fragmented social setting. Thus, La Mujer Obrera managed to coordinate the collaboration of public and private groups to revitalize the local garment industry. In similar fashion, Socorro Enterprises and Unite El Paso strove to consolidate bases of power to contend with nonlocal developments. These collaborative efforts were seriously undermined by the pervasive subordination of the local to the nonlocal.

The altered relation of global and local magnitudes is closely related to the shuffling of multiple parameters with uncertain outcomes and levels of intervention. The passage from space to hyperspace implicit in the transition from an industrial to an information society bridges and divides as much as the border region between the United States and Mexico. Concurrently, diverse configurations and overlapping spaces have resulted in some of the social breakthroughs generated by the civil rights movement in the last five decades in many social and geographical areas of the country. The border zones alluded to by Rosaldo map the conflicting delineations of these breakthroughs for those who have managed to overcome the initial barriers of exclusion. Tellingly, many proponents of the allegorical image of the border celebrated the image of the border as a cognitive referent in uncertain new parameters of inclusion. Yet, what about those left behind?

This book has addressed conceptual and empirical challenges to understand the specter of change, the polarizing interplay of breakthroughs and displacements. By citing various instances of the border region's alienated instrumentality, I have described diverse effects of globalization on El Paso to illustrate the persistent production of the region as a frontier. The illustration is neither a paradigm, nor a metaphor. It is simply a case study that helps to clarify the border enigma as well as the mind-boggling development of globalization. Its ethnographic focus is on local responses to the challenges and opportunities derived from the increasingly direct integration of the city into wider flows of exchange and transit. My hope is to offer an alternative view of the border to counter the reifying glow of the region as a site of mythic or stigmatic dimensions. In its current alluring appeal, stubbornly and advantageously perceived as "empty space," the border region as a whole is incongruously recognized and erased at the same time. This partial recognition allows for the exploitation of the region primarily for nonlocal interests. Seen as a site of transgression, the site is continually transgressed. Seen as a site of chaos, it becomes chaotic as its local boundaries and concerns are overridden. Local residents respond to these transgressions, to the alienating manipulation of their boundaries, at times by reinforcing those boundaries, but at other times by recreating and manipulating them.

My aim is to underscore the social and, therefore, the human dynamics of the site as a dislocated context. Given the spectral contours of transformations and the magnitude of their polarizing challenges, I show that the border region, as a specific site primarily defined as a crossroad, faces its own crossroad. I recognize, however, this challenge within the overall transformation of many, increasingly interrelated, settings. Beyond the drama of transgression, the thrill of innovations, and the shock of chaos, we need to acknowledge that globalization means a dynamic reformulation of difference and inequality. We need a new analytical prism for looking at the perplexing situation of the border and the overall spectral transformation of globalization in most other settings. New parameters of competition and community overflow our traditional categories, frames of reference, and geopolitical mappings. I hope that my illustrations of a few of the multiple situations of local residents contribute to a more inclusive perspective on the border region's challenges and opportunities. I also hope that, at least, the various situations highlighted lead to the recognition that the region is not "empty space" and that its residents are more than merely waiters and prostitutes, or emblematic motifs in a literary piece or news account. Nor should they be viewed as only maquiladora workers or displaced workers. Some of them are children and old people. Others are business owners, labor activists, public functionaries, and so forth. Ultimately, I aim to show that the border does not derive its peculiar identity from these "characters" or their alleged identities, but from its frontier conditions and the extent to which its residents live their lives at different levels of engagement with the overridden subordinated conditions of the city.

These conditions are seldom recognized in the much-too-common celebratory or stigmatizing accounts of the border. Yes, there *are* salient concentrations of undocumented workers, border patrol agents, drug smugglers, transient visitors, and the like. However, there are also, in Carmen Rocha's terms, *empresarios* and *barbajanes*. There are people like Alfredo Contreras, the native lawyer with a master's degree in public policy from Harvard, among dropouts, and other contrasts, such as between racist Euro-Americans and progressive Euro-Americans, or between Chicanos prejudiced against Euro-Americans and anti-Mexican Mexican Americans. This multiplicity overrides preconceived notions. For example, notions of hybridity restate the confluence while overshadowing persistent differences and asymmetries.

I proposed that the new differences and inequalities take place, in figurative and literal respects, in the reconfiguring relations of the social production of space. My emphasis on the city of El Paso as a distinct yet concrete context, a crossroad at a crossroads, shows that contiguity does not necessarily generate blending or even contact. The "spatial practices" producing the city as a frontier involve "new subjectivities" such as Steve Carmichael or Nick Herrez, who adeptly contend with ambiguity as pointed out by Gloria Anzaldúa. However, these gifted individuals also confront the overriding impacts of a contextual setup that undermines their efforts to create social cohesiveness or to obtain the city's "fair share" of public resources. Their context, however, also involves contrasting "representational spaces" manifested in the contrasting experiences of the site. These experiences range, for example, from the elite member that considered that "there were too many brown faces" in the leadership effort promoted by Unite El Paso and the perilous and demanding success of Marcela Torres's communications firm, to the limited options of Leticia Santiesteban and thousands of other laid-off garment workers.

Regarding "space of representation," as in the conceptualization of the region in policies such as NAFTA, the most alluring representations only recognize what is functional to their figurative use. Yet the concept of the border is different for the diverse residents, as well as for the endless array of other individuals related to the border, such as tourists, prospective crossers, maquiladora personnel, bureaucrats, and so forth. In addressing this great diversity, my critique is not so much the reifying selectivity or even the artificial reductionism of current representations. My concern is not their—inevitable—enunciative poverty, but their conceptual poverty. Failing to look at concrete dimensions, difference is abridged and asymmetries overshadowed by neglect, trivialization, or trite reiterations. Addressing these conceptual and descriptive pitfalls, I underscore "distant proximities" to highlight persistent divisions in spite of contiguity or interaction. I explain this persistence in terms of the interplay of these divisions and "alienated instrumentalities"—the subordination of local concerns to nonlocal interests. I argue that, beyond superficial blending, this subordination is intensified in the way international integration is proceeding on this continent, as opposed to the more socially oriented route pursued in the European Union. In my view, the alluring representations replicate the exploitation of "alienated instrumentalities" and contribute to the production of the border as a frontier.

The situation confronted by actual residents is very pertinent for analogous and interrelated situations in other sites. More than the bizarre or the romanticized pronouncements, the questions are of a different order. Toward that exploration, I look at the relation between otherness and being local, nonlocal, or global in a globalized setting. Who *is* local in the supposedly "bicultural setting" of El Paso? Who is binational in this increasingly militarized border city? Who belongs and who is recognized as belonging?

Belonging, as a functional claim to local prerogatives and entitlements, is becoming rapidly obsolete. Globalization entails wider scopes of both dislocation and opportunity. Legitimacy is decreasingly dependent on geopolitical demarcations and more on operational ones. The initiatives described in this book attempted to use the ongoing challenges and opportunities presented by globalization to formulate new orientations of the local economy and its role in global markets. In the shifting parameters of competition and community, Carmen Rocha attempted to revitalize the garment industry. Clifford Crawford tried to develop a binational industrial zone. Marcela Torres sought to foster a technically proficient middle class. The Hispanic Chamber aimed to develop an institutional vehicle for including that emergent middle class. David Miller promoted the development of the "North American high-tech manufacturing region." And Unite El Paso endeavored to cultivate coherent and inclusive local leadership.

The question persists: who is the local in this overridden setting? Is the local the displaced worker or the border patrol agent? Is Clark Pereira, born in El Paso, more local than Roberto Ruiz, who was born in Ciudad Juárez? Are these two founders of the Hispanic Chamber more local than David Miller or Clifford Crawford, who were born elsewhere in the United States? Is John Oliver, born and raised in West Texas, less local than Steve Carmichael, a fourth-generation, fully bicultural Euro-American self-proclaimed *paseño de aquí y de alla* (from here and there)? Is Justice Chavira or businesswoman Marcela Torres more representative of the city's women than Mayor Iber or Leticia Santiesteban, a displaced worker protesting the La Vista Grande event? Does globalization make these ethnic, class, gender, age, regional, and national differences immaterial or irrelevant? Immaterial when—and to whom? Significant when—and to whom? Addressing these questions entails acknowledging the new spatial dimension of social living in a globalized environment. Thus, it inherently entails the dynamic interplay of space and reconfiguring parameters of otherness.

Are the individuals involved in these initiatives locals? The meaning of being local is being operationally altered by globalization, as most social beings are uprooted in the reconfiguring impacts of globalization. This uprooting is particularly vivid in the border's frontierlike context. In the dislocated conditions of the city, in its perplexing interplay of operating as a bridge and a barrier, the city is socially fragmented. Thus, each initiative appears as a disjointed yet related piece of a kaleidoscope. Consequently, the extent to which each initiative has managed to assert any degree of control or ownership on local developments varies. As such, assessing their progress toward their goals is a complex and inconclusive task. To begin with, in El Paso, such progress was curtailed or at least qualified by the power discrepancy between local and nonlocal entities, as well as by the asymmetries among the different local groups. Their respective accomplishments were made precarious not only by the speed of change, but by the magnitude of the discrepancies involved and by the site's stubborn fragmentation into distant proximities. The city's pervasive subordination and its "social disintegration"—in Arthur Gunter's words—erected formidable barriers to all these collective projects, obstructing efforts to alter the terms of the global integration of the site, its frontier condition itself.

The collective agendas are not extinct, even though their initial momentum has dwindled or their accomplishments remain partial. The situation of displaced workers and the overall poverty in the city have continued to worsen in spite of the work of La Mujer Obrera, and the efforts of labor advocates to formulate or pursue new plans seemed to wane by 1997. In November 2001, La Mujer Obrera had managed to bring to fruition its five-point program for the community development it had advocated for close to a decade. That month its "marketplace" and restaurant were open to the public as a cooperative, giving employment to about fifty of the displaced workers. Unfortunately, as significant as this accomplishment was, as with all the other initiatives, contrasting magnitudes dwarf the immediate accomplishments. Those fifty workers are not even one percent of the displaced workers. Likewise, the High Fashion Institute is no longer in existence. Notwithstanding the overwhelming magnitude of the challenges it faced every step of the way, through the years, La Mujer Obrera offered workers much-needed resources and logistical guidance to meet immediate needs—including extra funds for job training.

Membership in the Hispanic Chamber has steadily increased, and its right to exist is undisputed, no longer provoking ethnic backlashes. Overall, Mexican Americans are no longer seen as unfit for high positions in the city. Since the early 1990s, they have had most of the seats in the city council and three of the five major terms have been served by two Mexican American mayors. Unite El Paso experienced a similar situation in which their accomplishments went beyond the specific group. On the one hand, the initial momentum of Unite El Paso was arrested by draconian measures taken by the border patrol, and the court of inquiry remains unresolved. As with La Mujer Obrera, however, the accomplishments of Unite El Paso have not withered. One of the most salient manifestations has occurred in the political arena. In 1991, the architect of the court of inquiry, Alfredo Contreras, was elected mayor of the city. His election furthered the group's goal for cohesive leadership. Based on many years of close friendship, the coordination between the offices of Mayor Contreras and Senator Carmichael most likely allows them to bring their shared vision for the city to more efficient fruition.

The two initiatives related to business projects discussed here also show diffuse and contradictory parameters. These complexities make it difficult to assess their accomplishments. In our last interview, Torres expressed disappointment that the momentum of Latina entrepreneurs had slowed down. However, the Socorro Enterprise project was again in operation, albeit at a smaller scale. Important infrastructure foundations—a new well and a port of entry—were already in operation. Finally, Miller's initiatives were less widely discussed in local circles as the impetus generated by NAFTA subsided from public attention. Miller's vision of high-tech operations has begun to be realized in the sophisticated research and design departments of maquiladora conglomerates consolidated—at least for the time being—in Ciudad Juárez.

Proficiency and resourcefulness, however, have translated into partial and individual successes. In the kaleidoscopic fragmentation of the site, individual outcomes coincide and contrast at once. In general, the leaders of these initiatives have maneuvered effectively in the global context. They belong to diverse networks that spread through other cities, countries, and continents. Pereira commutes between offices in El Paso and Austin to conduct his real estate operations. Carmichael is in his second term as a state senator. Torres continues with her communications firm, selling maquiladora directories around the world. Rocha left El Paso for national and international projects. Miller, now a partner in a private firm, continues to promote binational business operations that are spreading throughout Mexico and the United States.

Ultimately, the distances between these individual and collective outcomes reflect the differential effects of the alienating context. Parallels among the five initiatives do not equate to symmetries or correspondences. Points of coincidence and overall similarities are overridden by severe incongruities and disparities. The hardships encountered by Torres as a small business owner are not the same as the perils facing Santiesteban and other displaced workers. Crawford's capital investment was considerably greater than Miller's. Likewise, the outcomes of the political ambitions of Carmichael and Pereira sharply contrast. Similarities and asymmetries coexist, but do not necessarily lead to coalescing or cohesion. Sometimes, however, as the Hispanic Chamber of Commerce and Unite El Paso attest, such cohesive potential is recognized despite class or ethnic divides.

Regardless of the individual breakthroughs and the innovative character of their initiatives, the risk of impending doom was not averted. If anything, poverty and social chaos continue to expand. Compounding these risks, the intermediary role of the site is uncertain given the new dimensions and scope of NAFTA, in particular, and of globalization, in general. With direct exchanges among different regions of the two countries, the border may be bypassed. For example, for visitors from the north, the appeal of Mexico's tourist sites is no doubt challenged by increasingly available escapades or short visits to Mexico's interior, which are offered through all-inclusive packages. For visitors from the south, NAFTA has made U.S. products available at the stores in their own cities. Until now, there has been no evident decrease in these activities in El Paso. However, ever longer lines at the crossing bridges and ever more chaotic situations, including environmental pollution, threaten the continuation of the flow of visitors and transactions. Likewise, successive layoffs in both cites, El Paso and Ciudad Juárez, periodically bring to mind the images of doom painted by maquiladora promoters in the early 1980s regarding infrastructure problems.

A Crossroad at a Crossroad II

A Taoist story talks about the winds of the north and the south meeting at the house of chaos. After ages, they come to appreciate chaos's hospitality and decide to show their appreciation by straightening up its disarranged quarters. In spite of their heartfelt good intentions, their good deed kills chaos—for chaos cannot survive in order. The border, however, does not require chaos, and the social costs of the chaos need to be recognized and attended to. As the countries of the north and the south intensify their contact at and beyond the border region, let us hope that the complex character of the dividing line is finally recognized so that it can be transcended or transformed at a lower human cost.

Instead of a so-called paradigm, the border region suggests to me the image of a sphere situated at the dividing line between the United States and Mexico. The sphere operates as a play of mirrors. Internally, the concave surfaces of the sphere reflect each edge—each city—on the divide. Externally, the convex surfaces reflect each country. I believe that the image of a sphere allows us to recognize the simultaneously distorting and elucidating function of the border region in its frontier condition. As a sphere on the dividing line, the internal walls of the bubble reflect an inverse view of the opposite side. For example, Ciudad Juárez presents a distorted reflection of El Paso and vice versa. The distortion arises from the concave walls of the sphere: Looking south, residents on the U.S. side inadvertently see themselves. As in the panoramic view of Ciudad Juárez from Samudio's library tour, the exposure to the shantytowns across the river reflects El Paso's own shantytowns, areas that most of its residents refuse to acknowledge. Denied or rejected in their marginality, as Staudt illustrates, *colonia* residents in both cities cross the international divide to capitalize on both markets, just as maquiladora companies and promoters do, but with very discrepant resources and official support.

On the concave surfaces, the sphere reflects each country to itself. Mexico looks north and sees its own distorted image on the border, as does the United States looking south. This mixture of discovery and familiarity—of recognition and erasure—derives from the allure of the region in terms of its legendary stature and its stereotypes (representation of space), the experience of the curio shop or the shopping mall (representational spaces), and the manipulation of boundaries by the maquiladora industry or the undocumented worker (spatial practices). Currently, as the proximity between the two countries intensifies, the sphere is about to burst. This imminent implosion is fed by the unresolved overlap of hierarchies and power imbalances and shifts in which the complicated convergence of the two countries, simplistically mischaracterized by the notion of *mestizaje* or hybridity, alters the parameters of their relationships and constitutencies.

Lefevbre's conceptualization of the social construction of space allows us to see the complex and dynamic accounts and actions that, at once, reflect and reinforce the disjointed condition of the region. In the region's ever expanding overlappings, multiple contacts and exchanges override perilous delineations and yield, more often than not, uneven concatenations. The drama of these concatenations lends the hyperreal overtones of the appeal of the image of the border. An allegory for hybridity and transgression, the figure commands a strong capacity of circulation. It capitalizes on widely publicized dramas about undocumented crossings, drug dealing, maquiladora operations, and shantytowns. This publicity conflates with the legendary repute of the region as a site of chaos and crime, and it corroborates rushed impressions from brief trips to any border town's curios market or other tourist trap. These impressions from selective exposures create a place of controlled ambiguity in which the alien and the familiar touch and even converge but seldom blend. In this undefined place, the shock from the disruptions of globalization are indirectly apprehended, but not comprehended. The image functions as a cognitive buffer zone. The border remains the border, the space beyond, always open as a frontier, a territory of slash and burn where anxieties and desires are projected. It is also the space of freedom as transgression, of manipulated maneuvers through unsettled or undefined parameters.

In these undefined parameters, the border region emerges in the public mind as an "entity that is neither Mexico, nor the United States." I argue that this proclamation has much to do with blurring perspectives that fail to recognize the magnitude of changes. These changes, in fact, go beyond trade agreements, labor flows, or cultural blending per se. At a much deeper level, the challenge is to contend with these ambiguities related to the specter of change and their oxymoron-like overlaps of breakthroughs and displacements. The depth and magnitude of these juxtapositions bring to mind Michel Foucault's claim of a new ordering principle in Western thought. I believe that to step beyond the mesmerizing mirages suggested by the specter of change, we need to acknowledge the epochal transition we may be witnessing and the challenge it means to our ways of making sense of the world. Notions of borders and hybridity only enunciate and simplemindedly reiterate the shock the reconfiguration manifests.

In a book suggestively titled *The Order of Things*, Foucault traces a shift in the sense of the world. He talks about classical and modern epistemes to point to the contrasting "ordering principles" of each period. By episteme, in short, he refers to the cognitive orientation defining each epoch. In his view, in antiquity, knowledge was formulated in terms of similarities and contiguities. In the modern period, in contrast, the sense of "order" was defined primarily in terms of distinctions and separations. Thus, the homophonic character of ancient languages, such as Hebrew, in which a given feature of the object invoked is emulated in its assigned word, gave way to languages with no inherent correspondence between the referent, the word, and the reference, the object. Likewise, in painting and sculpture, earlier attempts for more accurate representation eventually subsided and abstract styles came to dominate most schools. Or in medicine, homeopathic approaches, the idea of healing through the body's own balances, have been overshadowed by allopathic interventions. In many additional areas, the earlier coherence of systems of communication, representation, and beliefs generated by analogies and emulations were debunked by analytical systems based on distinctions and contrasts. That epistemic transition has unfolded through centuries and, according to Foucault, is being brought to an end.

After tracing the gradual transition of these two epistemes, Foucault ends his book heralding a new epistemic epoch. Yet, he does not describe the new episteme because, in his view, its manifestations are still too new to be properly recognized. He only ventures to state that it may resemble a mixture of the two preceding ones. Paradoxically, this new episteme would encapsulate or perhaps even reconcile the contrast between similarities and differences. Apparently, the very logic distinguishing contrasts and analogies would be transcended while also being asserted at once. As far-fetched as the logic of this oxymoron-like arrangement may seem, it is nevertheless vividly suggested in perplexing new configurations of social, aesthetic, and international arrangements. Wholesomely defined as postmodernism, these new configurations bridge digressing or incongruent developments, styles, and settings. In architecture and the other arts, previous canons and differentiations in terms of styles and periods are overrun by a new aesthetic of juxtapositions and capricious mixtures with apparently little regard for functions or expectations (Harvey 1989). Significantly, Foucault's insight into the disconcerting, compounded character of the emergent episteme is analogous to a disconcerting trend in our perception and experience of history noted by Baudrillard (1994, 111). Twenty years after Foucault's claim, this other French theoretician points to the deeply ambigious sociopolitical character of the hyperreal. He illustrates this character in reference to an "acceleration" in the vertiginous flows and spectacularity of events, on the one hand, and a slowing down in the relevance or transcendance of those events in our minds on the other. In a similarly overwhelming disorientation effect, the instantaneous confluence of incongruent or at least disjointed profusion of developments oversaturates our capacity to make sense of the world and thus to effectively intervene for most of us (108).

Baudrillard, with his characteristic play of words, points out that the intensification of "difference," given the widening scopes of information from many places at once, generates, in turn, "indifference." The more we learn about the misfortune of many, for example, the more callous we become. As the magnitude of shock or indignation becomes greater, the more insensitive we train ourselves to be in order to cope. At the same time, our need for sensation brings us to seek ever more intense thrills or shocks (108). This is clearly manifested in the allure of the border image. The more dramatic or gruesome its dislocation and the more tragic events or conditions, the greater the massive appeal is. Yet, the appeal is seldom engaged with actions that respond to the dramatic situation or, even less, conditions of the site. Instead, as with the little extra tip or the purchase of the curio shop trinket from the first visit to the border, the shock, the thrill, and the guilt rapidly subside for the tourist. However, the complex conditions of the local residents persist. Much of this situation is unrecognized in the perception that nonlocal visitors and accounts emphasize and exploit. Thus, the border is at once highlighted and overshadowed, much in the same way that history, according to Baudrillard, accelerates and slows down. Baudrillard's analytical engagement corresponds to the epochal magnitude of change heralded by Foucault's epistemic shift. The latter's cognitive emphasis is insightfully materialized in the former's recognition of transcendental developments and our perceptions of them. Thus, the hyperreal representation of the border propagates beyond the specific site into the allegorical (i.e., "paradigmatic).

La Frontera and the Frontier: *¿Un Final Feliz?*

In the morass of iconoclastic and flexible reconfigurations of national arrangements produced by global integration, reformulations of international parameters suggest the new "ordering" principle envisioned by Foucault. As a postmodernist icon, the image of the border region crystallizes the perplexing new "order of things" only too well and with, by now, very limited analytical value and a high sociopolitical cost for the region.

It would be naive on my part to think that a handful of ethnographic accounts will dispel the compelling appeal of the allegoric or dramatic function of the border image. As I mentioned before, important shifts and "evidence" fuel such appeal. Along with the shock of globalization and the drama of the border region and its legendary repute, the passage from space to hyperspace reinforces the fetish and its cognitive use. At this mesmerizing level, however, I would like to enter fully the mythical realm of the hyperreal. I do so in terms of the epochal shifts pointed out by Foucault regarding our cognitive orientation to make sense of the world. In this bigger-than-life dimension, the new order envisioned in the new episteme helps to highlight the overlap of two deeply rooted senses of the two countries for their respective citizens. For the United States, it is the image of the frontier. For Mexico, it is *la Frontera.*

At the emblematic level, which is the realm of meaning where the allegorical image of the border gains its appeal, the two images contain historic and symbolic asymmetries ingrained in the nation-building myths of both countries. While sharing a common Latin cognate, the words *frontera* and *frontier* are seldom translated into each other (i.e., into English from Spanish or vice versa). The word *border,* which is not etymologically proximate, is used as the English equivalent of *frontera.* In turn, the word *frontier* with its English connotations does not exist in Spanish. As with the countries themselves, the two images increasingly overlap, yet do not merge. Beyond their etymology, the words *frontera* and *frontier* are unconnected, separated by the sociopolitical distance created by a defined historical event with dramatic yet contrasting meanings for each country—the U.S. invasion of Mexico in the middle of the nineteenth century. Each term conveys distinct sociopolitical resonances because each is written from a different perspective and situation.

Frontera, as understood in Mexico, refers to a political delimitation of simultaneous contiguity and separation. In that sense, *La frontera* is a buffer zone through which the centralist orientation of the Mexican state has attempted to protect its territory and institutions from the expansionist tendencies of the United States (which cost Mexico half its territory). This deeply held attitude is clearly expressed in a statement allegedly made by Porfirio Díaz, president of Mexico at the turn of the twentieth century: "Poor Mexico, so far from God and so close to the United States"—which now is a popular saying in Mexican folklore. At the same time, most Mexicans throughout the decades have reached avidly for U.S. products and for some selective cultural manifestations—movies, music, fashion, and so forth. Until now, many of these transactions have taken place through the mediation of the border region in the form of border commerce, immigration flow, or the high concentration of maquiladoras. However, as NAFTA demonstrates, the integration of Mexico and the United States is not static or uniform. In this dynamic and complex integration, the character and extent of the region's function are uncertain. Will NAFTA make the traditional linking role of the border region obsolete by facilitating direct exchanges between diverse areas of the two countries? Will border cities become ghost towns if the maquiladora plants relocate to other regions of Mexico, Latin America, or the world?

These uncertain outcomes are closely related to the notion of frontier. The frontier image is as deeply ingrained in the U.S. imagination as *La Frontera* is in Mexico's collective unconscious. However, the frontier evokes and enacts the opposite ethos. It connotes the expansionist orientation of the United States, which, according to Frederick Jackson Turner, defined its national character. In Turner's view, which has been fundamental in American studies and historiography for more than a century, the frontier contributed to the country's enterprising individuality and, consequently, to its democratic spirit:

> Up to our own day [1893] American History has been in a large degree the history of the colonization of the Great West. The existence of an area of free land, its continuous recession, and the advance of American settlement westward, explains American development. (Turner 1994, 2)

With fateful mythical overtones, Turner attributed the development of democratic institutions to the frontier, which as a practically inextinguishable land reservoir, allowed the common folk access to a significant degree of autonomy. That freedom allowed them to escape the encroachment of European aristocratic institutions. He noted a constant reenactment of the country's institutional development in its geographical expansion:

> In the case of most nations, however, the development has occurred in a limited area; and if the nation has expanded, it has met other growing peoples whom it has conquered. But in the case of the United States we have a different phenomenon. Limiting our attention to the Atlantic coast, we have the familiar phenomenon of the evolution of institutions in a limited area, such as the rise of representative government; the differentiation of simple colonial governments into complex organs; the progress from primitive industrial society, without division of labor, up to manufacturing civilization. But we have in addition to this a recurrence of the process in each western area reached in the process of expansion. (2–3)

Implicit in this mythmaking formulation is the perception of the border as "empty space," as part of the "wild west." Likewise, Turner's emphasis on a recurrent interplay between the old and the new, the "primitive" and the "civilized," prefigures the current celebration of hybridity and "new worlds":

> Thus American development has exhibited not merely an advance along a single line, and a new development for the area. American social development has been continually beginning over again on the frontier. This perennial rebirth, this fluidity of American life, this expansion westward with its new opportunities, its continuous touch with the simplicity of primitive society, furnish the forces dominating American character. (3)

In the traditional image of the term, evoked by Turner, frontiers are areas where the uncivilized and the civilized meet. Aside from obvious first world/third world or Euro-American–Mexican stereotypes, the perception of the "uncivilized" border coexists with its "empty space" and "wild west" characterizations. Interestingly, Turner's thesis acquired its dramatic overtones out of his observations about the end of the frontier. In his view, it was extinguished around the end of the 1880s. The epochal dimension of his pronouncement added dramatic overtones to his fateful and myth-making thesis. Similar overtones can be picked up in more recent descriptions of the border region. Contrasting with Turner's claim about the end of the frontier, yet with similar epic-sounding overtones, the border is today proclaimed to be still a place of chaos and transgression of transcendental significance: a "laboratory of postmodernity" (García Canclini on Tijuana), "the laboratory of our future" (Bowden on Ciudad Juárez), and "the future of Postmodernity" (Gómez Montero on the border).

Contrary to Turner's thesis, the frontier did not end in the nineteenth century. As the dominant U.S. powers reconfigured their relationships in the aftermath of the Civil War, the expansionist drive took on a different character and moved at a different rate. As geographical and institutional confines were officially demarcated, the edges of the country became reservoirs for the expansionist momentum. The official story claims that it was primarily redirected into internal affairs and territories. However, Turner's claims aside, the United States launched a war on Spain for its colonial possessions four years after his pronouncement. In addition, U.S. capital and intervention found their way into Mexico, particularly into its northern hinterlands. In fact, it was during the *Porfiriato,* the Mexican Revolution and its long aftermath, that the U.S.–Mexican border was a launching area, a meeting ground, and a stepping-stone for trends that have never been unidirectional, stopped, or completely controlled.

Amid these multiple and irregular developments, the frontier/*frontera* overlap implodes the border region. This implosion creates a persistent chaos and dislocation, perpetuating the dislocating subordination of the region in the three respects highlighted by Lefebvre. In all three senses, the border remains the space beyond, always open as a frontier, a territory of slash and burn where anxieties and desires are projected. It is, in fact, the space and now the hyperspace of manipulated maneuvers through unsettled or undefined parameters. While open, nevertheless, the border is not an empty space—at least as yet.

Works Cited

AFSC-ILEMP (American Friends Service Committee—Immigration Law Enforcement Monitoring Project). 1990. *Human Rights at the Mexico–U.S. Border.* Second Annual Report. March.

———. 1992. *Sealing Our Borders: The Human Toll.* Third Report of the Immigration Law Enforcement Monitoring Project (ILEMP). February.

Anzaldúa, Gloria. 1987. *Borderlands/La Frontera: The New Mestiza.* San Francisco: Spinsters/Aunt Lute Book Company.

———. 1998. "Chicana Artists: Exploring Nepantla, e/ Lugar de la Frontera." In *The Latino Studies Reader: Culture, Economy and Society,* edited by Antonia Darder and Rudolfo D. Torres. Oxford: Blackwell Inc.

Baake, Ken. 1990. "On 'Maquila' Celebration, Some Are in Mourning." *El Paso Herald Post,* 20 April.

Barrera, Mario. 1979. *Race and Class in the Southwest.* Notre Dame: Notre Dame University Press.

Barrett, Richard E., and Soomi Chin. 1987. "Export-oriented Industrializing States in the Capitalist World System: Similarities and Differences." In *The Political Economy of the New Asian Industrialism,* edited by Frederic C. Deyo. Ithaca: Cornell University Press.

Barry, Tom, and Beth Sims. 1994. *The Challenge of Cross-Border Environmentalism: The U.S.–Mexico Case.* Albuquerque: Resource Center Press.

Bartra, Roger. 1993. Introduction to *Warrior for Gringostroika.* St. Paul: Graywolf Press.

Baudrillard, Jean. 1983. *Simulations.* New York: Semiotext(e), Inc.

———. 1994. *The Illusion of the End.* Stanford: Stanford University Press.

———. 1998. *Paroxysm: Interviews with Philippe Petit.* New York: Verso.

Bauman, Zygmunt. 1998. *Globalization: The Human Consequences.* New York: Columbia University Press.

Beck, Ulrich. 1992. *Risk Society.* London: Sage Publications.

Bhabha, Homi K. 1994. *The Location of Culture.* New York and London: Routledge.

Bluestone, Barry, and Bennett Harrison. 1982. *The Deindustrialization of America.* New York: Basic Books.

Bohanan, Paul, and Fred Plog. 1967. *Beyond the Frontier: Social Process and Cultural Change.* New York: Natural History Press.

Bourdieu, Pierre. 1979. *Algeria 1960.* Cambridge: Cambridge University Press.

———. 1987. *Outline of a Theory of Practice.* Cambridge: Cambridge University Press.

Bowden, Charles. 1989. *Red Line.* New York: Penguin.

———. 1996. "While You Were Sleeping: In Juárez, Mexico, Photographers Expose the Violent Realities of Free Trade." *Harper's Magazine,* 44–52.

———. 1998. *Juárez: The Laboratory of Our Future.* New York: Aperture.

Brannon, Jeffrey T. 1989. "Fuerza de trabajo en la industria maquiladora." Paper prepared at the "Seminario: La Industria Maquiladora," June 5–7, at the College of Mexico, Mexico City.

Cardenas, Gilbert. 1988. "The Changing U.S.–Mexico Border Region: Implications for the Hispanic Labor Force." In *The Hispanic Experience in the United States: Contemporary Issues and Perspectives,* edited by Edna Acosta-Belen and Barbara R. Sjostrom. New York: Praeger Publishers.

Carnoy, Martin, Hugh M. Daley, and Raul Hinojosa Ojeda. 1993. "The Changing Economic Position of Latinos in the U.S. Labor Market Since 1939." In *Latinos in a Changing U.S. Economy,* edited by Rebecca Morales and Frank Bonilla. Newbury Park, Calif.: Sage Publications, 1993.

Cavanagh, John. 1992. *Trading Freedom: How Free Trade Affects Our Lives, Work, and Environment.* San Francisco: The Institute for Food and Development Policy.

Chambers, Iain. 1990. *Border Dialogues: Journeys in Postmodernity.* London and New York: Routledge.

Chavez, Leo R. 1992. *Shadow Lives: Undocumented Immigrants in American Society.* Fort Worth: Harcourt Brace Jovanovich College Publishers.

Chen, Xiangming. 1995. "The Evolution of Free Economic Zones and the Recent Development of Cross-National Growth Zones." *International Journal of Urban and Regional Research* 19, no. 4: 593–62.

City of El Paso, Texas. 1990. *Census Profiles from Summary Tape File 3A.* Department of Planning and Research. Table 1.

———. 1992. *Census Profiles from Summary Tape File 3A.* Department of Planning, Research, and Development.

Clifford, James, and George E. Marcus, eds. 1986. *Writing Culture: The Poetics and Politics of Ethnography.* Berkeley and Los Angeles: University of California Press.

Coalson, George. 1952. "Mexican Contract Labor in American Agriculture." Cited in Mario Barrera, *Race and Class in the Southwest.* Notre Dame: Notre Dame University Press, 1979.

Coyle, Laurie, Gail Hershatter, and Emily Honig. 1982. *Workers of Farah: An Incomplete History.* El Paso: Reforma.

Crowder, David. 1991. "Let's Start New Hispanic Traditions: Letters to the Editor." *El Paso Times,* 24 March.

———. 2000. "Unite El Paso Gets Advice—'Just Keep Doing What You're Doing.'" *El Paso Times.*

D'Antonio, William V., and William H. Form. 1965. *Influentials in Two Border Cities.* Notre Dame: University of Notre Dame Press.

Davis, Mike. 2000. *Magical Urbanism.* London and New York: Verso.

Deleuze, Gilles, and Félix Guattari. 1987. *A Thousand Plateaus: Capitalism and Schizophrenia.* Minneapolis: University of Minnesota Press.

Dunn, Timothy J. 1996. *The Militarization of the U.S.–Mexico Border, 1978–1992: Low-Intensity Conflict Doctrine Comes Home.* Austin: Center for Mexican-American Studies, University of Texas.

Economist. 1998. "Good Fences: Berlin, Buffalo, Narva and Other Liminal Places." December 19, 19–22.

Featherstone, Mike, ed. 1992. *Global Culture: Nationalism, Globalization, and Modernity.* London: Sage Publications.

"Fed Probe Finds Violations in Local Garment Industry." 1990. *El Paso Herald Post,* August 10.

Fernández, Raul. 1977. *The U.S.-Mexican Border: A Socio-Political Profile.* Notre Dame: University of Notre Dame Press.

———. 1989. *The Mexican-American Border Region: Issues and Trends.* Notre Dame: University of Notre Dame Press.

Fernández-Kelly, María Patricia. 1983. *For We Are Sold, I and My People: Women and Industry in Mexico's Frontier.* Albany: State University of New York Press.

Foucault, Michel. 1972. *The Archaeology of Knowledge and the Discourse on Language.* New York: Pantheon Books.

Fried, Jonathan. 1994. "Operation Blockade: A City Divided." A Report from the American Friends Service Committee's Immigration Law Enforcement Monitoring Project (ILEMP), July.

Friedman, Jonathan. 1992. "Being in the World: Globalization and Localization." In *Global Culture: Nationalism, Globalization, and Modernity,* edited by Mike Featherstone. London: Sage Publications.

Frobel, Folker, J. Heinrichs, and O. Kreye. 1980. *The New International Division of Labour.* Cambridge: Cambridge University Press.

Fuentes, Annette, and Barbara Ehrenreich. 1983. *Women in the Global Factory.* Boston: South End Press.

García, Mario T. 1981. *Desert Immigrants: The Mexicans of El Paso, 1880–1920.* New Haven: Yale University Press.

———. 1998. *The Making of a Mexican-American Mayor: Raymond L. Telles of El Paso.* El Paso: Texas Western Press, 1998.

García Canclini, Néstor. 1995. *Hybrid Cultures: Strategies for Entering and Leaving Modernity.* Minneapolis: University of Minnesota.

García Canclini, Néstor, and Patricia Safa. 1989. *Tijuana: La Casa de Toda la Gente.* Mexico City: INAH/ENAH/Programa Cultural de las Fronteras UAM-Iztapalapa/Conaculta.

Garreau, Joel. 1981. *The Nine Nations of North America.* New York: Avon Books.

Giddens, Anthony. 2000. *Runaway World: How Globalization Is Reshaping Our Lives.* New York: Routledge.

Gómez Montero, Sergio. 1994. *The Border: The Future of Postmodernity.* San Diego: San Diego State University Press.

Gómez-Peña, Guillermo. 1991. "A Binational Performance Pilgrimage." *The Drama Review* 35, no. 3.

———. 1993. *Warrior for Gringostroika.* St. Paul: Graywolf Press.

Gray, John. 1998. *False Dawn: The Delusions of Global Capitalism.* New York: New Press.

Halebsky, Sandor. 1995. "Urban Transformation and Survival Strategies." In *Capital, Power, and Inequality in Latin America,* edited by Sandor Halebsky and Richard L. Harris. Boulder, Colo.: Westview Press.

Hancock, David. 1986. "6 Teens Arrested in Beating Death." *El Paso Times,* 20 April.

Harvey, David. 1989. *The Condition of Postmodernity: An Inquiry into the Origins of Cultural Change.* Oxford: Basil Blackwell Ltd.

Herzog, Lawrence A. 1990. *Where North Meets South: Cities, Space, and Politics on the U.S.–Mexico Border.* Austin: Center for Mexican American Studies/University of Texas.

Heyman, Josiah McC. 2002. "U.S. Immigration Officers of Mexican Ancestry as Mexican Americans, Citizens and Immigration Police." *Current Anthropology* 43, no. 3 (June): 479–507.

Hicks, D. Emily. 1991. *Border Writing: The Multidimensional Text.* Minneapolis: University of Minnesota Press.

Hogue, Angela, and Dianne Carol. 1983. "The Rich 1,000 Juarenses Prove Not All Are Poor," in "Special Report—The Border," *El Paso Herald Post,* summer, 63.

Houtum, Henk van. 2000. "Theoretical Concepts in European Border Studies." Paper presented at the Annual Meeting of Association for Borderland Studies, San Diego, California, April.

Jones, Del. 1991. "City Leaders Talk Free Trade." *El Paso Times,* 7 April.

Jordan, David C. 1990. *Economic Outlook for the El Paso and Las Cruces Metropolitan Statistical Areas.* El Paso, Texas: El Paso Electric Company.

King, Tom. 1990. "Smiling Takes Less Effort Than Always Shouting 'Racism.'" *El Paso Herald Post,* 22 September.

Krishnamurti, J. 1969. *Freedom from the Known.* San Francisco: Harper San Francisco.

Kruszewski, Z. Anthony, Jacob Ornstein-Galicia, and Richard Hough. 1992. *Politics and Society in the Southwest: Ethnicity and Chicano Pluralism.* Boulder, Colo.: Westview Press.

Laclau, Ernesto, and Chantal Mouffe. 1985. *Hegemony and Socialist Strategy: Towards a Radical Democratic Politics.* London: Verso.

Latino Institute. 1994. *NAFTA and Latinos in Chicago.* Chicago: Latino Institute.

Lefebvre, Henri. 1991. *The Production of Space.* Cambridge: Basil Blackwell, Inc.

Letter to the Editor. 1990. "Denies Chamber Mixers Conflict Was Deliberate." *El Paso Herald Post,* 4 October.

Limón, José E. 1994. *Dancing with the Devil: Society and Cultural Poetics in Mexican-American South Texas.* Madison: University of Wisconsin Press.

Lorey, David E. 1999. *The U.S.–Mexican Border in the Twentieth Century: A History of Economic and Social Transformation.* Wilmington, Del.: Scholarly Resources Inc.

Madsen, William. 1973. *The Mexican-Americans of South Texas.* New York: Holt, Rinehart and Winston, Inc.

"Maquila: La Vista Grande." 1990. *El Paso Herald Post,* 19 March.

Márquez, Benjamin. 1985. *Power and Politics in a Chicano Barrio.* Lanham, Md.: The University Press of America.

Martínez, James. 1990. "Garment-factory Protesters Released from Jail." *El Paso Herald Post,* June 30.

Martínez, Oscar J. 1978. *Border Boom Town.* Austin: University of Texas Press.
———. 1988. *Troublesome Border.* Tucson: University of Arizona Press.
———. 1994. *Border People.* Tuczon: University of Arizona Press.
McWilliams, Carey. 1948. "The El Paso Story." *The Nation,* July 10.
Michaelsen, Scott, and David E. Johnson. 1997. *Border Theory: The Limits of Cultural Politics.* Minneapolis: University of Minnesota Press.
Michie, Donald. 1986. *Maquila Inputs.* Ciudad Juárez, Mexico: Desarrollo Economico.
Montero, Sergio Gómez. 1994. *The Border: The Future of Postmodernity.* San Diego: San Diego University Press.
Nathan, Deborah. 1991. *Women and Other Aliens: Essays from the U. S.–Mexico Border.* El Paso: Cinco Punto Press.
Neuman, Gerald L. 1996. *Strangers to the Constitution: Immigrants, Borders, and Fundamental Law.* Princeton: Princeton University Press.
Old, Joe. 1986. "Citizen: Border Patrol Roughed Me Up." *El Paso Herald-Post,* 24 July.
———. 1993a. "Dreaming the Future and Living the Unity: El Paso Makes Strategic Choices." El Paso: Unite El Paso, unpublished.
———. 1993b. "Unite El Paso, Tu Comunidad." El Paso: unpublished.
Omi, Michael, and Howard Winant. 1994. *Racial Formation in the United States.* New York: Routledge.
Ortíz, Victor M., and Marc Zimmerman. 1998. "Metaphorical Erasures and Lucid Transpositions of the Border Image: A Review Article." *Journal of the Midwest Modern Language Association* 31, no. 2: 79–95.
Ortíz-González, Victor M. 1993. *Market Identities: Local Entrepreneurship and Global Economic Integration.* Ph.D. diss., Stanford University.
Peach, James T. 1985. "Income Distribution in the U.S.–Mexico Borderlands in the U.S. and Mexico." In *Borderland Development and the National Economies,* edited by Lay James Gibson and Alfonso Corona Renteria. Boulder, Colo.: Westview Press.
Peña, Gerardo Devon. 1997. *The Terror of the Machine.* Austin: University of Texas Press.
Pendleton, Scott. 1993. "Environmental Toll of the Maquilas." *The Christian Science Monitor,* January 6, 10.
Pérez, Janet. 1990. "Plan Aims to Keep Garment Industry from Coming Apart at the Seams." *El Paso Times,* May 2, 1A.
Perrucci, Carolyn C., Robert Perrucci, Dena B. Targ, and Harry R. Targ. 1988. *Plant Closings: International Context and Social Costs.* New York: Aldine de Gruyter.
Piore, Michael J., and Charles F. Sabel. 1984. *The Second Industrial Divide: Possibilities for Prosperity.* New York: Basic Books, Inc.
Plaza, Tina. 1993. "Let's See Some Papers." *The Progressive* 57, no. 4 (April): 18–22.
"Que Demandarán por las Revisiones Vejatorias." 1986. *Diario de Juarez,* 6 November.
Rabinow, Paul. 1986. "Representations Are Social Facts: Modernity and Postmodernity in Anthropology." In *Writing Culture: The Poetics and Politics of Ethnography,* edited by James Clifford and George E. Marcus. Los Angeles: University of California Press.
Reich, Robert B. 1991a. "Who Is Them?" *Harvard Business Review* (March–April).
———. 1991b. *The Work of Nations.* New York: Vintage Books.

Robertson, Roland 1992. *Globalization: Social Theory and Global Culture.* London: Sage.

Romero, Mary. 1992. *Maid in the U.S.A.* New York: Routledge.

Rosaldo, Renato. 1989. *Culture and Truth: The Remaking of Social Analysis.* Boston: Beacon Press.

Rothstein, Richard. 1993. "NAFTA and Its Aftershocks." *The American Prospect* 12 (winter).

Ruíz, Vicki L., and Susan Tiano. 1987. *Women on the U.S.-Mexico Border: Responses to Change.* Boston: Allen and Unwin.

Saldívar, José David. 1997. *Border Matters: Remapping American Cultural Studies.* Los Angeles: University of California Press.

Sassen, Saskia. 1990. "Economic Restructuring and the American City." *Annual Review of Sociology* 16: 465–90.

———. 1994. *Cities in a World Economy.* Thousand Oaks: Pine Forge Press.

Savage, William Jr., and Steven I. Thompson. 1979. *The Frontier: Comparative Studies.* Norman: University of Oklahoma Press.

Scharrer, Gary. 1991. "Bill Makes Non-payment of Wages a Felony." *El Paso Times,* 28 May.

Schmidt, Samuel. 1995. "Planning a U.S.–Mexican Bi-National Metropolis: El Paso, Texas–Ciudad Juárez, Chihuahua." In *North American Cities and the Global Economy: Challenges and Opportunities,* edited by Peter Karl Kresl and Gary Gappert. Thousand Oaks, Calif.: Sage Publications, Inc.

Soja, Edward W. 1989. *Postmodern Geographies: The Reassertion of Space in Critical Social Theory.* New York and London: Verso.

Spener, David, and Kathleen Staudt. 1998. *The U.S.–Mexico Border: Transcending Divisions, Contesting Identities.* Boulder, Colo.: Lynne Rienner Publishers, Inc.

Spybey, Tony. 1996. *Globalization and World Society.* Cambridge: Polity Press.

Staudt, Kathleen. 1998. *Free Trade! Informal Economics at the U.S.–Mexico Border.* Philadelphia: Temple University Press.

Stoddard, Ellwyn R. 1976. "A Conceptual Analysis of the 'Alien Invasion' Institutionalized Support of Illegal Mexican Aliens in the U.S." *International Migration Review* 1976 (summer): 157–89.

———. 1987. *Maquila: Assembly Plants in Northern Mexico.* El Paso: Texas Western Press.

Suro, Roberto. 1998. *Strangers among Us: Latino Lives in a Changing America.* New York: Vintage.

Tabuenca Córdoba, María Socorro. 1997. "La Frontera Textual y Geografica en dos Narradoras de la Frontera Norte Mexicana: Rosina Conde y Rosario Sanmiguel." Ph.D. diss., State University of New York at Stony Brook.

Tiano, Susan. 1994. *Patriarchy on the Line: Labor, Gender, and Ideology in the Mexican Maquila Industry.* Philadelphia: Temple University Press.

Timmons, W. H. 1990. *El Paso: A Borderlands History.* El Paso: Texas Western Press.

Todorov, Tzvetan. 1992. *The Conquest of America.* New York: Harper Collins.

Towers, George William. 1991. "Colonial and Economic Restructuring in El Paso, Texas." Ph.D. diss., University of Arizona.

Turner, Frederick Jackson. 1994. "The Significance of the Frontier in American History." In *Where Cultures Meet: Frontiers in Latin American History,* edited by

David J. Weber and Jane M. Rausch. Wilmington, Del.: Jaguar Books on Latin America no. 6, A Scholarly Resources, Inc.

van de Ende, Arthur, and Henk A. Haring. *Sunbelt Frontier and Border Economy: A Field-Work Study of El Paso.* El Paso: Center for Inter-American and Border Studies.

Van Maanen, John. 1988. *Tales of the Field: On Writing Ethnography.* Chicago: University of Chicago Press.

Vargas, Lucinda. 1990. *The Maquiladora Export Industry: The Recent Past in Maquiladora Industry Analysis.* Vol. 3, no. 2. Philadelphia: CIEMEX-WEFA.

———. 1997. "NAFTA and Jobs" *Business Frontier,* issue 1. Publication of the El Paso Branch of the Federal Reserve Bank of Dallas.

———. 1998a. "El Paso's Labor-Mismatch Dilemma." *Business Frontier* 1. El Paso Branch—Federal Reserve Bank of Dallas.

———. 1998b. "El Paso's Labor-Mismatch Dilemma." *Business Frontier* 4. El Paso Branch—Federal Reserve Bank of Dallas.

Velde, M. van der, and Henk van Houtum. 2000. *Borders, Regions, and People.* London: Pion.

Velez Ibáñez, Carlos G. 1996. *Border Visions: Mexican Cultures of the Southwest United States.* Tucson: University of Arizona Press.

Vila, Pablo. 1998. "The Competing Meanings of the Label 'Chicano' in El Paso." In *The U.S.–Mexico Border Transcending Divisions, Contesting Identities,* edited by David Spener and Kathleen Staudt. Boulder, Colo.: Lynne Rienner Publishers, 1998.

———, ed. 2003. *Ethnography at the Border.* Minneapolis: University of Minnesota Press.

Villareal, Robert E., and Olga Mapula. 1991. "Latino Participation and Municipal Politics in a Border City." In *Latinos and Political Coalitinos: Political Empowerment for the 1990s,* edited by Robert Villareal and Norma G. Hernández. New York: Greenwood Press, 1991.

Welchman, John C. 1996. *Rethinking Borders.* Minneapolis: University of Minnesota Press.

Wilson, David. 1997. *Globalization and the Changing U.S. City.* Thousand Oaks, Calif.: Sage Periodicals Press.

Index

American Anthropological Association (AAA), 14
Arau, Alfonso, x
Alienated instrumentality, xxxi–xxxii, xxxvi, 26, 72, 99, 101, 139, 145–46; definition of, 144, 148
Anzaldúa, Gloria, xxiii–xxiv, xxxvi, 3, 11–14, 16–18, 34, 40, 147; and the border as an open wound, 11–12, 34; new subjectivity, 12, 44–45

Barrera, Mario, 52–53
Barry, Tom, 4
Baudrillard, Jean, 9, 11, 18, 154–55; the hyperreal, 9–11, 14, 18; the real, 9, 11
Bauman, Sigmund, xxix–xxx, 20, 39; tourists, xxix–xxx; vagabonds, xxix–xxxi
Border(s) xx, xxiv, xxxi, xxxii, 3, 5, 11, 18, 147; aesthetic characterization of, ix; "Border Brujo," ix; as bridge and barrier, xvii, xix, xxxiv, 10, 34–35; as empty space, 21, 146, 158; as hybrid space, 8; and identity, xiii, 12, 44–45; as a sphere, 152; borderland paradigm, xxiv, 6, 11–14, 19, 25, 40, 42, 152; Democratic party, 105; transit zone, xii, xv, xxi, 11, 21; and U.S.–Mexico integration, xvii–xix. *See also* Frontera; Frontier
Border cities, xvii; demographics, 24–25; economic indicators, 142–43; economic integration, 44–45, 69, 73, 130–31; networks, 44–45; poverty in, xvii, 143
Border crossers, x–xi, 48, 50–51, 53
Border image, xii, xxiii, xxxvii, xxxviii, 7–8, 11–12, 17, 20, 22, 26, 40, 155
Border patrol, x, 33, 38, 69, 71
Border region, xxxi, xxxii, xxxiii, xl, 3, 12, 15–16, 19–20, 142, 155
Border zones, 14, 16
Bowden, Charles, xxiv, 3, 158
Bracero Program, xviii
Bush, George H. W., 103, 111, 115, 138

Chavez, Cesar, 128, 131
Cisneros, Henry, 123
Ciudad Juárez, xxii, xxiv, 1; demographics, 42–43
Civil rights movement, xiii, 19, 145

Diaz, Porfirio, 156
Distant proximities, xxx, 8, 25, 28, 99, 101, 119, 144–45, 149; use of the term, 148
Dunn, Timothy, 6

Earll, Duncan, 6
El Paso, xx, xxiii, xxv, xxxiv; Border Patrol and, 33; Chamber of Commerce, 107, 109, 111–14;

Economic Development Corporation, 107, 139; Minority Business Council, 107, 112; demographics of, 36–39, 42–43, 48, 116–17; Economic and Work Force Development Committee, 139, 147; economy and, xxi, xvi–xvii, 23–24, 48; Greater El Paso Chamber of Commerce, 111, 115; Hands Across the Border, 44; Hispanic Chamber of Commerce, xxvi, xxvii, xxxvii, 101, 103, 106, 108, 110–11, 113–14, 117, 139, 148
Eliot, T. S., 26
Engels, Friedrich, xv
enunciative poverty, 8, 148; episteme, 153–54, 156; epistemic shift, 153–55
Euro-American, xl, 1–2, 10, 36, 39–40, 105, 107, 109, 119
European Union: comparison to NAFTA, 141–42, 144, 148

Fernández, Raul, 3
Flexible accumulation, xxxvii
Foucault, Michel, 8–9, 18–19, 153–56
Freire, Paolo, 84
Frontera, xxxviii, 156, 158
Frontier, xi–xii, 34, 146, 152, 156, 158; explanation of use of the term, 144, 156–57

García Canclini, Néstor, xxiii, 11, 15–18; on Tijuana, 158
García, Mario, 3
García Marquez, Gabriel, 14
Garment industry, 99, 145; garment workers, xxvi, xxix, 74, 76, 88–90, 101, 117, 147; High Fashion Institute, 85–86, 150; and relocations, 74, 76–77, 87–88, 90, 100; and viability of, 84–85, 87; working conditions, 82, 85
Garreau, Joel, xxiii, 3; MexAmerica, xxiii
Globalization, xiii, xv, xxviii–xix, xxxii, xxxviii, 15, 26, 28, 30, 39, 101, 120, 144, 146, 155; definition of, xv; and proliferation of borders, 141
Gómez Peña, Guillermo, xxiii–xxiv, 3
GOP, 70
Government agencies: Department of Defense, 97; Department of Economic Development, 43, 115; Drug Enforcement Administration (DEA), 22, 64; Environmental Protection Agency, 22; Federal Bureau of Investigation (FBI), 64; Food and Drug Administration, 22; North American Development Bank, xix; Panama–Pacific U.S. Commission, 108. *See also* Immigration and Naturalization Service

Harvey, David, xxviii, xxxiii, 19; space-time compression, xxviii
Herzog, Lawrence A., 6
Heyman, Josiah McC., 6
High Fashion Institute. *See* Garment industry
Hicks, Emily, 14
Hispanic Leadership Institute, 105
Huerta, Dolores, 128
Hybridity, xxxii, 3, 9, 20–21, 147, 152–53
Hyperreality, 15, 18, 22; definition of, 9
Hyperreal, 9–11, 14, 18
Hyperspace, xxxi, 9, 18, 20, 145, 155; definition of, xxxiii

Ibáñez, Velez, 6
Immigration, 49; immigrants, 29, 48–49
Immigration and Legal Enforcement Monitoring Project (ILEMP), 55, 65–66
Immigration and Naturalization Service, xxxvi, xxxviii, 32–33, 48, 50–70, 131; and abuses, 54–68; Joint Task Force Number 6 (JTF6), 64; and militarization of, 65–66, 69; Operation Alliance, 64; Operation Blockade, 69–70, 131, 134

Institutional Revolutionary Party (PRI), 58

Jodorosky, Alejandro, X

Kennedy, Edward, 45
Krishnamurti, J., 26
Kundera, Milan, 31

La Mujer Obrera, xxvi, 74–75, 81–90, 99–100, 138, 145, 149
Lefebvre, Henri, xx, xxiv, xxviii, xxxiii, xxxv, xxxvi, 9, 34, 72, 98, 152, 159; Representation of Space, xxi, xxxv, 17, 99, 152; representational spaces, xx, xxviii, xxxii, xxxiii, xxxvi, 3, 9–10, 13, 17, 20, 30, 34, 72, 147, 152; representation of space, xxiv, xxvi, xxxii, 3, 10–11, 14, 17, 27–28, 147; spatial practices, xi, xx, xxiii, xxxii, xxxiii, xxxvi, xxxvii, 10, 147, 152
League of Immigration and Border Rights Education (LIBRE), 55, 57–60, 62–63

Madsen, William, 104
Maquiladora, 5, 10, 19, 42, 73, 76, 80–81, 97; industry, xviii–xix, 23, 42, 45, 68, 73, 90–91, 94–95, 106, 116, 119–20; relocations, 100, 106–7, 117, 120; workers, 20, 73; working conditions, 82, 120
Martínez, Felix, 108–9
Martínez, Oscar J., 3, 6
Marx, Karl, xv, 20; and fetishism 20
Mestizaje, 12, 152
Mexican Americans, xxxix, 104–7, 109; and stigma, 71
Mexican Revolution, xxii, 158. *See also* El Paso
Moyers, Bill, xxiii, 33, 51
Murrieta, Joaquin, 3

NAFTA. *See* North American Free Trade Agreement

Nahuatl, 12
Nathan, Deborah, 3
National Action Party (PAN), 58
Neoliberal optic, xix, 10
New subjectivities, xxxi, 12, 29, 147
North American Free Trade Agreement (NAFTA), x, xv, xvi, xviii, xix, xxii, xxiii, xv, xxvi, xxx, 10, 32, 45, 48, 68, 74, 76, 78, 80, 86–88, 95–96, 103, 114, 116, 120, 138, 142, 147, 150–51, 156; comparison to European Union, 141–42, 144, 148; Trade Adjustment Assistance Program and, 87

Otherness, 41; definition of, 27–28

Palafox, José, 6
PAN (National Action Party), 58
Paredes, Don Américo, 3, 14
Plaza, Tina, 68
Polarization (social), xvi, xxviii, xxix, xxx, xxi, xxxiii, 25–26, 32, 38, 71, 119, 144–45; economic policies of, 143, 145
Porfiriato, 122, 158
Postmodernism, 154
PRI (Institutional Revolutionary Party), 58
Progressive, The (magazine), 68
Prohibition, 4, 13
Pullman, George, 94

Reagan, Ronald, 4
Reich, Robert, xxviii, xxix, 19; more abstract form of capitalism, 19
Richards, Ann, 32
Rosaldo, Renato, xxiii, xxxvi, 11, 14–18, 28
Ruíz, Vicki, 3

Safa, Patricia, 15
Sagan, Carl, 141
Saldívar, José, xxiv, 6–7, 14
Schmidt, Samuel, 3–5
Sims, Beth, 4

Simulacra, 11, 14, 17–18, 22; of knowledge, 20
Soviet Union, 141
Specter of change, xv, xxv, 19, 22, 145, 153
Specter of revolution, xv, xvii, xxxiii, xxxvi, 11, 26
Spener, David, 6, 8
Staudt, Kathleen, 6, 8, 42
Stoddard, Ellwin, 3, 6, 53

Tabuenca, Socorro, 6–7
Taoist story, 151–52
Tijuana, xxiii, 13, 15, 17; as border symbol, 24
Tourists, 1, 17, 20
Trade Adjustment Assistance Program. *See* North American Free Trade Agreement
Turner, Frederick Jackson, 157–58; U.S. national character, 157
Twin Plant News (magazine), xxviii, xxix
Twin Plant Wives Association, 73

Unite El Paso, xxvi, 106, 118–19, 121, 123–27, 129–34, 137–39, 145, 148

Vila, Pablo, 6–7, 71

War on Drugs, 4

Victor M. Ortíz-González was born in El Paso and raised in Ciudad Juárez. He is director of the Mexican and Caribbean studies program at Northeastern Illinois University.